Also by *Yankee Magazine*

Yankee Magazine's
New England Innkeepers' Cookbook

Yankee Magazine's
CHURCH SUPPERS &
POTLUCK DINNERS
COOKBOOK

❧

Yankee Magazine's

CHURCH SUPPERS &
POTLUCK DINNERS
COOKBOOK

Edited by Andrea Chesman
and the Editors of *Yankee Magazine*

VILLARD · NEW YORK

Yankee Magazine's Church Suppers & Potluck Dinners Cookbook
Edited by Andrea Chesman and the editors of *Yankee Magazine*
Design by Jill Shaffer
Illustrations by Pamela Carroll
Cover design by J Porter
Cover art by Joyce Patti

Copyright © 1996 by Yankee Publishing, Inc.

All rights reserved under International and Pan-American Copyright Conventions.
Published in the United States by Villard Books, a division of Random House, Inc., New
York, and simultaneously in Canada by Random House of Canada Limited, Toronto.

VILLARD BOOKS is a registered trademark of Random House, Inc.

ISBN: 0-679-43208-6

Printed in the United States of America on acid-free paper
9 8 7 6 5 4 3 2
First Edition

Acknowledgments

*T*HE EDITORS are deeply indebted to all the churches and community organizations who so generously contributed their recipes; to Susan Gagnon and her team of home cooks—Lea Banks, Gini Barss, Donna Bergeron, Carolyn Black, Tom Black, Ruth Bohrer, Suzanne Bosiak, Beth Browning, Colin Browning, Christine Burritt, Jean Camden, Stacy Chansky, Susan Chumas, Linda Clukay, Betsy Davis, Leslie DeGraff, Patricia Dodge, Mary Gagnon, Helen Goodwin, Carol Gove, Lori Hill, Julia Houk, David Jokinen, Kurt Jones, Jill Lowell, Theresa Maier, Jean Mayberry, Carolyn Muller, Elaine Pettit, Marie Procaccini, Lisa Rucinski, Blair Weidig, and Leslie Zimmer—who tested the recipes included here and whose family and friends told us these were the best of the lot; and to Carla Richardson, whose professional cooking expertise was invaluable in reviewing the recipes for feeding crowds.

We also greatly appreciate the contributions of Lori Baird, who worked on everything from compiling mailing lists to recipe selection and testing to permissions gathering, and who wrote many of the sidebars as well; Jill Shaffer, who designed the text, and J Porter, who designed the cover; Pamela Carroll, who created the inside art, and Joyce Patti, who provided the cover illustration; Faith Hanson, copy editor; Barbara Jatkola, proofreader; Nancy Bishop, who maintained the database of all the organizations, individuals, and recipes involved; Tony Lechtman, who assisted with permissions gathering; and Elise Earl, who compiled the index.

Finally, our sincere thanks to Andrew Krauss, Beth Pearson, Leta Evanthes, and Daniel Rembert at Villard, without whose efforts this book would never have seen the light of day.

CONTENTS

Introduction

CHURCH AND COMMUNITY SUPPERS are as much a part of the New England landscape as maple trees and snow. Rarely does a week go by when some church or organization doesn't put up a hand-lettered sign announcing a chicken pie supper or a ham and bean supper—fund-raisers that are popular with locals and tourists alike. Where else can you go to rub shoulders with neighbors and strangers in such an easy, convivial atmosphere? Where else can you have coffee poured for you by the local politicians and wanna-bes? And where else can you get such a wonderful spread of Yankee home cooking?

The only other place where the cooking is so varied is a potluck. The main difference between a potluck and a church supper is that no money changes hands at a potluck and you are expected to bring a dish yourself. But once you're there, the same good food and congenial atmosphere predominate.

Potlucks have become a standard way for both formal and informal groups to gather. Not only are potlucks a popular time-saving and budget-stretching option for entertaining, they have also become standard practice for community groups that want a little time to socialize. We know of several monthly contradances that begin with potlucks. Organizations may start quarterly meetings with dessert potlucks. And hockey players and their families may have a potluck at the end of the winter to celebrate the beginning of sleep-in season for all those who have faithfully turned out for 5 AM rink time.

Like most things New England, there is a seasonality to many of these gatherings. Fall is the time of chicken pie suppers, game suppers, and apple pie festivals. The long, cold winter brings roast turkey dinners, soup suppers, and smorgasbords. Spring is ushered in with ham and bean suppers, at which the new crop of maple syrup often adds important flavoring to the beanpot. Ham and beans, in fact, continue to be the main course of choice all the way through the strawberry festivals, when luscious strawberry shortcakes replace the familiar wedges of pie for dessert. Summer is a time of salad suppers, at which the tables are filled with the bounty of a hundred kitchen gardens. And firemen are famous for putting the fire to the grill all summer, earning chicken leg by chicken leg enough money to help pay for that new pumper.

There is just as much seasonality to the occasion for potlucks—the first day of school, the beginning or end of a sports season, annual meetings, holiday get-togethers, and so on. But because potlucks are potlucks, there's no telling what the food will be. In the Old West, it was a cowboy tradition to bring raw ingredients to a potluck—a hunk of beef, a sack of beans. These offerings were dumped into a giant pot and simmered all day. At the end, everyone enjoyed the luck of the pot. Today's New England potlucks follow the tradition of the "carry-in" or "covered-dish" supper: you are expected to bring a dish already cooked and ready to serve.

Some hosts and organizers may ask for a specific contribution—a dessert or a cooked vegetable, for example—while others prefer really to "take potluck." The amazing thing is that such casual attitudes almost always prove right. Somehow, enough hot dishes come, enough salads, enough desserts—though everyone has a tale of at least one potluck where everyone brought dessert or no one brought dessert. We've even heard of one summer gathering where everyone brought potato salad!

Good cooks are by nature a generous lot; that's certainly what we found when we put out a call for recipes tried and tested at church suppers and potlucks. The cooks we've talked to seem to enjoy preparing food for a potluck or community supper as much as the diners enjoy their efforts. For one thing, it's easier to prepare one dish than a whole meal! But it's also fun to have a chance to bring in your best dish and delight in an enthusiastic response.

When Yankee Publishing had its own book division, one of the most popular cookbooks it ever published was the *Yankee Church Supper Cookbook*—a unique title featuring simple but delicious New England fare from locally famous home cooks. If church suppers were a fading tradition, or a quaint Yankee custom that survived only in the literature presented to tourists, we might have stopped with that one volume. But community suppers continue to thrive! This tradition, born of Yankee hospitality and generosity, lives on. Friends and neighbors are just as happy to gather as ever, and just as pressed for time.

The recipes in this volume reflect how New Englanders eat today. They include pesto from the garden as well as fill-you-up casseroles, fresh vegetables, lots of flavorful herbs, plenty of pasta—and an abundance of fruit and chocolate in the desserts.

We have gathered a great collection of recipes here, representing many cooking styles. Some of the recipes are masterpieces of scratch cooking, every ingredient fresh. Others rely on the convenience of cream of mushroom soup to make the sauce in a hot dish or Cool Whip to provide the perfect creamy texture in a dessert. Whatever the ingredients, the recipes fall mainly into this category: easy, affordable, family-pleasing recipes that feature readily available ingredients—no last-minute trips to the gourmet shop required.

Just as our small towns and neighborhoods in New England have become more diverse, so has our cooking. And so, the recipes in this collection include everything from a Portuguese fish stew to Greek shish kebabs to Swedish coffee breads. Of course, you'll also find traditional Yankee classics such as pot roast, baked beans, fish chowder, corn bread, apple pie, Boston cream pie, and many other regional favorites.

All the recipes were submitted by veterans of community suppers and potlucks throughout New England. The most appealing-sounding ones were tested by a team of home cooks who proved the worth of each and every recipe by feeding them to their often-finicky families. When one tester wrote, "My picky seven-year-old asked for seconds!" we realized what a break-through recipe we had on our hands. We gave vegetable recipes to a vegetable hater, and when she loved a dish, we knew we had another winner. Of course, *everyone* loved the desserts.

The recipes that passed muster with our testers were then edited to forestall any uncertainty in the kitchen, and winnowed down once again to provide as much variety as possible in the limited space available.

Along the way, we picked up plenty of tips on how to organize a potluck and how to guarantee the success of a pancake breakfast. And we couldn't resist including some of our favorite church disaster stories, too. So whether you're organizing a community pancake breakfast, planning the family supper, or simply looking for a good read, in these pages you just might find the answer to your prayers . . .

APPETIZERS

PPETIZERS at a church supper? Well, you probably won't find a special table with dips and spreads, but seek out those suppers that call themselves smorgasbords and you are likely to find everything from guacamole to zucchini bread. Smorgasbords often offer the most scrumptious eating of any church supper.

Appetizers are always welcome at potlucks, especially when you aren't certain when the main course will be put on the table. In the flurry of greeting old friends who haven't been seen since the last potluck, finger foods whet the appetite and give the hosts a chance to organize the table. Besides, as we learned from these recipes, appetizers make for truly delicious eating.

GUACAMOLE

MAKES 4 TO 6 SERVINGS

This recipe is perfect (and so simple!) just as it is, but for a little variety, try adding chopped tomato, curry powder, chili powder, or Tabasco sauce.

1 cup mashed avocado (2 medium-size avocados)

1½ teaspoons grated onion

1 teaspoon salt

1 tablespoon lemon juice

Mix together all the ingredients. Serve at once or chill in an airtight container for a few hours, then serve. Pass chips or crackers on the side.

Susan Mulford
NEWTON KINGDOM HALL
BELMONT, MASSACHUSETTS

HUMMUS

MAKES ABOUT 3 CUPS

This Middle Eastern classic is superb with warmed pita pockets cut into triangles. Or serve it as a dip with vegetables or as a spread for crackers.

2 cans (15 or 19 ounces each) chickpeas, rinsed and drained

1 small garlic clove

½ cup chopped fresh parsley

6 tablespoons lemon juice

6 tablespoons olive oil

1 teaspoon salt

¼ cup grated onion

¼ cup sesame tahini

Combine all the ingredients in a food processor and process until smooth. Let stand for at least 30 minutes before serving. Hummus can be made a few days in advance and stored in an airtight container in the refrigerator.

Susan Mulford
NEWTON KINGDOM HALL
BELMONT, MASSACHUSETTS

HERBED CHEESE SPREAD

MAKES 10 TO 12 SERVINGS (3 CUPS)

Here's a wonderful recipe for entertaining—easy to make ahead of time and always popular with guests. It is delicious served with whole-wheat or whole-grain crackers.

2 packages (8 ounces each) cream cheese, at room temperature

½ cup (1 stick) butter, at room temperature

2 garlic cloves, minced

¼ teaspoon dried dillweed

¼ teaspoon dried basil

¼ teaspoon dried marjoram

¼ teaspoon dried thyme

¼ teaspoon dried oregano

¼ teaspoon black pepper

¼ teaspoon salt

Combine all the ingredients in a food processor and process until smooth. Spoon into a crock or bowl. Serve with crackers. This spread can be frozen for up to one month.

Lucile Edwards
CHESTER HISTORICAL SOCIETY
CHESTER, NEW HAMPSHIRE

Pineapple-Cheese Ball

Makes 10 to 12 servings

When time is at a premium, this easy-to-make recipe is a perfect option. If by some chance there are leftovers, just reshape it, wrap it tightly in plastic wrap, and refrigerate it until you're ready to serve it again.

2 packages (8 ounces each) cream cheese, at room temperature

1 can (8½ ounces) crushed pineapple

¼ cup finely chopped green bell pepper

2 tablespoons finely chopped onion

2 cups chopped walnuts

In a food processor or by hand with a fork, beat the cream cheese until smooth. Mix in the pineapple, green pepper, and onion. Reserve 1 cup of the nuts and mix in the remaining 1 cup of nuts. Shape the mixture into a ball, roll it in the reserved nuts, and refrigerate until well chilled. Serve with crackers.

Peggy Willey Fogg
Thetford Academy Alumni Association
Thetford, Vermont

Potluck Pit Stops

POTLUCKS ARE MEANT to be casual, and that usually means that people end up scattered about, chatting in small groups. Set up "dining stations" around the house where you think folks might congregate (or where you *want* them to congregate). Clear off end tables, mantels, bookcases, even footstools, and place baskets of napkins, coasters, and utensils close by. That way your guests know where it's OK to assemble (and where it's not), and everything they need will be at their fingertips.

GARLICKY CREAM CHEESE DIP
MAKES 6 TO 8 SERVINGS (1 CUP)

Our tester served this at a small gathering and received rave reviews. If you're watching fat intake, try substituting a reduced-fat cream cheese in place of the regular cream cheese and skim milk in place of the half-and-half, and serve with raw vegetables rather than crackers.

3 garlic cloves, finely minced

1 package (8 ounces) cream cheese, at room temperature

2 to 3 tablespoons half-and-half or milk

1½ tablespoons finely chopped fresh chives

In a food processor or by hand with a fork, beat the garlic, cream cheese, and half-and-half until smooth. Fold in 1 tablespoon of the chives, mixing gently. Spoon into a bowl or crock and garnish with the remaining ½ tablespoon chives. Chill for 2 hours before serving with an assortment of crackers and sliced fresh vegetables.

Lea Bohrer
THE GREENFIELD GOURMET CLUB
GREENFIELD, MASSACHUSETTS

Blue Corn Chips with Goat Cheese, Corn, and Tomato Salsa

Makes 6 servings

Quick to prepare and lighter than standard nachos, this dish is especially good with corn fresh from the garden or farm stand. What makes these nachos truly stand out is the innovative use of goat cheese. If goat cheese isn't available at your supermarket, try looking in a health food store.

½ cup white corn, frozen or freshly cooked

1 cup tomato salsa (bottled or homemade)

30 blue corn chips

8 ounces creamy fresh goat cheese (such as a *fromage blanc*)

1 head lettuce, shredded

Mix the corn with the salsa. Spoon into a small serving bowl. Cover and refrigerate until serving time. Place the corn chips on a foil-lined baking sheet. Dot each chip with 1 teaspoon of goat cheese. Cover and refrigerate until serving time.

Shortly before serving, preheat the oven to 300°F. Bake the chips for 10 minutes or until the cheese is melted. Mound the shredded lettuce on a serving platter. Place the bowl of salsa in the center of the platter. Arrange the chips on the lettuce in a circular pattern.

Debbie Weisberg
Debbie Weisberg Associates
Newton Center, Massachusetts

Stuffed Mushrooms
Makes 4 to 8 servings

Who can resist a stuffed mushroom? Pass a tray of these at your next party and watch them disappear. Stuffed mushrooms are great to make ahead and reheat just before serving. Serve them as an appetizer or a side dish.

1 package (10 ounces) mushrooms
¼ cup (½ stick) butter or margarine
1 celery stalk, finely chopped
1 medium-size onion, finely chopped
¼ cup bread crumbs
¼ teaspoon salt
⅛ teaspoon pepper

Preheat the oven to 350°F. Clean the mushrooms. Remove the stems and set the caps aside. Finely chop the stems.

In a medium-size skillet, melt the butter over medium heat. Add the chopped mushroom stems, celery, and onion and sauté until the onion is limp and transparent, about 5 minutes. Stir in the bread crumbs, salt, and pepper.

Stuff the mushroom caps with the sautéed mixture and bake for 12 minutes. Or microwave at 50 percent power for 6 minutes, turn, and cook for another 6 minutes. Serve warm.

Cora LaRochelle
Auburn Group of Worcester County Extension Service
Auburn, Massachusetts

CRAB DIP

MAKES 8 TO 10 SERVINGS

Tasty and easy to prepare—even less of a hassle if you make it ahead and refrigerate or freeze it until it's needed. The contributor notes that her family, having experimented with many types of crackers, recommends Ritz as the best complement for the dip.

½ cup (1 stick) butter, at room temperature

1 package (8 ounces) cream cheese, at room temperature

2 cups grated American cheese (approximately ½ pound)

1 container (16 ounces) sour cream

1 heaping tablespoon minced dried onion

1 package (14 to 16 ounces) frozen crab meat and/or imitation crab meat

Preheat the oven to 350°F. Mix together all the ingredients in a large casserole dish. Bake, uncovered, for 45 to 60 minutes, until the mixture is bubbling and the top is browned. Stir before serving hot with crackers.

Emily Murray
FIRST UNITARIAN UNIVERSALIST CHURCH OF MILFORD
MILFORD, MASSACHUSETTS

CRAB FARCIE

MAKES 5 SERVINGS

Crab dips are always popular, and this is a very tasty one. Serve this delicious dip with crackers or thin slices of French bread.

2 tablespoons butter, melted

¾ cup dry bread crumbs

1 can (6 ounces) crab meat, drained and shredded

½ cup heavy cream

2 tablespoons fresh lemon juice

Lemon wedges, to garnish (optional)

Fresh parsley sprigs, to garnish (optional)

Preheat the oven to 350°F. Lightly butter a small baking dish.

Mix together the butter and bread crumbs. Reserve about half for the topping and combine the rest with the crab meat, cream, and lemon juice. Spoon into the baking dish, top with the reserved bread crumbs, and bake for 20 to 30 minutes, until golden. Serve hot, garnished with lemon and parsley if desired.

Adapted from a recipe submitted by Eleanor F. Cassidy
DIGHTON HISTORICAL SOCIETY, INC.
DIGHTON, MASSACHUSETTS

There is no love sincerer than the love of food.
—George Bernard Shaw, *Man and Superman* (1903)

Potluck Politeness

*A*LL POTLUCK ATTENDEES have to do is show up with a pan of brownies, eat lots of food, and head home, right? Wrong! If that's been your strategy in the past, you may be sitting at home wondering why you haven't been invited back. Here are some etiquette pointers for would-be guests:

⋆ Let the host know ahead of time if you'll need refrigerator, stovetop, or oven space.

⋆ Heat the food you're taking to serving temperature *before* you leave home. It saves time once you arrive at your destination, and it keeps the food from sitting at room temperature (and increasing the risk of spoilage) for long periods of time. You may have to reheat the dish once you arrive.

⋆ Take along any utensils you will need to serve your dish. Chances are that your host won't have enough to go around. (We heard about one potluck at which the soup had to be served with teacups.)

⋆ If your dish needs special serving or carving, be on hand to perform your duty when the time comes.

⋆ If your dish is hot, bring along a trivet to protect your host's table.

⋆ Finally, don't dash home once you're finished eating; help clean up. It's the surest way to secure a repeat invitation.

LOX I GELS (JELLIED SALMON)

MAKES 8 TO 12 SERVINGS

A Swedish dish that's terrific on a hot summer night and easily doubled for a larger crowd. Serve this as an appetizer with crackers, or place on a bed of lettuce and serve it as a salad or light luncheon dish.

2 pounds fresh salmon fillets (or more)

4 cups cold water

2¼ teaspoons salt (or less)

1 bay leaf

2 whole allspice berries

3 to 4 fresh dill sprigs

2 envelopes unflavored gelatin

6 tablespoons cold water

Hard-boiled eggs and more fresh dill, to garnish

Wipe the salmon fillets with a clean, damp cloth. Place them in a heavy saucepan with the water, salt, bay leaf, allspice, and dill. Bring to a boil and skim off any foam that forms on the surface. Reduce the heat and simmer gently for 10 to 15 minutes or until the fish flakes easily when pierced with a fork.

Carefully remove the fish from the broth. Remove any skin and bones. Flake with a fork to make uniform-size pieces. Place the salmon in a 4-cup mold.

Strain the broth through cheesecloth so the jelly will be as clear as crystal when cold. Pour 3 cups of the strained broth into a clean saucepan and bring to a boil. Dissolve the gelatin in the 6 tablespoons of cold water. Add to the heated broth. Pour over the fish and add a few sprigs of dill.

Chill in the refrigerator for several hours or overnight. When you are ready to serve, unmold onto a serving platter and garnish with sliced hard-boiled eggs and fresh dill. Serve with vinegar.

Adapted from a recipe submitted by Lorraine Jepson
GUSTAF ADOLPH LUTHERAN CHURCH
NEW SWEDEN, MAINE

ORIENTAL CHICKEN WINGS
MAKES 6 TO 8 SERVINGS (24 PIECES)

Chicken wings just disappear from the table! This recipe is quick, easy to make, and loved by adults and children alike. If your family enjoys munching on chicken wings, they will be very happy when you serve this as a main dish with rice.

12 whole chicken wings

¼ cup dark brown sugar

¼ cup soy sauce

¼ cup water

1 tablespoon Worcestershire sauce

1 tablespoon dry sherry

1 teaspoon lemon juice

1 teaspoon ground ginger

1½ teaspoons cornstarch

Remove and discard the wing tips from the chicken and cut each remaining wing in half at the joint.

In a large nonreactive bowl or zippered plastic bag, combine and mix all the remaining ingredients except the cornstarch. Add the chicken; stir to coat. Refrigerate overnight, stirring once. Drain and reserve the marinade.

Preheat the oven to 350°F. Arrange the chicken in a single layer on a greased baking sheet and bake for 20 to 25 minutes or until browned and done.

Just before serving, bring the reserved marinade to a boil and boil for 5 minutes. Combine the cornstarch with a tablespoon of cold water to make a thick paste. Add to the marinade and cook until thickened. Serve with the warm chicken as a dip.

Mildred K. Ladd
BRENTWOOD HISTORICAL SOCIETY
BRENTWOOD, NEW HAMPSHIRE

SOUPS, CHOWDERS, AND STEWS

*I*T SHOULD COME as no surprise that we were able to find plenty of wonderful recipes for warming, hearty soups and stews. New England is famous for its "nine months of winter and three months of poor sledding." On cold wintry days, there's nothing more satisfying than sitting down to a steaming bowl of soup or a hearty serving of stew. Of course, the weather does heat up in the summer, which is why we are happy to lead off with a couple of delicious chilled fruit soups.

As you might expect, you'll find plenty of good chowder recipes in this chapter, too. Fish chowder is one of those quintessential New England dishes. The word may come from the French word for the caldron (*chaudière*) into which Breton sailors threw their catch of the day, or it may come from an old Cornwall or Devonshire word, *jowter*, meaning "fish peddler." Whatever the origin, New Englanders have been making chowders since the 1730s. We think you will enjoy our selection.

BLUEBERRY-CRANBERRY SOUP

MAKES 8 SERVINGS

A great soup for an elegant summer dinner. The recipe is based on a Swedish dish for which lingonberries normally would be used. If you can find any, use them. Otherwise, cranberries make a fine American adaptation to this dish. This soup keeps very well, and leftovers are wonderful stirred into plain or vanilla yogurt.

4 cups water

3 tablespoons quick-cooking tapioca

½ cup white sugar

¼ teaspoon salt

2 sticks cinnamon, 1½ inches long

1 teaspoon grated lemon zest

⅓ cup lemon juice

1½ cups fresh or frozen unsweetened blueberries

1 can (16 ounces) whole-berry cranberry sauce

Sour cream, to garnish

In a medium-size saucepan, combine all the ingredients except the cranberry sauce and sour cream. Over medium-high heat, bring the mixture to a boil, stirring constantly; then reduce the heat and simmer, stirring constantly, for 5 minutes. Remove from the heat and stir in the cranberry sauce. Cover and refrigerate until well chilled. Serve cold, with a dollop of sour cream.

Gretchen Holm
CORNISH HISTORICAL SOCIETY
CORNISH, NEW HAMPSHIRE

Cold Strawberry Soup

MAKES 8 TO 10 SERVINGS

Cool and refreshing—this soup is a winner during strawberry season.

2 quarts fresh strawberries
1 cup white sugar
2 cups water
¼ cup fresh lemon juice
Grated zest of 1 lemon
2 cups Rhine wine

In a food processor or blender, purée the berries. Set aside.

In a small saucepan, combine the sugar and water. Boil for 10 minutes to make a sugar syrup. Cool. Add the berries to the cooled syrup. Stir in the lemon juice and zest. Chill well. Just before serving, stir in the wine.

Carolyn Muller
ST. PETER'S EPISCOPAL CHURCH
WESTON, MASSACHUSETTS

Beautiful Soup, so rich and green,
Waiting in a hot tureen!
Who for such dainties would not stoop?
Soup of the evening, beautiful Soup!
Soup of the evening, beautiful Soup!
Beau—ootiful Soo—oop!
Beau—ootiful Soo—oop!
Soo-oop of the e—e—vening,
Beautiful, beautiful Soup!

—Lewis Carroll, *Alice in Wonderland* (1865)

Fruit Root Soup
Makes 6 servings

Inspired by a traditional Finnish recipe, this soup is delicious served either as an appetizer or as a main course with a hearty dark bread and a sharp cheese.

2 tablespoons olive oil

1 medium-size onion, chopped

3 medium-size parsnips, peeled and sliced

4 to 5 medium-size carrots, sliced

1 sweet potato, peeled and sliced

1 ripe pear, peeled, cored, and chopped

2 cans (14 ounces each) chicken or vegetable broth

2 cups water

½ cup white wine or apple cider (or juice)

1 teaspoon black pepper

¼ teaspoon ground cloves

¼ teaspoon ground nutmeg

¼ teaspoon ground ginger

¼ teaspoon ground cumin

In a large saucepan or stockpot, heat the olive oil over medium-high heat. Add the onion, parsnips, carrots, sweet potato, and pear and sauté for 10 to 15 minutes. Add the broth, water, wine, and all the spices. Simmer for 20 minutes. Let cool slightly, then purée in a food processor or blender until smooth. Serve hot.

Susan Gagnon
Hopkinton Cookie Exchange
Hopkinton, New Hampshire

VEGETABLE CHOWDER
MAKES 6 TO 8 SERVINGS

An absolutely terrific chowder made with vegetables and cheese and flavored with tomatoes. Served with a salad and a loaf of hot, crusty bread, this makes a very complete winter dinner—and a great alternative for those who don't eat meat.

2 cups diced and peeled potatoes

1 cup diced celery

1 onion, finely diced (or 1 tablespoon dried onion)

2 teaspoons salt

3 cups water

¼ cup (½ stick) butter or margarine

¼ cup all-purpose white flour

1 teaspoon dry mustard

3 cups milk

1 tablespoon steak sauce

4 slices American cheese, diced

1 can (28 ounces) tomatoes, chopped

Pepper to taste

In a large saucepan or stockpot, combine the potatoes, celery, onion, salt, and water. Cover and bring to a boil; then reduce the heat and simmer until the potatoes are tender, about 15 minutes.

In another saucepan, melt the butter over medium heat. Add the flour and mustard and mix them into the butter to form a paste. Stir in the milk and steak sauce and blend until smooth. Stir in the cheese and continue stirring until the cheese is completely melted. Then add this mixture to the vegetables. Add the tomatoes and pepper and heat through; do not allow the soup to boil. Serve hot.

Marguerite R. Curtiss
WOMEN OF THE MOOSE (LOYAL ORDER OF MOOSE)
KEENE, NEW HAMPSHIRE

THE WELL-PREPARED HOST

*W*HAT EXACTLY is the potluck host responsible for? It can vary from dinner to dinner, but here are some general guidelines:

Utensils. Guests ought to bring their own serving tools, but the host should provide eating utensils. Plastic is handy, but it's not very sturdy (or environmentally friendly).

Pots and pans, oven and burner space. For those who need to reheat food.

Refrigerator and freezer space. For beverages, salads, ice cream—the usual.

Plates and napkins. If you are a frequent potluck host, you may want to purchase a set of heavy plastic picnic ware. It's colorful and it saves wear and tear on your good china. And fabric napkins are less expensive than paper ones in the long run, as well as kinder to the environment.

Condiments. Salt, pepper, ketchup, mustard, mayonnaise, salsa, and so on.

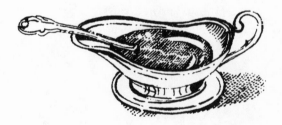

Zucchini-Potato Soup

MAKES 8 SERVINGS

Very different, very flavorful, and very good—a big hit even with those who aren't normally fond of soups. Be sure to follow the directions carefully when adding the eggs and lemon juice; otherwise the mixture is likely to curdle.

5 cups chicken broth

1 pound zucchini (4 small), thinly sliced

1 large potato, thinly sliced

1 large onion, thinly sliced

3 eggs

2 tablespoons lemon juice

Salt and pepper to taste

In a large saucepan, bring the broth to a boil. Add the zucchini, potato, and onion. Reduce the heat and simmer, covered, for 15 minutes.

In a small bowl, beat the eggs. Add the lemon juice and ½ cup of the broth. Stir into the soup. Increase the heat to medium and heat for 1 minute, stirring constantly; do not boil. Season to taste with salt and pepper and serve immediately.

Cora LaRochelle

AUBURN GROUP OF WORCESTER COUNTY EXTENSION SERVICE
AUBURN, MASSACHUSETTS

CREAM OF BROCCOLI SOUP
MAKES 8 TO 10 SERVINGS

For once, a vegetable soup that's not puréed! This one has plenty of flavor and plenty of texture, and it makes a wonderful lunch when served with an herb bread and a fruit dessert. If you prefer an even stronger flavor, try substituting a sharper variety for all or part of the cheese.

6 cups water

10 ounces fresh or frozen chopped broccoli

¾ cup finely chopped onion

2 cups shredded American cheese

2 teaspoons salt

2 teaspoons white pepper

1 teaspoon garlic powder

1 cup milk

1 cup light cream

¼ cup butter

½ cup cold water

⅓ cup all-purpose white flour

In a large saucepan, bring the water to a boil. Add the broccoli and onion; boil for 10 to 12 minutes. Add the cheese, salt, pepper, and garlic powder. Cook over medium heat, stirring constantly, until the cheese melts. Add the milk, cream, and butter. Heat to boiling, stirring constantly.

Add the water to the flour and mix until smooth. Add slowly to the hot soup, stirring rapidly. Continue to cook, stirring constantly, until the soup is the consistency of heavy cream. Serve hot.

Natalie Marko
NEW ENGLAND HISTORIC GENEALOGICAL SOCIETY
BOSTON, MASSACHUSETTS

DORSET BLACK BEAN SOUP
MAKES 8 TO 10 SERVINGS

A good soup that's low in fat. Great with a glass of red zinfandel and a fresh baguette.

1 pound dry black beans

Water

6 cups defatted chicken, vegetable, or ham broth

1 bay leaf

1 large or 2 medium-size onions, chopped

1 celery stalk, including leaves, chopped

2 green bell peppers, chopped

1 large tomato, peeled and chopped

1 to 3 garlic cloves, minced

6 serrano chili peppers (or to taste)

1 can (6 ounces) tomato paste

¼ teaspoon hot pepper sauce

¼ teaspoon black pepper

2 tablespoons Worcestershire sauce

Lemon slices, to garnish

Wash the beans. Combine with water to cover in a large saucepan or stockpot and soak overnight.

The next morning, drain the beans. Combine the beans with 2 cups water, the broth, and the bay leaf. Bring to a boil; then reduce the heat and simmer for 1½ hours. Add the remaining ingredients, except the lemon slices, and simmer for 2 hours.

Remove the bay leaf. Blend the soup in a blender for a smooth soup or mash the beans with a potato masher for a chunky soup. Serve hot, garnishing each bowl with a slice of lemon.

Peggy Gilbert
DORSET HISTORICAL SOCIETY
DORSET, VERMONT

EASY BLACK BEAN SOUP

MAKES 6 TO 8 SERVINGS

This is a great soup—zesty, flavorful, and not too "beany." Because it is prepared with canned beans, it is very quickly made. Serve it with sourdough bread for a hearty lunch or supper.

1 tablespoon olive oil

1 cup chopped onion

2 to 4 large garlic cloves, minced

2 cans (16 ounces each) peeled tomatoes, with liquid

2 cans (15 ounces each) black beans, drained and rinsed

1½ cups canned or homemade chicken broth

2 teaspoons ground cumin

¼ cup thinly sliced scallions, to garnish

½ cup chopped tomatoes, to garnish

½ cup sour cream, to garnish

In a medium-size saucepan, heat the oil over medium heat. Add the onion and garlic and sauté for 5 minutes, until the onion is tender.

In a blender or food processor, combine the tomatoes with liquid and three-quarters of the beans. Process until smooth. Add to the sautéed onion along with the remaining black beans, broth, and cumin. Cook over low heat for about 15 minutes, stirring occasionally.

Serve the soup hot, topping each bowl with a sprinkling of scallions and chopped tomatoes and a dollop of sour cream.

Lea Bohrer
THE GREENFIELD GOURMET CLUB
GREENFIELD, MASSACHUSETTS

13-BEAN GOOD-LUCK SOUP
MAKES 8 TO 10 SERVINGS

The parishioners of the Church of the Epiphany in Southbury, Connecticut, routinely package the dried (bean) part of this recipe in 2-cup plastic-bag portions and sell it at church activities—along with the recipe, of course. This is a very good soup that's also very simple to make, and it can easily be doubled and frozen. Feel free to experiment with different combinations of beans, but the folks in Southbury recommend always including black-eyed peas for good luck.

2 cups mixed dried beans (including black-eyed peas)

Water

2 tablespoons salt

1½ cups bite-size pieces lean baked ham (about ½ pound) or 1-pound meaty ham bone or ham hock

2 large onions, sliced

2 cups chopped celery

1 can (28 ounces) tomatoes, chopped

1 red bell pepper, chopped

Salt and pepper to taste

Wash the beans. Cover with water; add 2 tablespoons salt. Soak overnight.

The next day, drain the beans and combine with 2 quarts water in a large saucepan or stockpot. Add the ham and boil for 1½ to 3 hours, or until the beans are fully cooked and tender. Add the onions, celery, tomatoes, red pepper, and salt and pepper to taste. Simmer for at least 30 minutes, until the vegetables are cooked. Serve hot.

Dorothy Johnson
CHURCH OF THE EPIPHANY
SOUTHBURY, CONNECTICUT

Solianka (Fish Soup)

Makes 6 to 8 servings

Our testers absolutely raved about this! Because it can be served either slightly warm or piping hot, it's great for guests at any time of year.

1 cup chopped onions

1 bay leaf

2 to 3 sprigs fresh parsley

3 teaspoons salt

6 cups water

2½ pounds salmon steaks (or substitute halibut or haddock)

4 to 6 tablespoons (½ to ¾ stick) butter

1 to 2 cups chopped onions

2 medium-size cucumbers, peeled, halved, seeded, and chopped into ½-inch cubes

4 tomatoes, peeled, seeded, and coarsely chopped

1 quart clam juice or other fish broth

½ teaspoon white pepper

2 tablespoons chopped black olives, rinsed

2 tablespoons chopped fresh parsley, fennel, or cilantro

20 pitted black olives

1 lemon, thinly sliced

In a large saucepan or stockpot, combine the 1 cup chopped onions, bay leaf, parsley, salt, and water. Cover and bring to a boil over high heat. Add the fish. Reduce the heat and simmer, uncovered, for about 6 minutes, or until the fish is firm to the touch. Remove the fish and cut into 1-inch chunks. Strain the broth through a fine sieve, pressing down on the onions to extract all the juice. Set aside.

Wipe out the saucepan and melt the butter in the pan. Add the 1 to 2 cups chopped onions and sauté until the onions are soft but not brown, about 5 minutes. Then add the cucumbers and tomatoes and simmer for about 10 minutes. Add the reserved fish broth and 1 quart clam broth or other fish broth, along with the remaining ingredients. Simmer for about 15 minutes. Then add the fish and continue simmering until the fish is warmed through. Serve hot or warm.

B. W. Amaral, M.D.
Boscawen Historical Society
Boscawen, New Hampshire

CREAMY TUNA-POTATO SOUP
MAKES 6 TO 8 SERVINGS

Even our doubting tester discovered that this simple recipe produced great results. A terrific emergency supper on a night when you're snowbound or you've just run out of time to get to the store. And since the leftover soup is quite thick, it's great served over toast points for a quick lunch.

1 tablespoon margarine or butter

¼ cup chopped scallions, diced onions, or snipped chives

2½ cups grated raw potatoes or frozen hash browns

3 cups chicken stock or broth

1 can (13 ounces) evaporated milk

2 cans (6 ounces each) tuna, drained

1 teaspoon dried dillweed

½ teaspoon fresh-ground pepper

Salt to taste

Melt the butter in a large saucepan. Add the scallions and sauté until limp, about 3 minutes. Add the potatoes and broth. Bring to a boil and cook until the potatoes are tender, about 5 minutes. Stir in the remaining ingredients and heat through. Serve hot.

Dijit Taylor
HOPKINTON CONGREGATIONAL CHURCH
HOPKINTON, NEW HAMPSHIRE

༺ఓఓ༻

Whoever tells a lie cannot be pure in heart—and only the pure of heart can make a good soup.
—Ludwig van Beethoven, 19th-century composer

༺ఓఓ༻

Baked Fish Chowder

Makes 4 to 6 servings

An outstanding recipe for chowder that's quick to make and very easy because it's all made in the oven. There's no standing over a hot stove for this one. Thumbs up!

1 pound haddock or cod, cut in bite-size pieces

1 pound scallops

3 cups diced peeled potatoes or 8 small unpeeled red potatoes, diced

1 medium-size onion, sliced

¼ cup white wine

2 cups water

¼ cup (½ stick) butter

¼ cup all-purpose white flour

2 cups light cream or milk

Salt, pepper, and garlic powder to taste

Preheat the oven to 350°F.

In a 9-inch by 13-inch pan, combine the fish, scallops, potatoes, onion, wine, and water. Cover with aluminum foil and bake for 30 minutes.

Melt the butter in a medium-size saucepan over medium heat. Stir in the flour to make a paste. Add the cream or milk and stir until thickened. Add to the baking pan along with the salt, pepper, and garlic powder. Cover and continue baking for another 30 minutes. Stir well before serving.

Adapted from a recipe submitted by Vera Shinner
Women's Alliance, First Parish Congregation Unitarian Church
Kennebunk, Maine

Seafood Chowder

MAKES 6 TO 8 SERVINGS

The folks at Emmanuel Church report that they serve this chowder often at "polishing parties"—it's a very good chowder that fortifies the parishioners for polishing the altar brass.

3 slices bacon

1 onion, chopped

4 to 5 medium-size potatoes, peeled and diced

1 teaspoon salt

Water

¾ pound haddock or other firm white fish or 8 to 10 ounces imitation crab meat, cut in bite-size pieces

2 cans (6½ ounces each) tiny shrimp, drained and rinsed

2 cans (6½ ounces each) chopped clams

2 cans (12 ounces each) evaporated milk

1 teaspoon dried basil

1 teaspoon dried thyme

1 tablespoon chopped fresh parsley

Salt and pepper to taste

In a large saucepan, fry the bacon. Remove the bacon from the pan, pat dry, crumble, and set aside. Drain off all but 1 tablespoon of the bacon fat. Add the onion and sauté over medium heat until the onion is limp, about 5 minutes. Add the potatoes, salt, and water to cover. Cover and bring to a boil; boil for 5 minutes. Then add the fish and simmer for 5 minutes. Add the remaining ingredients and bring just to a boil. Remove from the heat. Add the crumbled bacon and serve hot.

Adapted from a recipe submitted by Norma C. Greene
EMMANUEL CHURCH
NEWPORT, RHODE ISLAND

Harvest Salmon Chowder
Makes 4 to 6 servings

Pretty in color, rich, thick, and flavorful. A great way to make use of the late summer harvest.

3 tablespoons butter

½ cup chopped onion

½ cup chopped celery

¼ cup chopped green bell pepper

3 garlic cloves, minced

1 cup peeled and diced potatoes

1 cup diced carrots

2 cups chicken broth or stock

1½ teaspoons salt

¾ teaspoon pepper

½ teaspoon dill seed

½ cup diced zucchini

½ cup diced yellow squash

1 can (15 ounces) salmon

1 can (12 ounces) evaporated milk

1 can (7 ounces) creamed corn

In a large saucepan or stockpot, melt the butter over medium-high heat. Add the onion, celery, green pepper, and garlic and sauté until translucent, about 5 minutes. Add the potatoes, carrots, broth, salt, pepper, and dill seed. Cover and simmer for 20 minutes. Add the zucchini and yellow squash and simmer for 5 minutes. Flake the salmon and add to the pot along with its liquid, the milk, and the corn. Heat through before serving.

Marianne Metcalf
St. Thomas Becket Church
Cheshire, Connecticut

Portuguese Fish Stew
Makes 6 to 8 servings

The contributor obtained this recipe from her husband's grandmother, Ermelinda Amaral. She in turn got it from her mother, Anna Pacheco, who was a caterer in São Miguel, Azores. Anna was a widow who supported a family of twelve and eventually managed to send all of them to the United States—bringing the final three, including Ermelinda, to Martha's Vineyard in 1889. The stew has an exotically sweet, spicy flavor. Serve it over rice, or add 2 cups of fish broth and present it as a soup with crusty rolls.

2 tablespoons olive oil

3 to 4 medium-size onions, finely chopped

2 to 3 pounds firm white fish, such as pollock or cod, cubed

1 cup peeled and deveined shrimp (optional)

1 cup scallops (optional)

1 cup chopped clams (optional)

1 can (28 ounces) crushed tomatoes

½ cup red wine

1 teaspoon salt

1 teaspoon freshly ground black pepper

1 teaspoon chopped fresh tarragon

1 teaspoon chopped fresh parsley

1 teaspoon dried dillweed

1 teaspoon crushed red pepper

1 tablespoon white sugar

2 teaspoons ground cinnamon

In a large saucepan or nonreactive Dutch oven, heat the olive oil over medium-high heat. Add the onions and sauté until soft, about 5 minutes. Reduce the heat to medium-low. Add the fish and other seafood, if using. Stir in the remaining ingredients. Cover and cook for about 1 hour. Taste and adjust the seasoning.

B. W. Amaral, M.D.
Boscawen Historical Society
Boscawen, New Hampshire

MULLIGATAWNY SOUP
MAKES 6 SERVINGS

This is an Indian soup adopted by the English and imported to Massachusetts by the contributor's husband. It's very easy to make, and the finished product made a big hit with our testers. Consider serving the soup over a bowl of rice for extra heartiness.

2 tablespoons butter

1 medium-size onion, sliced

1 medium-size carrot, diced

1 celery stalk, diced

1 green bell pepper, seeded and diced

1 medium-size apple, peeled and sliced

1 cup diced cooked chicken

⅓ cup all-purpose white flour

1 teaspoon curry powder

⅛ teaspoon ground mace

2 whole cloves

1 sprig fresh parsley

2 cups chicken stock or broth

1 cup chopped cooked or canned tomatoes

Salt and pepper to taste

Melt the butter in a large saucepan or stockpot over medium heat. Add the onion, carrot, celery, green pepper, apple, and chicken and sauté until the onion is tender. Gradually stir in the flour and curry powder. Then add the remaining ingredients and simmer, covered, for 30 minutes. Serve hot.

Natalie Marko
NEW ENGLAND HISTORIC GENEALOGICAL SOCIETY
BOSTON, MASSACHUSETTS

Peel-a-Pound Soup
Makes 6 to 8 servings

We love the old-fashioned name of this soup as much as we love the good old-fashioned flavor. It's a perfect way to use up leftover Thanksgiving turkey and eat some good-for-you vegetables.

½ to 1 pound green cabbage, cut in bite-size pieces

1 green bell pepper, chopped

2 celery stalks, chopped

2 medium-size onions, chopped

1 can (16 ounces) tomatoes, with liquid, chopped

3 bouillon cubes

1 teaspoon celery seeds

1 teaspoon dried basil

2 teaspoons dried oregano

½ teaspoon garlic powder

2 or more quarts water

Salt and pepper to taste

2 cups diced cooked turkey or beef

Combine all the ingredients in a large saucepan or stockpot, adding enough water to completely cover the vegetables. Bring to a boil, then reduce the heat and simmer for about 1 hour. Serve hot.

Ruth Southwick
Willington Baptist Church
Willington, Connecticut

STAY-A-BED SOUP

MAKES 6 TO 8 SERVINGS

A whimsical name for a delicious, easy-to-make soup. And it really is well named—once all of the chopping is done, you can leave this soup unattended for hours.

1 to 2 pounds stew beef (or substitute boned, skinless chicken breast, cut in bite-size pieces)

1 bay leaf

2 cups fresh, frozen, or canned peas

1 cup sliced carrots

2 onions, chopped

1 teaspoon salt

Pepper to taste

1 can (10¾ ounces) condensed Golden Mushroom Soup plus ½ can water

2 to 3 potatoes, sliced

Preheat the oven to 275°F. Combine all the ingredients in a roasting pan and bake for about 5 hours. Serve hot.

Ruth Southwick
WILLINGTON BAPTIST CHURCH
WILLINGTON, CONNECTICUT

⁓✧⁓

Of Soup and Love, the first is best.
—Thomas Fuller, *Gnomologia* (1732)

⁓✧⁓

Main Dish Minestrone

Makes 6 to 8 servings

A flavorful soup, made mostly from ingredients that are already on the kitchen shelf. Serve with a fresh, crusty bread for a hearty meal.

1 tablespoon olive oil

½ pound sweet or hot Italian sausage, crumbled

1 large onion, chopped

1 garlic clove, minced

½ cup chopped celery

½ cup chopped carrot

½ cup chopped green bell pepper

1 can (16 ounces) whole tomatoes

4 cups chicken stock or broth

2 cups shredded cabbage

2 tablespoons chopped fresh parsley

½ teaspoon dried basil

1 bay leaf

Pinch dried thyme

½ cup uncooked elbow macaroni

1 cup cooked kidney beans

Freshly grated Parmesan cheese (optional)

In a large saucepan or stockpot, heat the oil. Add the sausage and cook until browned. Drain off all but 1 tablespoon of the fat. Add the onion, garlic, celery, carrot, and green pepper and sauté until the vegetables are soft, about 5 minutes. Add the tomatoes with their liquid, chicken stock, cabbage, and herbs. Bring to a boil, cover, and simmer for 30 minutes. Add the macaroni and beans and cook until the macaroni is tender, about 30 minutes. Remove the bay leaf before serving. Sprinkle each serving with Parmesan cheese, if desired.

Adapted from a recipe submitted by Jean Caird
St. Brendan's Catholic Woman's Club
Colebrook, New Hampshire

SWEDISH CABBAGE SOUP WITH MEATBALLS
MAKES 6 TO 8 SERVINGS

In New Sweden, Maine, they call this Kol-Soppa och Frikadellar. *Whatever you call it, it's a good hot soup that warms the bones and soothes the soul. This authentic version begins with making soup stock from lamb. However, you can take a shortcut with canned beef stock and have a wonderful soup that's ready in 30 minutes. For a heartier variation, add 1 cup fine egg noodles 5 minutes before serving. Serve the soup piping hot, accompanied by Swedish rye bread.*

2 to 4 pounds lamb stew meat or lamb flank

Water

1 celery stalk, including leaves, cut in chunks

1 carrot, cut in chunks

Salt and whole peppercorns to taste

A few allspice berries

1 large green cabbage, cut into bite-size pieces

1 pound ground chuck

1 egg

½ small onion, finely chopped

1 teaspoon salt (or less)

¼ teaspoon pepper

In a large saucepan or stockpot, cover the lamb with cold water. Add the celery and carrot. Bring to a boil and simmer for about 4 hours, removing any foam that forms at the top. Remove the meat and reserve for hash or some other use. Refrigerate the broth overnight to allow the fat to harden and rise to the surface.

The next day, skim off the fat from the broth. Add salt and peppercorns to taste along with the allspice berries and cabbage. Cover and simmer on low heat for 15 minutes.

To make the meatballs, combine the ground chuck, egg, onion, salt, and pepper. Form into very small balls. Bring the soup to a boil and drop the meatballs one by one into the boiling soup. Cover and simmer for another 15 to 20 minutes. Serve very hot with Swedish rye bread.

Lorraine Jepson
GUSTAF ADOLPH LUTHERAN CHURCH
NEW SWEDEN, MAINE

Shepherd's Stew

Makes 6 servings

Quick and easy to prepare—and very good, too.

1 pound sweet or hot Italian sausage, sliced

1 large onion, chopped

6 potatoes, peeled and diced

1 cup sliced celery, including leaves

2 cans (16 ounces each) whole tomatoes

¼ cup chopped fresh parsley

1½ cups beef broth or stock (or 2 beef bouillon cubes dissolved in 1⅓ cups water)

1 bay leaf

½ teaspoon dried thyme

¼ teaspoon pepper

Juice of ½ lemon (optional)

Salt to taste

In a large saucepan or nonreactive Dutch oven, brown the sausage over medium heat. Add the onion and sauté until transparent, about 5 minutes. Add the remaining ingredients and bring to a boil. Reduce the heat and simmer, uncovered, for 45 to 60 minutes, or until the potatoes are tender. Remove the bay leaf before serving. Serve hot.

Priscilla Geer

Handel Society, Dartmouth College Department of Music
Hanover, New Hampshire

CHUCKIE'S TORTELLINI AND SAUSAGE STEW
MAKES 6 TO 8 SERVINGS

An outstanding stew that's perfect for those nights when every member of the family needs to eat at a different time—it makes a lot, can be reheated over and over, and gets even better each time. The contributor says she got the recipe from a friend, Chuckie, "who learned in his bachelor days how to impress the ladies with a few culinary delights handed down from his mom." Anyone who wants to make an impression on a member of the opposite sex should have a few recipes as good as this one.

1 pound sweet or hot Italian sausage (turkey sausage may be used)

1 cup chopped onion

4 garlic cloves, minced

10 cups beef broth or stock

½ cup water

1 cup dry red wine

2 cans (28 ounces each) peeled tomatoes, chopped

1 can (8 ounces) tomato sauce

1 cup thinly sliced carrots

1½ teaspoons dried oregano

1½ teaspoons dried basil

2 small zucchini, sliced

1 green bell pepper, chopped

2 cups dry tortellini pasta

3 tablespoons dried parsley

Remove the casings from the sausage and cut into bite-size pieces. Brown the sausage in a large saucepan or nonreactive Dutch oven. Remove the sausage with a slotted spoon and set aside. Drain off all but 1 tablespoon of the fat.

Add the onion and garlic to the saucepan and sauté over medium-low heat until soft and translucent, about 5 minutes. Return the sausage to the pot along with the broth, water, wine, tomatoes, tomato sauce, carrots, oregano, and basil. Bring to a boil, then reduce the heat and simmer, uncovered, for 30 minutes.

Skim off any fat that rises to the top of the pot. Stir in the zucchini, green pepper, tortellini, and parsley. Simmer, covered, for 45 minutes or until the pasta and vegetables are tender.

Dianne R. Duncan
WALPOLE HISTORICAL SOCIETY
WALPOLE, NEW HAMPSHIRE

ENGLISH BROWN STEW
MAKES 6 TO 8 SERVINGS

This stew has a touch of sweetness and is not too spicy for young palates, but grownups love it, too. Served with dumplings, muffins, or homemade bread, it's delicious on a cold winter evening.

2 pounds London broil, cubed

2 large onions, diced

2 large potatoes, peeled and diced

3 carrots, diced

3 to 4 stalks celery, chopped

2 garlic cloves, minced

1 cup tomato juice or 1 tablespoon tomato paste

1 tablespoon Worcestershire sauce

2 tablespoons lemon juice

2 tablespoons white sugar

1 tablespoon ground allspice

1 tablespoon mild paprika

3 tablespoons beef fat or 2 tablespoons vegetable oil

3 tablespoons all-purpose white flour

Salt and pepper to taste

Put the meat in a large saucepan or nonreactive Dutch oven and cover with water. Bring to a boil, then reduce the heat to a simmer, skimming off any foam that rises to the top. When the broth is clear, add the vegetables, tomato juice, Worcestershire sauce, lemon juice, sugar, allspice, paprika, and more water if needed to cover the meat. Simmer until the vegetables are done and the meat is tender, about 2 hours.

In a small saucepan, heat the beef fat or oil. Stir in the flour until you have a smooth paste and cook, stirring constantly, for 1 to 2 minutes. Remove ½ to 1 cup of the broth from the stew and stir into the flour mixture until you have a thick gravy.

Then pour the gravy into the stew. Add salt and pepper and correct the seasonings. Serve hot.

Lucile Edwards
CHESTER HISTORICAL SOCIETY
CHESTER, NEW HAMPSHIRE

SURF AND BARNYARD STEW
MAKES 4 SERVINGS

A quick and easy one-pot dinner that's relatively low in fat. For an interesting variation, try substituting venison sausage for the turkey sausage. Either way, this rich dish is a real winner.

1½ tablespoons vegetable oil

1 cup finely chopped onions

1½ cups chopped green bell pepper

3 garlic cloves, minced

1 cup rice

½ cup chicken broth or stock

1 can (16 ounces) diced tomatoes

2 tablespoons tomato paste

½ teaspoon salt

¼ teaspoon pepper

1 bay leaf

½ teaspoon crushed Italian seasoning

½ teaspoon chili powder and/or a few drops Tabasco sauce (optional)

½ pound smoked turkey sausage (Polish kielbasa), peeled, halved, and sliced ½ inch thick

¾ pound cooked, peeled shrimp

In a large saucepan or nonreactive Dutch oven, heat the oil over medium heat. Add the onions, green pepper, garlic, and rice and sauté until the onions are soft and the rice looks dry and translucent, about 5 minutes. Add the broth, tomatoes, tomato paste, and seasonings. Bring to a boil, then reduce the heat and simmer for 15 minutes, until the rice is cooked. Add the sausage and return to a boil; then reduce the heat and simmer for 7 to 8 minutes. Stir in the shrimp and cook long enough to heat through. Remove the bay leaf and serve.

Adapted from a recipe submitted by Marcia Cassin
WOMAN'S CLUB OF CONCORD
CONCORD, NEW HAMPSHIRE

SALADS AND DRESSINGS

S ALAD SUPPERS are a fairly recent development in the history
of church suppers, but they are gaining in popularity, especially in summer, when many kitchen gardens are bursting
with tempting fresh vegetables. Summers can be hot in this part of
the country, and no one feels like spending hours in the kitchen
when the temperature and humidity levels soar sky-high. For that
matter, at the end of a hot day, most people are interested in eating
light, cool foods, like these salads.

In this chapter, you'll find a lovely low-fat version of the familiar spinach salad as well as an absolutely delightful spinach and
strawberry salad. We have pasta salads and three very different
potato salads, including a deliciously sophisticated one that starts
with roasted potatoes. And, of course, we have a couple of those
ever-popular gelatin salads, which always look so pretty on a buffet
table. In short, we have assembled in this chapter a mix of traditional and innovative recipes that reflect that state of culinary art in
New England today.

SPINACH-STRAWBERRY SALAD
MAKES 4 TO 6 SERVINGS

Not your usual spinach salad, but a winning combination of strawberries and spinach tossed with a crunchy sweet-sour poppy-seed dressing. This goes over big, even with those who aren't usually tossed-salad fans. It's bright and pretty, too—perfect for a quick lunch or supper, or for a small party.

½ cup white sugar

2 tablespoons sesame seeds

1 tablespoon poppy seeds

1½ teaspoons minced onion

¼ teaspoon Worcestershire sauce

¼ teaspoon paprika

½ cup vegetable oil

¼ cup cider vinegar

1 bag (10 ounces) fresh spinach

1 pint strawberries, sliced thin

In a blender, combine the sugar, sesame seeds, poppy seeds, onion, Worcestershire sauce, paprika, oil, and vinegar. Blend well. If the dressing seems thick, add a few drops of water.

Remove the stems from the spinach and tear the leaves into bite-size pieces. Arrange them on individual salad plates or in a salad bowl. Arrange the strawberries on top. Drizzle the dressing over the strawberries and serve.

FLORENCE GRISWOLD MUSEUM
LYME HISTORICAL SOCIETY
OLD LYME, CONNECTICUT

MARY'S SPINACH SALAD
MAKES 4 TO 6 SERVINGS

Here's a delightful twist on the familiar spinach salad. It's made with a non-fat tomato-based dressing that complements the salad quite well and looks very appealing on the buffet table. Both the salad and the dressing can be made in advance and then tossed together right before serving.

SALAD

1 pound spinach

½ onion, thinly sliced

1 carrot, grated

2 hard-boiled eggs, quartered

5 slices bacon, fried crisp and crumbled

1 to 1½ cups croutons

DRESSING

½ cup honey

¼ cup water

¼ cup cider vinegar

¼ cup ketchup

2 tablespoons minced onion

1 teaspoon Worcestershire sauce

Wash the spinach and drain well. Tear into bite-size pieces. Combine with remaining salad ingredients. Combine the dressing ingredients in a jar and shake well. Just before serving, pour the dressing over the salad and toss to mix.

Mary Gagnon
ST. ISAAC JOGUES CHURCH
EAST HARTFORD, CONNECTICUT

Apple-Almond Salad

Makes 8 servings

We thought this light, refreshing salad made a terrific accompaniment for pork. Cortland apples hold their color best in the salad, but any tart, firm variety will do.

¼ cup salad oil

2 tablespoons white sugar

2 tablespoons malt or cider vinegar

¼ teaspoon salt

⅛ teaspoon almond extract

6 cups torn mixed greens

3 medium-size apples, cut into wedges

1 cup thinly sliced celery

2 tablespoons sliced scallions

⅓ cup slivered almonds, toasted

In a screw-top jar, combine the oil, sugar, vinegar, salt, and almond extract. Cover the jar and shake well until the sugar and salt are dissolved. Chill in the refrigerator for several hours.

Just before serving, combine the greens, apple wedges, celery, and scallions in a salad bowl. Sprinkle with the almonds. Pour the dressing over the salad and toss. Serve immediately.

Alice Veraguth
East Dover Baptist Church
East Dover, Vermont

SEVEN-LAYER SALAD

MAKES 10 TO 12 SERVINGS

You'll find this attractive salad on buffet tables throughout New England. It looks just great when you assemble it in a clear glass bowl. This is a salad that must be made about 8 hours before serving, which makes it very convenient for church suppers and potlucks when you don't have time for a lot of last-minute preparations.

1 head lettuce, torn in bite-size pieces

1 cup diced green bell pepper

1 cup chopped celery

1 cup diced onion

1 package (10 ounces) frozen peas, thawed

2 cups mayonnaise (low-fat mayonnaise can be used)

1 tablespoon white sugar

6 slices bacon, fried crisp and crumbled

¾ cup grated Cheddar cheese

Place the lettuce in the bottom of a clear salad bowl. On top of the lettuce, layer the pepper, celery, onion, and peas in that order. Spoon the mayonnaise over the top to cover and seal the vegetables. Sprinkle the sugar, bacon, and cheese on top. Cover tightly with plastic wrap and refrigerate for 8 hours before serving.

Ruth L. Walker
FRIENDS OF THE DOVER PUBLIC LIBRARY
DOVER, NEW HAMPSHIRE

BROCCOLI SALAD

MAKES 6 TO 8 SERVINGS

Tired of the same old spinach salad? Here's a delicious alternative made with good-for-you broccoli. It incorporates the same flavors as the standard spinach salad, but it can be made up to a day in advance and won't wilt on the buffet table.

4 cups broccoli florets

4 hard-boiled eggs, thinly sliced

½ cup (or more) thinly sliced onion

10 slices bacon, fried crisp and crumbled

1 cup mayonnaise

¼ cup white sugar

3 tablespoons vinegar

Blanch the broccoli in boiling water to cover for 30 seconds. Remove the broccoli from the water and plunge it into ice water to stop the cooking. Drain well.

In a large bowl, combine the broccoli, eggs, onion, and bacon. In a small bowl, mix together the mayonnaise, sugar, and vinegar, whisking until the sugar is dissolved. Pour over the broccoli and mix gently. Refrigerate for 6 hours or overnight before serving. Just before serving, toss lightly.

Gladys Anderson
WILLINGTON BAPTIST CHURCH
WILLINGTON, CONNECTICUT

PENNY CARROT SALAD
MAKES 10 TO 12 SERVINGS

Carrots in a sweet-and-sour tomato dressing make a tasty salad that's easy to prepare. Perfect for a potluck because it's made ahead and holds up well on a buffet table, it's also good for bringing to a hot-weather picnic.

2 pounds carrots, peeled and sliced (about 6 cups)

1 red onion, thinly sliced

1 green bell pepper, cut in strips

1 can (8 ounces) tomato sauce

½ cup white sugar

½ cup wine vinegar

½ cup olive oil

½ teaspoon pepper

1 teaspoon salt

1 teaspoon dry mustard

Blanch the carrots in boiling water to cover for about 30 seconds. Plunge into ice water to stop the cooking. Drain well. In a large bowl, combine the carrots with the onion and green pepper.

In a separate bowl or in a blender, combine the remaining ingredients to make the dressing. Mix until well blended. Pour over the carrot mixture. Toss to mix well. Cover and chill before serving.

Adapted from a recipe submitted by Jane Golec
HARWINTON LIBRARY FRIENDS
HARWINTON, CONNECTICUT

Carrots with Dill Dressing

MAKES 4 TO 6 SERVINGS

Carrots and dill are a winning combination, but you can substitute tarragon if you prefer. This salad makes a wonderful accompaniment for hot or cold poultry dishes.

5 to 6 medium-size carrots, thinly sliced or julienned

½ medium-size onion, peeled and finely chopped

1 teaspoon finely chopped fresh dill or 1 tablespoon chopped fresh tarragon

¼ teaspoon freshly ground black pepper

½ teaspoon white sugar

¾ teaspoon salt

2 tablespoons peanut or corn oil

1 tablespoon red or white vinegar

Blanch the carrots in boiling water to cover for about 30 seconds. Plunge them into ice water to stop the cooking. Drain well. In a large mixing bowl, combine the carrots with the remaining ingredients. Chill well before serving.

Mary Gagnon
St. Isaac Jogues Church
East Hartford, Connecticut

LEA'S INDIAN SALAD
MAKES 4 SERVINGS

Serve this delicious yogurt-dressed vegetable combo as a salad or a mouth-cooling condiment with spicy food. We think it is terrific with highly spiced grilled chicken. The cumin adds an exotic flavor, but dill works a different, equally appealing magic. You can easily multiply this recipe to feed a crowd.

1 cucumber, peeled, seeded, and cubed

1 large ripe tomato, cubed

1 green bell pepper, cubed

1 celery stalk, cubed

½ to 1 cup plain low-fat yogurt

⅔ cup raw cashew nuts

1 teaspoon ground cumin (or more to taste)

Combine all of the vegetables in a medium-size bowl. Add the yogurt, cashews, and cumin and mix gently. Chill in the refrigerator for at least 1 hour before serving.

Lea Bohrer
THE GREENFIELD GOURMET CLUB
GREENFIELD, MASSACHUSETTS

❧

To make a good salad is to be a brilliant diplomat: one must know exactly how much oil one must put with one's vinegar.
—Oscar Wilde, 19th-century wit and writer

❧

CECI BEAN SALAD

MAKES 4 TO 6 SERVINGS

Whether you call them ceci beans, chickpeas, or garbanzos, these beans are tasty and good for you besides. This marinated bean salad makes a delicious dish that holds up well on a buffet table. It can be made in advance and keeps well for several days in the refrigerator.

1 can (19 ounces) chickpeas (ceci beans or garbanzos)

1 cup water

5 fresh or dried sage leaves

1 jar (3 ounces) pimientos, chopped

10 fresh parsley sprigs, leaves only, chopped

1 garlic clove, minced

½ cup olive oil

½ teaspoon salt

½ teaspoon pepper

3 tablespoons wine vinegar

1 teaspoon prepared mustard

4 whole green scallions, diced, or 3 tablespoons minced sweet onion

In a medium-size saucepan, combine the beans and their liquid with the water. Simmer gently for 15 minutes. Drain, place in a warm bowl, cover, and keep warm while you prepare the dressing.

Combine all the remaining ingredients in a small bowl and mix well. (Note: If you're using dried sage leaves, soak them in the wine vinegar for about 15 minutes before combining with the other ingredients.)

Pour the dressing over the warm beans. Let stand for at least 30 minutes before serving.

Mary Gagnon
ST. ISAAC JOGUES CHURCH
EAST HARTFORD, CONNECTICUT

Potluck Primer

ONE REASON potluck dinners are so popular is that the work is divided up among lots of people; the host doesn't have to spend the evening in the kitchen or waiting on everyone else.

The amount of planning that goes into the supper is up to the host: those who don't like surprises may want to assign dishes to guests. One host we know prepares a main entrée—turkey or lasagna—and asks her guests to provide side dishes and desserts. Other hosts—in the true spirit of potluck—prefer to leave the menu to chance (in which case you may end up with eight desserts, but who would complain?). What usually happens, though, is that once your guests receive the invitation they'll call to ask what kinds of dishes you need. So once the calls start coming in you may want to keep track of who's contributing what.

If you have friends who don't cook, ask them to provide beverages or munchies such as crudités, pretzels, or chips. That goes for the host, too, because that's the best part of potluck. You don't have to be a cook to put one on.

Marinated Vegetables
Makes 8 to 12 servings

A colorful dish that's easy to prepare and always welcome at a potluck or hot-weather picnic. It's a good make-ahead recipe, too, that keeps for several days in the refrigerator.

½ head cauliflower, in small pieces

2 cups bite-size broccoli florets and stems

2 carrots, sliced

2 celery stalks, sliced 1 inch thick

1 small onion, sliced

1 green bell pepper, cubed

¾ to 1 cup stuffed green olives or pitted black olives, drained

¾ cup white or wine vinegar

½ cup salad oil

2 tablespoons white sugar

1 teaspoon salt

½ teaspoon pepper

½ to 1 teaspoon dried oregano or mixed salad herbs

¼ cup water

Bring a large pot of water to a boil. Add the cauliflower and broccoli and blanch for 1 minute. Drain, then immediately plunge into cold water to stop the cooking. Drain well.

In a large salad bowl, combine all the vegetables with the olives. In a small bowl or jar, mix together the vinegar, oil, sugar, salt, pepper, herbs, and water. Mix well. Pour over the vegetables. Cover the bowl and refrigerate for 8 to 24 hours before serving.

Adapted from a recipe submitted by Barbara Little
Good Shepherd Lutheran Church
Rutland, Vermont

POTATO SALAD
MAKES 12 TO 14 SERVINGS

An excellent treatment of an old favorite.

8 cups cubed cooked potatoes

1½ cups chopped celery

6 hard-boiled eggs, chopped

⅔ cup chopped radishes

½ cup chopped scallions

1 cup chopped green bell pepper

1 teaspoon salt

Dash pepper

1⅓ cups Miracle Whip salad dressing

2 tablespoons prepared mustard

Cherry tomato halves, to garnish

In a large bowl, combine the potatoes, celery, eggs, radishes, scallions, green pepper, salt, and pepper. Combine the salad dressing and mustard and add to the potato mixture. Mix lightly. Chill before serving. Garnish with cherry tomato halves.

Maude R. Larsen
WALPOLE HISTORICAL SOCIETY
WALPOLE, NEW HAMPSHIRE

Much virtue in herbs, little in men.
—Benjamin Franklin, *Poor Richard's Almanack* (1734)

HOT GERMAN POTATO SALAD

MAKES 15 SERVINGS

For those who prefer their potato salad warm, this is a wonderful choice on a buffet table.

20 medium-size potatoes

¾ pound bacon (21 slices)

¾ cup wine vinegar

1 tablespoon salt

½ teaspoon pepper

2 cups thinly sliced scallions

In a heavy pot, cover the potatoes with water. Bring to a boil and cook until the potatoes are tender, about 40 minutes. Drain the potatoes. When cool enough to handle, peel and cut into ½-inch cubes. Return the potatoes to the pot.

Fry the bacon until crisp. Remove from the pan, reserving the bacon grease. Drain the bacon, then crumble. To the bacon grease in the pan, add the vinegar, salt, and pepper. Heat over medium heat until bubbling. Remove from the heat.

Pour the dressing over the potatoes. Reserve some scallions and bacon for a garnish and add the remainder to the potatoes. Toss lightly to mix. Cover and let stand for 45 minutes to absorb the seasoning.

Just before serving, set the pot over moderate heat and heat for about 10 minutes. Turn out into a serving bowl. Top with the reserved bacon and scallions and serve.

Janet D. Johnson
THE CHURCH OF THE GOOD SHEPHERD
ACTON, MASSACHUSETTS

Roasted Potato Salad

Makes 4 servings

Our testers loved this low-fat alternative to the traditional potato salad. Besides being easy to make and delicious, it can be served warm, at room temperature, or cold, which makes it perfect for every occasion from picnics to cabin fever potlucks.

2 pounds small red potatoes, halved or quartered

2 tablespoons olive oil

Several pinches dried thyme

1 green bell pepper, cut in thin strips

1 medium-size sweet white onion, cut in ½-inch slivers

½ red bell pepper, cut in thin strips

2 tablespoons white wine vinegar

½ teaspoon salt

¼ teaspoon black pepper

Preheat the oven to 400°F. Toss the potatoes with 1 tablespoon of the olive oil and a pinch of thyme. Place in a single layer in a roasting pan and roast for 15 minutes. Meanwhile, combine the green pepper and onion with the remaining oil and a pinch of thyme. Add to the potatoes after 15 minutes, loosening the potatoes and stirring the mixture. Continue roasting, stirring occasionally, until the potatoes are browned and tender and the onion begins to caramelize at the edges, about 45 minutes. Spoon into a large bowl and let cool slightly.

Combine the red pepper, vinegar, salt, pepper, and another pinch of thyme. Add to the potato mixture. Serve the salad warm, cold, or at room temperature.

Sylvia Martin
East Dover Baptist Church
East Dover, Vermont

SPINACH PASTA SALAD
MAKES 10 TO 12 SERVINGS

A colorful summer salad that's full of flavor. Try adapting it to use up whatever is on the pantry shelf—tomato instead of pimiento, green olives instead of black ones, perhaps a different cheese.

8 ounces corkscrew spinach pasta

1 can (8½ ounces) artichoke hearts, drained and sliced

¾ cup pitted black olives

½ cup chopped pimiento, drained

1 medium-size red onion, chopped

1 ounce provolone cheese, cubed

1 ounce Cheddar cheese, cubed

⅓ cup white wine vinegar

¼ cup salad oil

2 tablespoons honey

¾ teaspoon dried basil

½ teaspoon dried dillweed

½ teaspoon garlic powder

½ teaspoon pepper

¼ teaspoon salt

Cook the pasta according to the package directions. Rinse and drain well.

In a large mixing bowl, combine the pasta, artichoke hearts, olives, pimiento, onion, and cheeses. Toss to mix. In a screw-top jar or small mixing bowl, combine the remaining ingredients. Shake or whisk to mix well. Pour over the pasta mixture. Toss to coat. Cover and refrigerate for several hours or overnight before serving.

Dottie Rowe
BRENTWOOD HISTORICAL SOCIETY
BRENTWOOD, NEW HAMPSHIRE

ITALIAN-STYLE PASTA SALAD
MAKES 4 TO 6 SERVINGS

We loved this refreshingly different pasta salad made with vermicelli instead of the usual shells or twists. And the combination of artichokes, ham, and cheese make this attractive salad particularly rich and tasty.

4 ounces vermicelli or spaghetti

1 jar (6 ounces) marinated artichoke hearts

1 very small zucchini, halved and thinly sliced

1 carrot, shredded

¼ pound thinly sliced and chopped cooked ham

1 cup shredded mozzarella

2 tablespoons grated Parmesan cheese

2 tablespoons salad oil

2 tablespoons white wine vinegar

¾ teaspoon dry mustard

½ teaspoon dried oregano

½ teaspoon dried basil

1 garlic clove, minced

Cook the pasta according to the package directions and drain well. Drain the artichokes, reserving the marinade. Coarsely chop the artichokes.

In a large bowl, combine the pasta, vegetables, ham, and cheeses. In a small bowl or jar, combine the reserved marinade with the oil, vinegar, mustard, and herbs. Mix well. Pour the dressing over the pasta and toss to mix. Chill for several hours.

Christine Burritt
HENNIKER CONGREGATIONAL CHURCH
HENNIKER, NEW HAMPSHIRE

Tabouli Salad

Makes 12 to 15 servings

Not your typical tabouli salad, this is chunkier than most and full of luscious tomatoes. It's a refreshing dish, best made at the height of tomato season.

BULGUR MIXTURE

1 cup uncooked bulgur

¾ cup boiling water

⅔ cup minced scallions

¼ cup chopped fresh parsley

2 tablespoons chopped fresh mint

6 tablespoons olive oil

2 tablespoons lemon juice

1½ teaspoons salt

Dash pepper

TOMATO MIXTURE

2 pounds tomatoes, seeded and diced

1 cup sliced onions

1 cup diced and seeded cucumbers

½ cup sliced ripe olives

¾ cup diced green bell pepper

¼ teaspoon dried basil

¼ teaspoon dried oregano

¼ cup wine vinegar

½ cup olive oil

Salt and pepper to taste

CHEESE AND LETTUCE

12 ounces feta cheese, crumbled

Romaine lettuce or mixed greens

In a large bowl, combine the ingredients for the bulgur mixture. Cover and chill for at least 3 to 4 hours or overnight.

In a second large bowl, combine the ingredients for the tomato mixture. Cover and chill for at least 3 to 4 hours or overnight.

To serve, spoon some of the dressing from the tomato mixture over the feta cheese. Line a large salad bowl with the romaine or mixed greens. Combine the bulgur mixture with the tomato mixture and spoon on top of the lettuce. Sprinkle the cheese on top.

Esther L. Chandler
FRIENDS OF THE DOVER PUBLIC LIBRARY
DOVER, NEW HAMPSHIRE

Molded Coleslaw

Makes 4 to 6 servings

A make-ahead side dish that's not only tasty but also low in fat and calories. A food processor greatly speeds up the shredding process.

½ cup white sugar

2 envelopes unflavored gelatin

½ teaspoon salt

1 cup hot water

½ cup cider vinegar

2 tablespoons lemon juice

1½ cups cold water

2 cups shredded cabbage or a mixture of cabbage and carrots

1 cup finely diced celery

½ red or green bell pepper, finely chopped

Lettuce

Mayonnaise, regular or low-fat

The day before you plan to serve this coleslaw, combine the sugar, gelatin, and salt in a medium-size mixing bowl. Stir in the hot water and continue to stir until the gelatin is dissolved. Stir in the vinegar, lemon juice, and cold water. Chill in the refrigerator until the mixture just begins to set; it should mound slightly on a spoon. Fold in the vegetables and pour into a 4-cup mold. Refrigerate overnight.

To serve, unmold on a bed of lettuce and serve with mayonnaise.

Patricia S. Stephan
GOSHEN HISTORICAL SOCIETY
GOSHEN, NEW HAMPSHIRE

Cranberry Gelatin Salad

MAKES 6 TO 8 SERVINGS

This colorful salad simply sparkles on a buffet table!

1 package (3 ounces) cherry gelatin

1 cup boiling water

¼ cup cold water

¼ cup red wine

1 can (11 ounces) mandarin oranges, drained

1 can (16 ounces) whole-berry cranberry sauce

1 can (16 or 20 ounces) crushed pineapple, drained

½ cup coarsely chopped walnuts

At least 6 hours before serving, dissolve the gelatin in the boiling water. Add the rest of the ingredients. Pour into a 1½-quart mold and chill until set. To serve, unmold onto a serving platter.

Kathy Lengol
GOOD SHEPHERD LUTHERAN CHURCH
RUTLAND, VERMONT

THE PRETTY POTLUCK TABLE

*P*OTLUCK DOESN'T have to mean plain: there are lots of ways to spruce up your buffet table. A vase of fresh-cut flowers or a potted plant adds color and interest. Encourage your friends to bring their foods in pretty serving bowls and platters (everything doesn't have to match to be attractive), and set the table with a colorful runner or tablecloth. Use baskets lined with bright fabric napkins for utensils, rolls, cookies, and other desserts.

Chicken Salad

Makes about 12 servings

Blue cheese in a chicken salad? Well, why not? This tasty combination of flavors makes a delicious salad.

6 cups diced cooked chicken

¾ cup crumbled Roquefort or blue cheese

½ cup coarsely chopped walnuts

¾ cup olive oil

⅓ cup red wine vinegar

1 garlic clove, minced

½ cup chopped shallots or scallions

½ teaspoon salt

¼ teaspoon pepper

10 cups torn romaine lettuce (bite-size pieces)

4 avocados, sliced, to garnish

1 large red onion, sliced, to garnish

4 oranges, sliced, to garnish

Combine the chicken, cheese, and walnuts in a bowl. In a smaller bowl, combine the oil, vinegar, garlic, shallots, salt, and pepper. Whisk until well combined. Pour over the chicken and toss to mix. Arrange the lettuce on a platter. Mound the salad on top. Garnish with the avocados, red onion, and oranges.

Adapted from a recipe submitted by Martha McDonald
Harwinton Library Friends
Harwinton, Connecticut

Beef Arbuckle Salad

Makes 4 to 6 servings

Very quick and easy, and a great way to add variety to leftovers.

½ to ¾ pound leftover cooked roast beef, cut in strips

2 tablespoons fresh lemon juice

2 tablespoons minced onion

1½ cups sour cream

1 garlic clove, minced

2 teaspoons Dijon-style prepared mustard

Salt and pepper to taste

4 to 6 ripe beefsteak tomatoes, sliced

In a large bowl, combine the beef with the lemon juice, onion, sour cream, garlic, mustard, and salt and pepper. Arrange the tomatoes on a large serving platter and spoon the beef mixture on top.

Donald Novak
Mark Twain Library
Redding, Connecticut

Quick and Easy Salad Dressing

Makes 1⅓ cups

A good, simple dressing for a tossed salad or coleslaw. For extra zip on a tossed salad, try using a flavored vinegar, such as tarragon.

1 cup salad oil

½ cup vinegar

½ cup white sugar

Dash salt

½ teaspoon celery seeds

¼ teaspoon garlic salt

Mix all the ingredients together. Shake well before using.

Gladys Anderson
Willington Baptist Church
Willington, Connecticut

VEGETARIAN
MAIN DISHES

SOMEWHERE along the way, vegetarian cooking got a bad reputation; people said vegetarian foods were time-consuming to make and less than pleasurable to eat. Nothing could be further from the truth! In this chapter, you'll discover some wonderful pasta dishes made with herbs or fresh tomatoes or greens—good for you, delicious, and whipped together in no time. You'll also find recipes for absolutely mouthwatering beans, rice, and quiches.

Vegetarian dishes are always welcome at a potluck, because you never know what people's dietary restrictions will be. Some will appreciate the vegetarian offerings because they always eat vegetarian, and others will appreciate them as low-fat choices among the richer foods. But even among dedicated meat eaters, these flavorful recipes are sure to win fans.

PESTO PASTA
MAKES 4 TO 6 SERVINGS

Pesto sauce is easy to make, sophisticated, and delicious—great over pasta for a last-minute dinner party. Pesto can replace the sauce on a pizza, be baked into breads, or be incorporated in salad dressings. Extra pesto is easily frozen. In fact, during the basil season, you may want to buy bunches of basil at your local farmers market if you don't grow your own, multiply this recipe by as much basil as you have, and freeze the pesto in 1-cup containers (recycled yogurt containers work just fine).

2 cups basil leaves

½ to ¾ cup olive oil

2 garlic cloves

½ cup grated Parmesan cheese

2 to 4 tablespoons nuts (pine nuts or walnuts)

Pepper to taste

16 ounces dried pasta

Chop the basil in a blender or food processor. Add the oil and garlic and blend. Add the cheese and nuts. Blend. Add pepper to taste.

Meanwhile, cook the pasta in plenty of boiling salted water according to the package directions. Just before draining, add a few tablespoons of the pasta cooking water to the pesto to thin the sauce and warm it. Drain the pasta. Top with the pesto. Serve.

Adapted from a recipe submitted by Richard Caron
HARWINTON LIBRARY FRIENDS
HARWINTON, CONNECTICUT

PASTA WITH AGLIO E OLIO

MAKES 4 TO 6 SERVINGS

This earthy, simple, Italian garlic-and-oil sauce is delicious served over linguine or capellini, with a leafy green salad and warm, crusty bread to sop up the extra sauce.

16 ounces dried linguine or capellini

½ cup olive oil

3 to 4 large garlic cloves, finely minced

¼ teaspoon red pepper flakes or 1 hot chili pepper pod

3 tablespoons chopped fresh parsley

Cook the pasta in plenty of boiling salted water according to the package directions. Drain and place on a large, hot serving platter. Heat the oil in a small skillet and add the garlic and pepper. Just as soon as the garlic takes on a little color, pour the sauce over the pasta, add the parsley, and toss quickly. Serve at once.

Mary Gagnon
ST. ISAAC JOGUES CHURCH
EAST HARTFORD, CONNECTICUT

SOMETHING FOR EVERYONE

THESE DAYS you are likely to have at least one vegetarian in your potluck circle, so plan for at least one nonmeat entrée on the menu. There are all sorts of dishes that don't use any meat at all but that will please carnivores and herbivores alike, such as pasta, beans and rice, and meatless quiches.

Pasta with Fresh Tomato Sauce
Makes 4 to 6 servings

When tomatoes are in season, consider this impressive-looking, very color-ful pasta dish. The recipe doesn't require a lot of time in the kitchen, but the flavor is incredible. A perfect supper for a hot summer day.

1 to 1½ pounds fresh ripe tomatoes (4 or 5 large beefsteak-type tomatoes or 8 to 10 plum tomatoes)

½ cup olive oil

2 garlic cloves, thinly sliced

½ cup ripe or oil-cured black olives

Salt and freshly ground pepper to taste

Pinch red pepper flakes

2 to 3 tablespoons chopped fresh basil

16 ounces dried capellini or vermicelli

At least 2 hours before serving time, prepare the sauce. Remove the stems and cores from the tomatoes. Slice them in half through the stem end and squeeze out and discard the seeds, leaving as much moisture as possible in the tomatoes. Chop the tomatoes and place in a glass or porcelain bowl. Add the oil and toss lightly. Add the garlic, olives, salt and pepper, pepper flakes, and basil. Toss lightly. Set aside at room temperature to allow the flavors to develop.

Cook the pasta in plenty of boiling salted water according to the package directions. Place the drained pasta in a large serving bowl, add the tomato sauce, and toss well. Serve at once.

Adapted from a recipe submitted by Mary Gagnon
St. Isaac Jogues Church
East Hartford, Connecticut

Pasta with Greens and Feta

Makes 4 to 6 servings

Pasta and greens make a marvelous combination—a tasty and nutritious change of pace from the usual tomato sauce. The feta cheese adds just the right tang. You can make this year-round, with summer greens, such as spinach and Swiss chard, or winter greens, such as kale and escarole.

6 tablespoons olive oil

4 cups chopped onions

7 to 8 cups packed chopped mixed greens

12 to 16 ounces dried short pasta (radiatore is recommended)

8 to 12 ounces feta cheese, crumbled

Freshly grated Parmesan cheese

Salt and freshly ground black pepper to taste

In a large Dutch oven, heat the oil over medium heat. Add the onions and sauté until golden, about 10 minutes. Meanwhile, begin heating the water for the pasta. Add the chopped greens to the Dutch oven and stir until the greens begin to wilt. Cover and cook over medium-low heat for 10 to 15 minutes.

Cook the pasta according to the package directions. Drain, adding a few tablespoons of the cooking water to the greens. Reduce the heat under the greens to low. Add the cheese. Then add the pasta to the greens and mix thoroughly. Add the Parmesan cheese and salt and pepper to taste.

Adapted from a recipe submitted by Carol Vandertuin
East Dover Baptist Church
East Dover, Vermont

Baked Pasta with Fresh Tomatoes and Smoked Mozzarella

Makes 4 to 8 servings

Smoked mozzarella and ripe plum tomatoes make this summer pasta casserole unforgettable. A great dish for entertaining, it can be prepared a day ahead, refrigerated, and brought to room temperature before baking. Add a green salad and a bottle of wine for a spectacular dinner, or serve this special pasta dish as an appetizer or side dish for a larger meal.

4 tablespoons olive oil

1 red onion, chopped

3 garlic cloves, minced

5 plum tomatoes, seeded and chopped

16 ounces dried linguine or vermicelli

½ cup (1 stick) butter, melted

8 ounces smoked mozzarella cheese, cubed

¼ cup chopped fresh Italian parsley

Salt and freshly ground pepper to taste

1 cup fresh bread crumbs

In a skillet, heat 3 tablespoons of the oil over low heat. Add the onion and garlic and sauté for about 5 minutes or until the onion is transparent. Add the tomatoes and sauté for 5 minutes.

Meanwhile, cook the pasta in a large pot of boiling salted water according to the package directions. Drain and toss with the remaining 1 tablespoon olive oil. Place in a large mixing bowl.

Preheat the oven to 375°F.

Add ¼ cup of the melted butter, plus the tomato-onion mixture, the cheese, and the parsley, to the pasta. Toss well. Season to taste with salt and pepper. Spoon into a greased 2-quart casserole. Combine the remaining ¼ cup melted butter with the bread crumbs and sprinkle on top.

Bake for 20 to 25 minutes. Place under the broiler for 30 seconds to brown the bread crumbs just before serving.

Debbie Weisberg
Debbie Weisberg Associates
Newton Center, Massachusetts

Baked Ziti

MAKES 6 TO 10 SERVINGS

Ziti with carrots, peppers, and zucchini in a tasty cheese sauce. This is wonderful to take to a potluck, where it can be enjoyed as a vegetarian main dish or a side dish. Either way, we guarantee it will not leave you with leftovers.

16 ounces dried ziti

½ pound carrots, sliced

1 red or green bell pepper, julienned

1 onion, sliced

1 zucchini, sliced

2 cups grated Cheddar or Swiss cheese

¼ cup (½ stick) butter

¼ cup all-purpose white flour

3 cups milk

Salt and pepper to taste

Preheat the oven to 350°F. Butter a 9-inch by 13-inch baking dish.

Bring a large pot of water to a boil. Cook the ziti and carrots together for about 6 minutes. Drain well. Pour into the baking dish along with the pepper, onion, zucchini, and 1 cup of the cheese.

In a medium-size saucepan, melt the butter. Add the flour and whisk until you have a smooth paste. Slowly add the milk, whisking constantly. Turn the heat to low and cook for 12 to 15 minutes, whisking occasionally. Season to taste with salt and pepper.

Pour the sauce over the pasta and vegetables. Sprinkle the remaining cheese on top. Bake for 30 minutes or until bubbly.

Adapted from a recipe submitted by Clara E. Carsen
EMMANUEL CHURCH
NEWPORT, RHODE ISLAND

Broccoli-Noodle Casserole
Makes 4 to 8 servings

Whether you are in the mood for a vegetarian main dish or just an extra-tasty side dish, this broccoli, noodle, and cheese recipe is sure to please.

2 packages (10 ounces each) frozen chopped broccoli

8 ounces medium egg noodles

2 eggs, beaten

1 can (10¾ ounces) condensed cream of mushroom soup

1 cup grated sharp Cheddar cheese

1 cup mayonnaise

2 tablespoons minced onion

½ cup milk

Cracker crumbs

Cook the broccoli according to the package directions; drain. Cook the egg noodles according to the package directions; drain. Preheat the oven to 350°F.

In a large bowl, mix together the eggs, soup, cheese, mayonnaise, onion, and milk. Add the broccoli.

In a greased 2½-quart casserole, make several alternating layers of broccoli, sauce, and noodles, beginning and ending with broccoli. Top with cracker crumbs. Bake for 45 minutes. Serve hot.

Dorothy Traester
St. Peter's Episcopal Church
Oxford, Connecticut

Potluck with a Motif

*W*E KNOW ONE AVID potluck host who plans suppers around different activities. Before monthly contradances (a kind of folk dance usually held at the local town hall) she gives dinners at which her dancer pals—greenhorns and old pros—gather. And as the dinner progresses, not-so-seasoned dancers receive lessons in the finer points of contradancing from the veterans. Next time you're hosting a potluck, try planning it around a theme or one of your hobbies. Here are some suggestions:

⌁ Combine a potluck and Pictionary, Monopoly, Trivial Pursuit, or any other game you and friends enjoy playing.

⌁ Invite your guests to bring along their musical instruments and turn supper into a sing-along or jam session.

⌁ Ethnic foods are hot. Plan a potluck around a particular cuisine—Chinese, Indian, Italian, Mexican, Thai, Vietnamese—and turn it into a chance to learn more about different cultures. Have the kids (or the adults) in the group research the country whose cuisine you're enjoying and ask them to give short presentations about what they learn.

⌁ Choose one or two of your favorite (or favorite bad) movies to watch during dinner.

⌁ Potluck and take-out. Preferred by the "I-hate-to-cook" set. Everyone stops by his or her favorite take-out restaurant and brings one course of the meal.

CHEESY COUSCOUS
MAKES 4 TO 6 SERVINGS

Couscous, composed of little beads of semolina pasta, is an excellent comfort food with a distinctive flavor and texture. Combined with vegetables and cheese, it makes a great-tasting dish that caused even a picky seven-year-old to clamor for seconds. This is a very flexible recipe that can be adapted to whatever cheeses are available; try Swiss and Monterey Jack, Camembert and sharp Cheddar, or herbed Brie and Colby. Other vegetables can be used as well.

1 package (10 ounces) instant couscous

1½ cups chopped fresh broccoli

2 large carrots, grated

½ cup sliced black olives

5 garlic cloves, minced

½ cup mayonnaise (or more as needed)

½ cup crumbled feta cheese

1 cup grated Cheddar cheese

Grated Parmesan cheese

Paprika

Cook the couscous according to the package directions.

Steam the broccoli until just tender. Drain, plunge into cold water to stop the cooking, and drain well.

Preheat the oven to 350°F. In a mixing bowl, combine the couscous, broccoli, carrots, olives, garlic, mayonnaise, feta, and Cheddar. Mix well. Spoon into an ungreased 1½-quart casserole dish. Top with a sprinkling of Parmesan and paprika. Bake, covered, for 20 minutes or until heated through. Serve hot.

Lea Bohrer
THE GREENFIELD GOURMET CLUB
GREENFIELD, MASSACHUSETTS

Gado Gado

Makes 4 to 6 servings

Gado gado is an Indonesian recipe for a spicy peanut sauce; this version is rich but quite mild. It is served over a bed of rice topped with steamed vegetables. This is one of those recipes for which the measurements do not have to be precise—experiment and have fun!

2 tablespoons peanut oil

1 large onion, chopped

2 garlic cloves, minced

2 bay leaves

1 to 2 teaspoons ground ginger

¼ teaspoon cayenne pepper

1 tablespoon cider vinegar

2 tablespoons lemon juice

1 cup natural crunchy peanut butter

3 cups water

Salt to taste

3 to 4 cups hot cooked rice (1½ to 2 cups uncooked)

4 to 6 cups steamed vegetables (broccoli, carrots, snow peas, cauliflower, peppers, etc.)

In a medium-size saucepan, heat the oil over medium heat. Add the onion, garlic, and bay leaves and sauté until the onion is transparent, about 4 minutes. Add the ginger, cayenne, vinegar, lemon juice, peanut butter, water, and salt. Simmer over low heat until smooth and thickened, approximately 30 minutes. Remove the bay leaves.

Arrange the rice on a large serving platter. Top with the vegetables. Pour the sauce over the vegetables.

Adapted from a recipe submitted by Marilyn Rogers
Hopkinton Congregational Church
Hopkinton, New Hampshire

BLACK BEANS AND RICE
MAKES 4 TO 6 SERVINGS

Simple and very good. A very healthy choice for a family dinner.

2 teaspoons olive oil

2 onions, minced

2 green bell peppers, diced

3 garlic cloves, minced

2 cans (15 ounces each) black beans, drained and rinsed

2 teaspoons dried oregano

2 teaspoons balsamic vinegar

2 red bell peppers, diced

4 cups hot cooked rice

4 tomatoes, chopped

2 cups shredded cheese (Monterey Jack, sharp Cheddar, or a combination)

Hot sauce

In a large saucepan, heat the oil. Add the onions, green peppers, and garlic and sauté for 3 minutes. Add the black beans and oregano. Bring to a boil, then cook over medium heat for 5 minutes. Add the balsamic vinegar and remove from the heat. Stir in the red peppers.

To serve, place the rice in individual serving bowls and spoon the beans on top. Offer the tomatoes, cheese, and hot sauce on the side.

Theresa Maier
ANNUAL PERENNIAL CLUB
HENNIKER, NEW HAMPSHIRE

VEGETARIAN CHILI TOPPED WITH SPICY CORN BREAD
MAKES 6 SERVINGS

Great eye appeal—and great taste as well.

VEGETARIAN CHILI

2 teaspoons olive oil

1 teaspoon cumin seeds

1 green bell pepper, chopped

1 red bell pepper, chopped

½ jalapeño, chopped

1 to 2 celery stalks, chopped

1 teaspoon dried thyme

1 teaspoon chili powder

1 can (16 ounces) diced tomatoes

1 can (15 ounces) pinto beans or
    kidney beans, drained and rinsed

2 tablespoons tomato paste

1 cup fresh or frozen corn

2 teaspoons chopped fresh cilantro

Salt and pepper to taste

CORN BREAD

1 cup cornmeal

⅔ cup all-purpose white flour

2 teaspoons baking powder

½ teaspoon salt

½ cup water

½ cup milk

2 tablespoons egg substitute

1½ tablespoons vegetable oil

2 tablespoons honey

2 tablespoons chopped fresh cilantro

⅓ cup chopped black olives

½ cup shredded sharp Cheddar cheese

Heat the oil in a large, heavy skillet. Add the cumin seeds and sauté until lightly browned, about 1 minute. Add the bell peppers, jalapeño, celery, thyme, and chili powder. Cover and let stand for 3 to 4 minutes. Stir in the tomatoes, beans, and tomato paste. Cover and simmer for about 20 minutes. Add the corn and cook for another 5 minutes. Stir in the cilantro. Add salt and pepper to taste. Spoon into a 2-quart casserole.

Preheat the oven to 400°F.

In a large bowl, mix together the cornmeal, flour, baking powder, and salt. In a separate bowl, mix together the water, milk, egg substitute, oil, honey, and cilantro. Add to the dry ingredients and mix well. Spoon the batter over the chili, spreading to the edges of the dish. Sprinkle the olives and cheese over the batter.

Bake for 18 to 25 minutes, until the corn bread is golden. Let stand for 10 minutes before serving.

Adapted from a recipe submitted by
Eileen LaPierre
WOMAN'S CLUB OF CONCORD
CONCORD, NEW HAMPSHIRE

ITALIAN ZUCCHINI CRESCENT PIE
MAKES 6 TO 8 SERVINGS

Who can ever have enough recipes for zucchini? This one is easy, delicious, and highly recommended.

3 tablespoons margarine or butter

4 cups thinly sliced zucchini

1 cup chopped onion

½ cup chopped fresh parsley or 2 tablespoons dried

½ teaspoon salt

½ teaspoon pepper

¼ teaspoon garlic powder

¼ teaspoon dried basil

¼ teaspoon dried oregano

2 eggs, beaten

8 ounces mozzarella cheese, shredded (2 cups)

1 can (8 ounces) crescent dinner rolls

2 teaspoons prepared mustard

Preheat the oven to 375°F. In a large skillet, melt the margarine over medium heat. Add the zucchini and onion and sauté until the onion is golden, about 10 minutes. Remove from the heat. Stir in the parsley, salt, pepper, garlic powder, basil, and oregano. Combine the eggs and mozzarella and stir into the zucchini mixture.

Place the crescent rolls in an ungreased 10-inch pie plate. Press over the bottom and up the sides to form a crust. Spread the crust with the mustard. Pour the vegetable mixture into the crust. Bake for 18 to 20 minutes or until the center is set.

If the crust begins to brown before the center is set, cover with aluminum foil. Let stand for 10 minutes before serving.

Marilyn D. Serus
ST. PETER'S EPISCOPAL CHURCH
OXFORD, CONNECTICUT

Fresh Tomato Pie

Makes 4 servings

Incredibly easy to make, and it tastes wonderful! The cheese-mayonnaise mixture melts down over the vegetables, and the crust browns beautifully, so it makes a very attractive presentation. A great summer supper with bread and a green salad, or a nice appetizer any time of year.

2 cups Bisquick mix

¾ cup milk

4 medium-size tomatoes, sliced ¼ inch thick

1 green bell pepper, sliced

1 teaspoon dried basil

1 teaspoon dried chives

1 teaspoon dried parsley

1½ cups grated sharp Cheddar cheese

½ cup mayonnaise

Preheat the oven to 400°F.

Mix together the Bisquick and milk. Press into the bottom and up the sides of a greased 9-inch pie plate. Layer the tomatoes and green pepper in the pie plate, sprinkling each layer with the herbs. Combine the cheese and mayonnaise and spread on top. Bake for 20 to 35 minutes, until the crust and top are golden. Let stand for 10 minutes before serving.

Shirley Dunlap
HOPKINTON CONGREGATIONAL CHURCH
HOPKINTON, NEW HAMPSHIRE

BROCCOLI QUICHE

MAKES 6 SERVINGS

A great choice for brunch or supper. Broccoli quiche is delicious served with toasted French bread and slices of fresh tomatoes on the side.

1 package (10 ounces) frozen chopped broccoli

3 eggs

¾ cup light cream or milk

⅛ teaspoon salt

1½ cups shredded Monterey Jack cheese

1 can (8 ounces) sliced mushrooms, drained (optional)

1 unbaked 9-inch pie shell

Paprika

Preheat the oven to 350°F.

Cook the broccoli according to the package directions. Drain the broccoli, plunge it into cold water to stop the cooking, and drain well.

In a mixing bowl, beat the eggs, cream, and salt. Stir in the broccoli, cheese, and mushrooms, if using. Pour into the pie shell. Sprinkle with paprika.

Bake for 50 to 60 minutes or until a knife inserted near the center comes out clean. Let stand for 10 minutes before serving.

Kimberly Ereminas
HARWINTON LIBRARY FRIENDS
HARWINTON, CONNECTICUT

APPLE QUICHE

MAKES 6 SERVINGS

Fabulous! What a wonderful change of pace for brunch or lunch! Use an apple that will hold its shape when baked—Granny Smith, Golden Delicious, Rome, or Northern Spy will all work. Avoid McIntosh and Red Delicious.

5 to 6 large apples, peeled and sliced

1 unbaked 9-inch pie shell

1 cup shredded Cheddar cheese

2 eggs, beaten

1 cup evaporated milk

½ teaspoon salt

Dash nutmeg

Dash cinnamon

Preheat the oven to 350°F.

Place the apples in the pie shell. Sprinkle the cheese over the apples. In a small bowl, mix together the eggs, milk, salt, nutmeg, and cinnamon. Pour over the apples. Bake for 60 to 70 minutes. Let stand for 10 minutes before serving warm, or serve chilled.

Beth Lentz
HARWINTON LIBRARY FRIENDS
HARWINTON, CONNECTICUT

༺✿༻

The discovery of a new dish does more for the happiness of mankind than the discovery of a new star.

—Brillat-Savarin, 19th-century writer

༺✿༻

VEGETABLE-CHEESE BAKE
MAKES 6 TO 8 SERVINGS

Very easy, and very good. The herb stuffing mix adds a nice flavor, and the textures of the vegetables are terrific.

2 tablespoons vegetable oil

1 large onion, chopped

1 large green bell pepper, cubed

1 medium-size eggplant, cubed

8 ounces mushrooms, sliced

1 large tomato, chopped

1 teaspoon salt

¾ teaspoon dried thyme

⅛ teaspoon pepper

1 cup herb stuffing mix

12 ounces Swiss cheese, shredded

Preheat the oven to 350°F. Butter a 2-quart casserole dish.

Heat the oil in a large skillet over medium heat. Add the onion and green pepper and sauté for 3 minutes. Add the eggplant and mushrooms and sauté for 3 more minutes. Add the tomato and seasonings and cook for 1 minute.

Spread the stuffing mix in the bottom of the casserole. Layer half of the vegetable mixture over the stuffing. Sprinkle with 1 cup of the shredded cheese. Cover with the remaining vegetables. Bake, uncovered, for 30 minutes. Sprinkle with the remaining cheese and bake for 10 more minutes or until the cheese melts.

Barbara Ecke
ST. THOMAS BECKET CHURCH
CHESHIRE, CONNECTICUT

MAIN DISHES WITH FISH AND SHELLFISH

*T*HE DAYS OF WORKERS demanding contract concessions that limit the number of times they are served lobster or salmon are long behind us, but the tradition of Yankee seafood cookery lives on. It can be an expensive tradition these days; with a few exceptions, the recipes collected here are party dishes, special-occasion recipes for those times when you want to cook something really festive. Still, these are not complicated recipes, and casseroles—good for stretching to feed a crowd—dominate the table. On those occasions when nothing less than shrimp, scallops or salmon will do, turn to these pages and do it *right!*

VERMICELLI WITH WHITE CLAM SAUCE
MAKES 4 TO 6 SERVINGS

White clam sauce can be made with canned clams or fresh littleneck clams, depending on what is available to you. Either way, this pasta dish makes a great quick supper, served with crusty hot bread and a salad on the side. Be careful not to overcook the clams.

2 cans (6½ ounces each) minced clams or 1 cup freshly steamed and shucked clams

¼ cup olive oil

1 to 2 tablespoons butter

4 garlic cloves, crushed

2 to 3 tablespoons chopped fresh parsley

½ teaspoon salt

16 ounces dried vermicelli

Drain the clams and reserve the juice. Or measure out 1 cup of the clam-steaming liquid and set aside.

In a medium-size saucepan, heat the olive oil and butter over low heat. Add the garlic and simmer for about 3 minutes, just until the garlic begins to color; do not let the garlic turn brown or the sauce will taste bitter. Add the parsley, salt, and clam juice. Simmer for 10 minutes. Add the clams and cook just enough to heat through.

Meanwhile, cook the pasta in plenty of boiling salted water according to the package directions. Drain. Place the pasta in individual serving bowls and pour the sauce on top.

Adapted from a recipe submitted by Reverend David M. Blanchard
NORTH PARISH CHURCH OF NORTH ANDOVER, UNITARIAN UNIVERSALIST
NORTH ANDOVER, MASSACHUSETTS

Pasta with Red Clam Sauce
Makes 4 to 6 servings

This is truly delicious. The garlic can be increased to taste—use as much as you dare, the contributor advises, or as much as your close ones will tolerate.

2 cans (6½ ounces each) minced clams or 1 cup freshly steamed and shucked clams

¼ cup olive oil

1 to 2 tablespoons butter

4 garlic cloves (or more to taste), minced

2 to 3 tablespoons chopped fresh parsley

1 teaspoon dried oregano

1 teaspoon dried basil

1 teaspoon salt

¼ teaspoon pepper

1 can (28 ounces) Italian tomatoes

1 can (8 ounces) tomato sauce

16 ounces dried linguine or vermicelli

Drain the clams and reserve the juice. Or measure out 1 cup of the clam-steaming liquid and set aside.

In a large saucepan, heat the olive oil and butter. Add the garlic and simmer for about 3 minutes, just until the garlic begins to color; do not let the garlic turn brown or the sauce will taste bitter. Add the parsley, oregano, basil, salt, pepper, tomatoes, tomato sauce, and clam juice. Simmer for 45 minutes. Add the clams and cook just enough to heat through.

Meanwhile, cook the pasta in plenty of boiling salted water according to the package directions. Drain. Place the pasta in individual serving bowls and pour the sauce on top.

Adapted from a recipe submitted by Reverend David M. Blanchard
North Parish Church of North Andover, Unitarian Universalist
North Andover, Massachusetts

ANGEL HAIR PASTA WITH RED PEPPER AND ANCHOVY SAUCE

MAKES 4 SERVINGS

Great taste, great color, and very, very good. Something magical happens when you blend red peppers with anchovies—the distinct flavors meld and transform themselves into a new and wonderful taste. It's a good idea to refrigerate the peppers for at least an hour before roasting them; the flesh stays firmer and doesn't char as much.

4 red bell peppers

1 tablespoon olive oil

2 garlic cloves, minced

¼ teaspoon red pepper flakes (optional)

Salt and pepper to taste

4 anchovies, mashed into a paste

16 ounces angel hair pasta (capellini)

Freshly grated Parmesan cheese

To roast the peppers, place them under a broiler and broil, turning frequently, until well charred. Or roast them directly over the flames of a gas burner until well charred. Immediately place the charred peppers in a brown paper bag and seal. When the peppers are cool enough to handle, peel off the charred skin. Seed the peppers. Cut into 1-inch cubes.

In a large skillet, heat the olive oil over medium heat. Add the garlic and red pepper flakes and sauté for 1 minute, until the garlic is golden. Add the cubed red peppers and salt and pepper to taste and cook for about 10 minutes, stirring occasionally. Add the anchovies. Purée the sauce in a food processor or blender and keep warm.

Meanwhile, cook the pasta according to the package directions. Drain well. Pour the sauce over the pasta and toss well. Serve at once, passing the cheese at the table.

Theresa Maier
ANNUAL PERENNIAL CLUB
HENNIKER, NEW HAMPSHIRE

Lobster Newburg
Makes 4 to 6 servings

Coastal New England is renowned for its wonderful lobster dishes. This one was actually invented long ago in the famous Delmonico Restaurant in New York City. But no matter where it is served, it is a dish with great flavor, fantastic for entertaining because it is so easily made.

2 tablespoons butter

1 tablespoon all-purpose white flour

1⅓ cups cream (or use part milk)

2 cups (1 pound) cooked lobster meat

3 egg yolks, beaten

⅓ cup sherry

1 teaspoon salt

In the top of a double boiler over simmering water, melt the butter. Add the flour and blend to form a smooth paste. Add the cream and cook until thickened. Add the lobster meat. Stir in the eggs, sherry, and salt. Continue cooking until the sauce has thickened, about 3 minutes. Serve at once, in pastry shells or over rice or toast points.

Bertha Gray
CHEBEAGUE PARENTS ASSOCIATION
CHEBEAGUE ISLAND, MAINE

❦

*A truly destitute man is not one without riches,
but the poor wretch who has never partaken of a lobster.*
—Anonymous

❦

Shrimp Casserole

MAKES 8 SERVINGS

A great buffet dish. It should be made well ahead so the flavors have time to meld.

2 pounds cooked, peeled shrimp

6 slices white bread, torn in bite-size pieces

8 ounces cheese (Cheddar is recommended), grated

2 tablespoons butter, melted

3 eggs, lightly beaten

2 teaspoons dry mustard

2 cups milk

Butter a 2-quart casserole dish and layer with half the shrimp, half the bread, and half the cheese. Repeat for a second layer of each, ending with the cheese. Pour the melted butter over the cheese. Beat together the eggs, mustard, and milk. Pour over the casserole. Cover and refrigerate for at least 3 hours, preferably overnight.

Preheat the oven to 350°F. Bake, covered, for 1 hour. Serve warm.

Adapted from a recipe submitted by Rita Young
OUR LADY OF GOOD HOPE CATHOLIC WOMEN'S CLUB
CAMDEN, MAINE

LORD HAVE MERCY!

ONE ANXIOUS LITTLE GIRL singing the Lord's Prayer for the first time in front of her congregation belted out, "Lead us *into* temptation . . ."

SHRIMP AND RICE CASSEROLE
MAKES 4 SERVINGS

Shrimp and rice in a creamy tomato sauce with a nice, crispy top. This makes a great one-dish dinner.

2 tablespoons butter

¼ cup chopped onion

¼ cup chopped green bell pepper

1 pound cooked, peeled shrimp

1½ cups cooked white rice (¾ cup uncooked)

1 can (10¾ ounces) condensed tomato soup

1 cup light cream

¼ to ½ cup dry sherry

¼ teaspoon mace

1 teaspoon salt

Pepper to taste

½ cup chopped almonds

¼ cup dry bread crumbs

1 tablespoon softened butter

Preheat the oven to 350°F. In a small skillet, melt the 2 tablespoons butter over medium heat. Add the onion and green pepper and sauté until limp, about 4 minutes. Combine in a 2-quart casserole dish with the shrimp, rice, tomato soup, cream, sherry, and seasonings. Mix together the almonds, bread crumbs, and softened butter and sprinkle on top. Bake for about 25 minutes, until bubbly. Serve hot.

Adapted from a recipe submitted by Frances Todd
CHEBEAGUE PARENTS ASSOCIATION
CHEBEAGUE ISLAND, MAINE

SHRIMP CREOLE
MAKES 6 SERVINGS

This is a dish with southern origins but too good to leave out! Serve over a bed of fluffy white rice, accompanied by a green salad.

2 tablespoons butter

1 cup chopped onion

1 cup chopped green bell pepper

1 garlic clove, minced

2 cups stewed tomatoes

⅛ teaspoon paprika

Salt and pepper to taste

1 pound shrimp, peeled and deveined

In a large heavy skillet, melt the butter over medium heat. Add the onion, green pepper, and garlic and sauté until the pepper is tender, about 5 minutes. Add the tomatoes and seasonings and simmer for 5 minutes. Add the shrimp and simmer for 10 minutes. Serve hot.

Rosemary Purdy
ST. THOMAS BECKET CHURCH
CHESHIRE, CONNECTICUT

BAKED SCALLOPS
MAKES 6 SERVINGS

Our testers called this dish "easy and elegant—great dinner party fare."

2 pounds scallops

½ cup (1 stick) butter, melted

¼ cup grated Parmesan cheese

1 cup crushed Ritz crackers

1 tablespoon lemon juice

¼ teaspoon pepper

¼ teaspoon garlic salt

1 tablespoon dry vermouth

Preheat the oven to 325°F. Wash the scallops and pat dry. Place in a buttered 8-inch baking dish. Mix together the remaining ingredients and spoon on top of the scallops. Cover the dish and bake for 30 minutes. Serve hot.

Lynne Maxim
ST. ANDREW LUTHERAN CHURCH
ELLSWORTH, MAINE

MARINATED SCALLOPS

MAKES 4 SERVINGS

On the expensive side, like any scallop recipe, but very good. While the scallops marinate, you will have just enough time to make a salad and prepare the side dishes. Just before serving, cook the scallops; they'll be ready in a flash.

1 pound bay scallops (or substitute sea scallops cut in quarters)

⅓ cup dry vermouth

1 garlic clove, minced

Salt and pepper

½ cup dry bread crumbs

6 tablespoons (¾ stick) butter

Minced fresh parsley, to garnish

Lemon wedges, to garnish

Marinate the scallops in the vermouth, garlic, and salt and pepper for about 30 minutes. Drain and mix with the bread crumbs. Heat the butter in a large heavy skillet over medium heat. Add the scallops and sauté until they are cooked through, 3 to 4 minutes. Place on a warmed serving platter and garnish with the parsley and lemon wedges.

Joan Blanchard
NORTH PARISH CHURCH OF NORTH ANDOVER, UNITARIAN UNIVERSALIST
NORTH ANDOVER, MASSACHUSETTS

Scallops in Wine Sauce
Makes 4 servings

Absolutely wonderful! Easy to make, but tastes great—prepare it for guests or as a special treat for the family. If you can't find bay scallops, substitute sea scallops, but cut them in quarters.

½ cup water
⅓ cup dry white wine
1 teaspoon cider vinegar
1 pound bay scallops
2 tablespoons butter or margarine
2 tablespoons all-purpose white flour
⅓ cup mayonnaise
¼ teaspoon ground thyme
Salt and pepper to taste

In a medium-size saucepan, bring the water, wine, and vinegar to a boil. Add the scallops and simmer for 5 minutes. Drain and set aside; reserve the cooking liquid.

Wipe out the saucepan and return to the stove. Add the butter and allow it to melt over medium heat. Stir in the flour and cook for about 5 minutes, stirring constantly. Add the reserved cooking liquids and stir until thickened. Stir in the mayonnaise and thyme. Season to taste with salt and pepper. Add the scallops and serve at once or transfer to a double boiler and keep warm.

Gerald T. Littlefield
Chebeague Parents Association
Chebeague Island, Maine

Sherried Scallops

MAKES 4 SERVINGS

Another variation on the popular baked scallop dish. This one is flavored with sherry and uses cream of mushroom soup as a base. Very easy and very tasty—everyone who tried it loved it!

1½ pounds scallops

1 can (10¾ ounces) condensed cream of mushroom soup

¼ cup dry sherry

1 can (8 ounces) sliced mushrooms, drained

½ cup cornflake crumbs or dry bread crumbs

3 tablespoons grated Parmesan cheese

2 tablespoons butter

Preheat the oven to 350°F. Butter a 2-quart baking dish and arrange the scallops in it. Combine the soup, sherry, and mushrooms and pour over the scallops. Combine the crumbs and cheese and sprinkle over the casserole. Dot with the butter. Bake, uncovered, for 1 hour. Serve hot.

Carolyn Muller
ST. PETER'S EPISCOPAL CHURCH
WESTON, MASSACHUSETTS

TIME TO PRAY

*J*OHNNY—JUST A TOT—was suffering from a serious case of the fidgets during the church service one Sunday. Finally, after admonishing his son repeatedly, Johnny's father snatched him out of the pew and marched him out toward the back of the church. Just as father and son exited the sanctuary, Johnny shouted to the congregation, "You all pray for me, okay?"

FLOUNDER AND VEGETABLES SEALED IN SILVER
MAKES 4 SERVINGS

Elegant, easy to prepare, delicious to eat, and low in fat and cholesterol— what more could you ask for? This dish is perfect for dinner parties because, unlike many fish dishes, which tend to cool off fast, this one is kept hot by the foil wrapping while you get everyone to the table. If flounder is unavailable, substitute any firm white-fleshed fish.

2 tablespoons grated Parmesan cheese

¾ teaspoon dried basil

¼ teaspoon garlic powder

¼ teaspoon salt

¼ teaspoon pepper

1 large carrot, julienned

1 large leek, julienned

2 large mushrooms, thinly sliced

4 flounder fillets, about 5 ounces each

1 teaspoon minced fresh chives

1 teaspoon lemon juice

Preheat the oven to 400°F.

Combine the cheese and seasonings and set aside. In a medium-size saucepan, blanch the vegetables in boiling water to cover for 1 minute. Drain, plunge into cold water to stop the cooking, and set aside to drain thoroughly.

Cut 4 sheets of aluminum foil, each large enough to enclose a fillet. Coat each sheet with nonstick cooking spray. Lay a fillet in the center of each sheet. Arrange a quarter of the vegetables on top of each. Sprinkle with the cheese and seasoning mixture. Finally, top each with ¼ teaspoon chives and ¼ teaspoon lemon juice. Fold the foil over the fillets and crimp the edges to seal. Place the foil packets on a baking sheet and bake for 7 to 8 minutes. Transfer the packets to dinner plates and let the diners open their own.

Mary Gagnon
ST. ISAAC JOGUES CHURCH
EAST HARTFORD, CONNECTICUT

Quick Haddock Casserole

Makes 6 to 8 Servings

Fast and easy to put together, and everyone loves it. If haddock is not available, substitute any firm white-fleshed fish.

2 pounds haddock fillets

1 package (6 ounces) stovetop stuffing mix

½ cup (1 stick) margarine, melted

1 can (10¾ ounces) condensed cream of mushroom soup

Preheat the oven to 350°F. Cut the fillets into pieces that measure 2 inches by 3 inches. Place half the fish in the bottom of a 9-inch square baking dish. Combine the stuffing mix and melted margarine; set aside ½ cup. Spoon half of the remaining stuffing mix on top of the fish. Add another layer of fish and another layer of stuffing. Pour the soup over the casserole. Bake for 20 minutes. Spread the reserved ½ cup of stuffing over the top and bake for 10 minutes more. Serve hot.

Barbara B. Collier

Women's Alliance, First Parish Congregation Unitarian Church
Kennebunk, Maine

SALMON WITH BUTTER SAUCE
MAKES 4 SERVINGS

A sophisticated dish that you are just as likely to encounter in a restaurant as at your next potluck. If you can't find crème fraîche at your gourmet cheese store or health food store, you can make it yourself (at a fraction of the cost), but you will have to start it a day in advance (see note below).

BUTTER SAUCE

2 large shallots, minced

½ cup dry white wine

2 tablespoons crème fraîche

½ cup (1 stick) cold unsalted butter, cut into pieces

Salt and pepper to taste

FISH

1½ pounds center-cut salmon fillets with skin

½ teaspoon dried thyme

Salt and pepper

2 tablespoons unsalted butter

Fresh parsley sprigs, to garnish

To make the sauce, combine the shallots and wine in a small saucepan. Bring to a boil and simmer until the wine has almost completely evaporated. Stir in the crème fraîche. Bring the mixture to a boil, stirring constantly. Whisk in the butter, 1 piece at a time, lifting the pan from the heat occasionally to cool the mixture and adding each new piece of butter before the previous one has completely melted. (The sauce should not become hot enough to liquefy.) Add salt and pepper to taste. Keep the sauce warm in the top of a double boiler while you prepare the fish.

To cook the fish, sprinkle the fillets with the thyme, salt, and pepper. Melt the butter in a large heavy skillet. When the foam subsides, add the fish, skin side up, and cook for 2 minutes. Then turn and cook the other side for about 1 minute. Serve with the butter sauce and garnish with parsley.

NOTE: To make crème fraîche, combine 1 cup whipping cream with 1 teaspoon cultured buttermilk. Heat to 85°F. Cover and let stand at room temperature for 8 to 24 hours, until thickened. Store in the refrigerator.

Mary Gagnon
ST. ISAAC JOGUES CHURCH
EAST HARTFORD, CONNECTICUT

SALMON AND CORN CASSEROLE
MAKES 6 TO 8 SERVINGS

When unexpected guests arrive, this is a great casserole to whip up quickly with ingredients you are likely to have on hand in the pantry.

1 can (14¾ ounces) salmon, bones and skin removed

Milk

3 tablespoons butter

½ cup chopped onion

¼ cup chopped green bell pepper

2 eggs, beaten

2 cups shredded sharp Cheddar cheese

1 can (15 ounces) creamed corn

¼ teaspoon salt

½ teaspoon pepper

1¼ cups crushed crackers

Preheat the oven to 350°F.

Drain the salmon, pouring the liquid into a glass measuring cup. Flake the salmon and place in a large mixing bowl. Add enough milk to the measuring cup to make 1 cup of liquid. Add to the salmon.

Melt 2 tablespoons of the butter in a small skillet over medium heat. Add the onion and green pepper and sauté until limp, about 4 minutes. Add to the salmon, along with the eggs, cheese, corn, salt, and pepper. Mix well. Spoon into a 9-inch by 13-inch baking dish.

Melt the remaining 1 tablespoon butter and combine with the crushed crackers. Sprinkle over the top of the casserole. Bake for 45 minutes, uncovered. Serve hot.

Tillie Crowell
BANGOR NATURE CLUB
BANGOR, MAINE

QUICK AND EASY SALMON PATTIES
MAKES 4 TO 6 SERVINGS

A good recipe for a cold winter night, and the perfect last-minute supper when you don't have time to shop.

1 can (14¾ ounces) salmon, bones and skin removed

1 egg

⅓ cup minced onion

½ cup all-purpose white flour

1½ teaspoons baking powder

½ cup finely crushed crackers or dry bread crumbs

Crisco or canola oil for frying

Drain the salmon, setting aside 2 tablespoons of the liquid. In a medium-size mixing bowl, combine the salmon and 2 tablespoons liquid, the egg, onion, flour, and baking powder. Mix well. Form into small patties and coat the patties with the crushed crackers.

Heat the oil in a large heavy skillet. Fry the patties until golden brown on both sides, about 3 minutes per side. Drain well and keep warm while frying the remaining patties. Serve warm.

Adapted from a recipe submitted by Frances L. Calder
CHEBEAGUE PARENTS ASSOCIATION
CHEBEAGUE ISLAND, MAINE

Salmon Casserole

Makes 4 Servings

A quick, easy, and budget-conscious recipe. Mashed potato lovers will enjoy this casserole!

1 can (14¾ ounces) salmon, bones and skin removed

1 can (10¾ ounces) condensed cream of mushroom soup

1 tablespoon dried dillweed

1 tablespoon finely minced onion

6 medium-size potatoes, peeled, boiled, and mashed

5 saltine crackers, crumbled

1 tablespoon butter, melted

Preheat the oven to 450°F. Drain the salmon and flake into a greased shallow 2-quart baking dish. Spread the soup over the salmon. Sprinkle with the dillweed and minced onion. Pile mounds of mashed potatoes over the soup. Sprinkle with the crumbled crackers and drizzle with the melted butter. Bake for 25 minutes. Serve hot.

Adapted from a recipe submitted by Charlotte LaCrosse
Daughters of St. Bernard, St. Bernard's Church
Rockland, Maine

California Chicken

MAKES 4 SERVINGS

This one's a keeper! Easily prepared in less than 15 minutes, it tastes great—and all the ingredients are already on the kitchen shelf. Can be doubled or tripled for larger groups. Leftovers can be reheated and served over pasta, rice, or toast points.

1 can (6 ounces) tuna, drained

1 can (10¾ ounces) condensed cream of mushroom soup

1 can (8½ ounces) peas

1 can (8½ ounces) carrots

1 cup diced cooked potatoes

½ cup crushed crackers

2 tablespoons butter

Preheat the oven to 350°F. Butter a 2-quart baking dish. Mix together the tuna, soup, and vegetables. Place in a casserole, sprinkle with the cracker crumbs, and dot with the butter. Bake for 20 minutes or until heated through. Serve hot.

Elaine B. Varley
DIGHTON HISTORICAL SOCIETY, INC.
DIGHTON, MASSACHUSETTS

Main Dishes with Chicken and Turkey

WE ARE ALL eating more chicken and turkey these days, and it's no wonder. Both are low in fat and cholesterol and get high marks for their versatility. As everyone knows, you could cook chicken every night of the week for a year and never repeat a meal. As the price of seafood continues to rise and red meat remains dear in terms of health issues, chicken becomes the protein of choice.

Main dishes based on chicken and turkey are particularly good for potlucks because they are both economical and quick to make. Here's a collection of recipes that will be a welcome addition to any cook's repertoire. These dishes emphasize flavor and convenience and include plenty of casseroles that will stretch quite nicely for unexpected guests. In many of the recipes, a rich sauce guarantees that the chicken will remain moist and provides a gravy for a bed of rice, noodles, or mashed potatoes. In the back of this chapter, look for creative ways to use turkey leftovers.

Special Roasted Chicken
Makes 4 servings

A huge hit! The garlic, lemon, and rosemary flavorings are subtle but delicious, and the end product makes a beautiful presentation.

3-pound to 4-pound roasting chicken

Salt and pepper

1 lemon

5 garlic cloves, sliced in half
    lengthwise

1 tablespoon fresh or dried rosemary

1 teaspoon paprika

Preheat the oven to 350°F.

Wash the chicken and remove any loose fat and the giblet bag. Pat dry and sprinkle with salt and pepper inside and out. Place the chicken in a baking dish, breast side up. Wash the lemon thoroughly. Roll the lemon against a countertop several times to burst the juice sacs, making the lemon juicier. With a trussing needle or toothpick, poke 30 to 40 holes in the lemon. Place the lemon inside the chicken cavity. Close the opening of the chicken with toothpicks or a trussing needle. With a sharp knife, make an incision into the chicken breast with a garlic piece resting on the knife's edge. Push the garlic deeper into the chicken meat. Repeat all over the chicken until all the garlic pieces have been inserted. Generously sprinkle the chicken with the rosemary and paprika.

Roast for 20 minutes per pound. Baste once or twice while it roasts. Before serving, remove the lemon carefully; the juices will be hot.

Susan Gagnon
Hopkinton Cookie Exchange
Hopkinton, New Hampshire

CHICKEN CACCIATORE

MAKES 4 SERVINGS

This recipe arrived via Ellis Island with the contributor's father, Louis Janus Vici, around the turn of the century. Mr. Vici, his daughter reports, cut a dashing figure in World War I, serving in the Air Corps as a navigator, gunner, and bombardier in the back of a two-seater airplane. He was a great cook, too, if this recipe is any evidence. It takes some time, but it's a feast for family or friends, or to take to a housebound neighbor.

3-pound to 4-pound frying chicken, cut in pieces

Salt and pepper

3 tablespoons butter

1 tablespoon olive oil

1 medium-size onion, finely chopped

½ pound fresh mushrooms, sliced

2 tablespoons all-purpose white flour

½ cup dry white wine

2 tablespoons cognac

1 cup chicken broth

3 cups peeled, chopped tomatoes, drained

1 to 2 garlic cloves, minced

2 tablespoons chopped fresh parsley

2 tablespoons chopped fresh basil

½ teaspoon dried oregano

Season the chicken with salt and pepper. In a large Dutch oven, heat the butter and oil. Brown the chicken in the butter mixture. Remove and set aside.

Preheat the oven to 350°F.

Add the onion, mushrooms, and ½ teaspoon each of salt and pepper to the pan. Sauté until the onion is transparent, about 5 minutes. Stir the flour into the butter and cook, stirring constantly, until the butter is golden brown. Add the wine, cognac, broth, tomatoes, and garlic. Simmer for 10 minutes. Return the chicken to the pan.

Cover and bake in the preheated oven for 45 to 60 minutes, until the chicken is done. Remove the chicken and keep warm on a serving plate. Bring the sauce to a boil on top of the stove and cook until the volume is reduced to about 3 cups. Add the parsley, basil, and oregano. Serve with linguine.

Fredericka L. Jones
NEW ENGLAND HISTORIC GENEALOGICAL SOCIETY
BOSTON, MASSACHUSETTS

CHICKEN AND RICE LACONIAN

MAKES 4 TO 6 SERVINGS

Scrumptious! A Greek recipe that was brought to America by the contributor's father at the turn of the century, this is also a great dish for campers, because it's made all in one skillet and the ingredients are simple.

2 to 3 pounds chicken pieces with skins removed (8 to 10 thighs or 5 or 6 breasts)

Salt and pepper

2 tablespoons olive oil

1 medium-size onion, cut in thin slivers

2½ cups water

1 tablespoon dried oregano

5 tablespoons ketchup

1 cup uncooked long-grain white rice

1 red bell pepper, cubed

1 cup frozen peas

Wash the chicken and pat dry. Season with salt and pepper and set aside.

In a large, heavy skillet, heat the olive oil over low heat. Add the onion and sauté until limp, about 4 minutes. Add the chicken and cook until brown, about 15 minutes, turning frequently. You will have to do this in a few batches. As the pieces brown, remove them from the skillet and keep them warm. When the last piece is browned, wipe out the skillet with paper towels to remove any excess fat.

Return the chicken to the skillet. Combine the water, oregano, and ketchup and pour over the chicken. Bring to a boil, then simmer, covered, for 1 hour over very low heat (for boneless chicken reduce the cooking time to 30 minutes). Remove the chicken to a platter and cover to keep it warm.

Measure the liquid remaining in the skillet. Add enough water to measure 2 cups. Bring to a boil. Add the rice, stir, and return to a gentle boil. Add the red pepper and peas. Reduce the heat and simmer, covered, for about 14 minutes. Remove from the heat and let stand for 10 minutes. Serve with the chicken.

Adapted from a recipe submitted by Diane Speare Triant
THE HELLENIC WOMEN'S CLUB, EOK OF GREATER BOSTON
WELLESLEY HILLS, MASSACHUSETTS

French Chicken

Makes 4 servings

"Wow!" reported one young tester, whose mom has already passed the recipe on to several friends. This dish offers great flavor and an elegant presentation for very little effort. Serve any extra sauce over rice or buttered noodles for a fabulous meal.

3 tablespoons margarine

3 to 4 pounds chicken quarters

1 small onion, minced

1 teaspoon salt

¼ teaspoon black pepper

¼ teaspoon dried thyme

¼ teaspoon dried basil

¾ cup dry white wine

2 tablespoons sherry

1 cup light cream

Juice of ½ lemon

In a large skillet over medium heat, melt the margarine. Add the chicken, onion, salt, and pepper. Cook until the chicken is browned on both sides. Reduce the heat to low, cover, and cook for 20 to 30 minutes. Add the thyme, basil, white wine, and sherry and continue cooking for 15 minutes more, or until done.

In a small saucepan, bring the cream to a boil and cook to reduce the volume somewhat. Add the lemon juice.

Transfer the chicken to a serving dish. Add the hot cream to the pan juices and stir briefly over a hot burner. When well blended, pour over the chicken and serve.

Florence Griswold Museum
Lyme Historical Society
Old Lyme, Connecticut

TARRAGON CHICKEN
MAKES 4 TO 6 SERVINGS

The chicken is baked in an easy-to-make mushroom sauce flavored with tarragon. This makes a wonderful company meal. You might want to serve the chicken and sauce on a bed of rice or provide some crusty French bread for sopping up the delicious sauce.

¼ cup (½ stick) margarine, melted

3½ pounds chicken pieces

¼ cup all-purpose white flour

1 can (12 ounces) evaporated milk

1 can (10¾ ounces) condensed cream of mushroom soup

½ cup dry vermouth

1 can (8 ounces) sliced mushrooms, drained

1½ tablespoons dried tarragon

½ teaspoon salt

⅛ teaspoon pepper

Preheat the oven to 425°F. Pour the margarine into a 9-inch by 13-inch baking pan. Coat the chicken with the flour and arrange in a single layer, skin side down, in the baking pan. Bake, uncovered, for 30 minutes, turning the chicken once during baking.

Remove the chicken from the oven and pour off the excess fat. Reduce the oven temperature to 325°F. Combine all the remaining ingredients and pour the sauce over the chicken. Cover the pan with aluminum foil and continue to bake for 20 minutes. Serve hot.

Janet Crooks
ST. ANDREW LUTHERAN CHURCH
ELLSWORTH, MAINE

Chicken with Wine and Almonds

Makes 10 to 12 servings

The chicken cooks on a bed of rice with a creamy sauce flavored with wine, almonds, and cheese. This is a very easy to prepare one-dish meal that will feed a small crowd.

1¼ cups uncooked white rice

1 can (10¾ ounces) condensed cream of mushroom soup

1 can (10¾ ounces) condensed cream of celery soup

1 can (14 ounces) chicken broth

½ cup dry sherry or white wine

½ cup (1 stick) butter or margarine, melted

6 to 8 whole chicken breasts, skinned, boned, and split

3 ounces grated Parmesan cheese

3 ounces slivered almonds

Preheat the oven to 375°F. Spread the rice in the bottom of a 9-inch by 13-inch baking dish. Mix together the soups, broth, sherry, and melted butter. Pour 1 cup of this liquid into the rice and stir to evenly moisten the rice. Arrange the chicken pieces in a single layer over the rice. Pour the remaining liquid on top. Sprinkle the Parmesan cheese and almonds on top. Cover and bake for about 1 hour, until the chicken is done and the rice is tender.

Joy A. O'Meara
Harwinton Library Friends
Harwinton, Connecticut

DOUBLE OR NOTHING?

*Y*OU HAVE A RECIPE that serves five. You'd like it to serve fifty. So, you simply multiply all the ingredients by ten, right? Well ... maybe.

Recipes for baked goods—cakes and breads—should *never* be increased to serve more than they were originally intended to feed because those recipes are very exact formulas. If you have a cake recipe that serves eight and you want to double the yield, make two cakes rather than trying to double the recipe.

It's *generally* safe to double or triple the yields of other kinds of recipes. But there are a couple of rules of thumb to keep in mind:

❧ You probably don't have to double (or triple) the amount of herbs or spices in a recipe when you increase the rest of the ingredients. For instance, you may not want to double the amount of garlic called for in a recipe that already calls for two cloves. The flavor will probably be overpowering. Use the amount called for in the original recipe, then add a little more at a time, and keep tasting as you go. Remember, you can always add more, but you can't take it back.

❧ When you increase the yield of a recipe, you may also have to increase the cooking time. For instance, a 30-pound turkey must roast longer than a 15-pound bird. But not necessarily twice as long. Gauge doneness by the internal temperature of the food. (You'll need a good thermometer.) Moreover, foods cooked in a crowded oven (three pies in one oven rather than just one) will need an extra five to ten minutes (maybe more) to finish cooking.

Chicken with Artichokes
Makes 4 to 6 servings

An easy dish with lots of flavor. And since it takes only one pan, cleanup is easy, too. Serve with rice and a green vegetable.

4 whole chicken breasts, boned and split

½ cup Italian salad dressing

1 cup sliced mushrooms (canned or fresh)

1 can (8½ ounces) artichokes, quartered

1 cup chicken broth

1 teaspoon cornstarch

In a large heavy skillet, combine the chicken, salad dressing, mushrooms, artichokes, and broth. Cover and cook over medium heat until the chicken is cooked through, 20 to 25 minutes. Turn the chicken once during the cooking.

Remove the chicken, mushrooms, and artichokes to a warm serving platter and keep warm. Dissolve the cornstarch in a little water. Add to the liquid in the skillet, bring to a boil, and cook until the sauce is bubbly and thickened. Pour the sauce over the chicken and serve.

Adapted from a recipe submitted by Pamela La Mattina
Willington Baptist Church
Willington, Connecticut

CHICKEN, APPLE, AND CHEESE CASSEROLE
MAKES 6 SERVINGS

Outstanding! The combination of apples and Swiss cheese is lovely, and preparation is easy. Use Golden Delicious apples—or any other variety firm enough to hold up when cooked.

5 tablespoons butter or margarine, softened

3 medium-size apples, halved, cored, and sliced (3 cups)

2 large onions, thinly sliced (2 cups)

3 whole chicken breasts, boned, skinned, and split

1 teaspoon salt

¼ teaspoon pepper

½ cup shredded Swiss cheese

½ cup grated Parmesan cheese

¼ cup dry bread crumbs

½ teaspoon dried thyme

2 tablespoons brandy or apple cider

Preheat the oven to 350°F. Coat a 1½-quart baking dish with 1 tablespoon of the butter.

Melt the remaining 4 tablespoons butter in a large heavy skillet over medium heat. Add the apples and onions and sauté until the apples are tender, about 10 minutes. Spoon into the baking dish.

Rub the chicken with the salt and pepper and arrange over the apple-onion mixture. Combine the cheeses with the bread crumbs and thyme and sprinkle the mixture over the chicken. Drizzle the brandy over the cheese. Bake for 35 minutes or until the cheese is golden brown and the chicken is done.

Carolyn Muller
ST. PETER'S EPISCOPAL CHURCH
WESTON, MASSACHUSETTS

Mona's Chicken Casserole
Makes 4 to 6 servings

Chicken with mushrooms, peas, carrots, parsnips, and artichokes in a creamy wine sauce. This is a delicious casserole, filled with good-for-you vegetables. If you like, assemble it up to a day ahead of time and refrigerate it until you are ready to bake it. Serve with rice or noodles to enjoy with the extra sauce.

4 whole chicken breasts, boned, skinned, and split

1 cup sliced carrots

1 cup sliced parsnips

6 tablespoons (¾ stick) butter

8 ounces mushrooms, sliced

½ cup all-purpose white flour

1 can (15 ounces) chicken broth

1 cup white wine

1 cup regular or low-fat sour cream

Salt and pepper

1 cup frozen peas

1 can (14 ounces) artichoke hearts, drained and halved

Preheat the oven to 400°F. Arrange the chicken breasts in a shallow baking dish and bake for 30 minutes.

While the chicken is baking, blanch the carrots and parsnips in boiling water for 2 minutes. Drain and set aside.

In a medium-size saucepan, melt the butter over medium heat. Add the mushrooms and sauté until golden, about 5 minutes. Whisk in the flour to form a paste. Stir in the chicken broth and cook until smooth and thickened. Stir in the wine and any pan drippings from the baked chicken breasts. Remove from the heat and stir in the sour cream. Add salt and pepper to taste.

To assemble the casserole, combine the carrots, parsnips, peas, and artichokes with the sauce. Pour over the chicken in the baking dish. Reduce the oven temperature to 350°F. Bake for 40 minutes or until heated through.

Adapted from a recipe submitted by Mona Newkirk
Walpole Historical Society
Walpole, New Hampshire

Chicken Divine

MAKES 4 SERVINGS

This is the dish that is credited with introducing Americans to broccoli in the 1930s. You can't go wrong with this popular combination of chicken, mushrooms, and broccoli in a creamy rich sauce. It's especially good served with noodles.

2 packages (10 ounces each) frozen broccoli spears

½ lemon

2 whole chicken breasts, boned, skinned, and split

1 can (6 ounces) sliced mushrooms, drained

1 can (10¾ ounces) condensed cream of mushroom soup

1 cup sour cream

½ to ¾ cup dry sherry

Paprika

Preheat the oven to 350°F. Cook the broccoli according to the package directions until just tender. Drain well.

Butter a 2-quart casserole dish. Arrange the broccoli in the casserole and squeeze the lemon over the broccoli. Place the chicken on the broccoli. Combine the mushrooms, soup, sour cream, and sherry. Pour over the chicken. Sprinkle generously with paprika. Bake, uncovered, for 1 hour. Serve hot.

Margaret Newton
CHURCH OF THE EPIPHANY
SOUTHBURY, CONNECTICUT

Fast and Fancy Chicken
Makes 6 Servings

Topnotch! Very good flavor, moist, and just downright good. The mushrooms are optional, but they make a delicious addition. This chicken dish is perfect for a family dinner or a small party.

3 whole chicken breasts, boned, skinned, and split

6 slices Swiss cheese

4 ounces mushrooms, sliced (optional)

1 can (10¾ ounces) condensed cream of chicken or cream of mushroom soup

½ cup white wine (or ¼ cup milk and ¼ cup water)

2 cups herb stuffing mix

½ cup (1 stick) butter, melted

Preheat the oven to 350°F. Lightly grease a 9-inch by 13-inch baking dish.

Place the chicken in a single layer in the baking dish. Top each piece with a slice of cheese. Sprinkle the mushrooms over the cheese. Mix together the soup and wine and pour over the chicken. Spread the dry stuffing mix over the top. Drizzle the melted butter over the stuffing. Bake, uncovered, for 50 minutes. Serve hot.

Marge A. Cousens
Emmanuel Church
Newport, Rhode Island

Extra-Special Chicken

MAKES 6 SERVINGS

A simple dinner, rich in flavor.

1 package (4½ ounces) sliced dried beef, chopped

3 whole chicken breasts, boned, skinned, and split

6 slices bacon

1 can (10¾ ounces) condensed cream of mushroom soup

1 cup sour cream

Preheat the oven to 350°F. Run cold water over the dried beef. Drain and arrange in the bottom of a 9-inch by 13-inch baking dish. Place the chicken breasts on top of the beef and top each piece with a slice of bacon. Bake, uncovered, for 30 minutes.

Combine the soup and sour cream. Pour over the chicken. Bake for another 25 minutes. Serve hot.

Mary Jane Sears
WILLINGTON BAPTIST CHURCH
WILLINGTON, CONNECTICUT

Chicken Doble

MAKES 6 SERVINGS

Here's a simple dish that couldn't be tastier. Try red wine vinegar in place of the cider vinegar for a change of pace, and serve with rice.

2 pounds chicken thighs, skinned

2 garlic cloves, chopped

¼ cup soy sauce

¼ cup cider vinegar

½ cup water

Combine all the ingredients in a heavy 2-quart saucepan or Dutch oven. Bring to a boil and boil for 30 minutes. Reduce the heat and simmer for 15 minutes. Serve hot.

Larry Godin
CHEBEAGUE PARENTS ASSOCIATION
CHEBEAGUE ISLAND, MAINE

CHICKEN SATAY

MAKES 6 TO 8 SERVINGS

Skewered chicken flavored with peanuts and spices—this unusual dish is exotic enough to thrill the grownups, but mild enough for kids—perfect for a family cookout or a small outdoor party. Serve these with skewers of grilled vegetables—Vidalia onions, mushrooms, zucchini, and red bell peppers. Delicious!

3 pounds boneless, skinless chicken breasts, cut into cubes for skewers

¼ cup soy sauce

¼ cup orange juice

2 tablespoons vegetable oil

½ teaspoon red pepper flakes, crushed

1 garlic clove, minced

¼ cup peanut butter

2 tablespoons minced onion

1 teaspoon ground coriander

1 teaspoon ground turmeric

½ teaspoon ground ginger

¼ cup chopped fresh cilantro

Place the chicken in a large shallow bowl or baking dish. Combine the remaining ingredients and pour over the chicken. Marinate overnight in the refrigerator, turning a few times.

Prepare a fire in a grill or preheat the broiler. Thread the chicken onto skewers. Grill or broil the chicken for 5 to 7 minutes on each side. Serve hot.

Ursula Abbott
FIRST PARISH IN NEEDHAM, UNITARIAN UNIVERSALIST
NEEDHAM, MASSACHUSETTS

Chicken Hawaiian

Makes 4 servings

Enjoy a taste of Hawaii on a cold New England night. This is a good choice when unexpected company drops by because it can be easily extended by adding chunks of onions, mushrooms, bell peppers, carrots, or broccoli. Just steam or sauté the vegetables separately and add to the baking dish during the last 15 minutes of cooking. This is great served on rice.

2 whole chicken breasts, boned, skinned, and split

1 can (16 or 20 ounces) pineapple chunks in juice

¼ cup soy sauce

½ to 1 teaspoon ground ginger

2 tablespoons cornstarch

Place the chicken, whole or cut into bite-size pieces, in a shallow glass bowl or baking dish. Drain the pineapple. Mix the pineapple juice with the soy sauce and ginger. Pour the mixture over the chicken. Marinate the chicken for 30 to 60 minutes, or overnight in the refrigerator.

Preheat the oven to 400°F. Lightly grease a 9-inch by 13-inch baking dish. Remove the chicken from the marinade, place it in the baking dish, and sprinkle with the cornstarch. Bake for 20 to 25 minutes. Turn the chicken, cover with the pineapple chunks and remaining marinade, and bake for 15 minutes. Serve hot.

Adapted from a recipe submitted by Myrtle P. Rowland
St. Peter's Episcopal Church
Oxford, Connecticut

TERIYAKI-LEMON CHICKEN

MAKES 6 SERVINGS

Crispy on the outside, flavorful on the inside, these chicken breasts are great! Serve over rice for a good family supper or a small dinner party.

3 whole chicken breasts, boned, skinned, and split

¼ cup all-purpose white flour

2 to 4 tablespoons unsalted butter

⅓ cup teriyaki sauce

3 tablespoons lemon juice

1 teaspoon minced garlic

½ teaspoon white sugar

Roll the chicken in the flour to coat. Melt the butter in a large heavy skillet over medium heat. Add the chicken and brown on both sides, about 7 minutes per side. Remove the chicken to a plate and keep warm. Add the remaining ingredients to the skillet and mix well. Return the chicken to the skillet and simmer for 3 to 5 minutes. Turn the chicken and simmer for another 3 to 5 minutes, with the pan covered, or until the chicken is cooked through.

Cari Marchese
NORTH PARISH CHURCH OF NORTH ANDOVER, UNITARIAN UNIVERSALIST
NORTH ANDOVER, MASSACHUSETTS

SAVORY BUTTERMILK CHICKEN
MAKES 6 TO 8 SERVINGS

Meltingly tender chicken morsels with a crispy coating flavored with Parmesan cheese. Very good, and very little work. Use freshly grated Parmesan cheese for the best results.

1½ cups all-purpose white flour

⅔ cup grated Parmesan cheese

¾ teaspoon paprika

¾ teaspoon dried oregano

¼ teaspoon pepper

4 whole chicken breasts, skinned and split

1 cup buttermilk

¼ to ½ cup (½ to 1 stick) butter, melted

Preheat the oven to 350°F. Line a baking pan with aluminum foil for easy cleanup.

Mix the flour, cheese, and seasonings in a plastic bag. Dip the chicken in the buttermilk, then in the flour mixture. Arrange in a single layer in the baking pan. Drizzle the melted butter over the chicken. Bake for 50 minutes. Increase the oven temperature to 400°F and bake for another 10 minutes to make the crust crispy. Do not turn the chicken while it is baking. Serve hot.

Lee Ann Robinson
CHEBEAGUE PARENTS ASSOCIATION
CHEBEAGUE ISLAND, MAINE

Sesame-Seed Chicken

MAKES 4 SERVINGS

These tasty cutlets are especially popular with children, who love the crunchy coating made with sesame seeds. A dipping sauce made quickly with preserves, soy sauce, and garlic is a very pleasing accompaniment. Serve with rice and a green salad.

CUTLETS

¼ cup all-purpose white flour

2 eggs, beaten

2 tablespoons soy sauce

2 tablespoons water

1 cup dry bread crumbs

¼ cup sesame seeds

1 teaspoon paprika

½ teaspoon garlic salt

½ teaspoon salt

½ teaspoon pepper

1 pound chicken cutlets

Vegetable oil for frying

SAUCE

1 jar (10 or 12 ounces) apricot or peach preserves

1 to 2 tablespoons water

1 garlic clove, minced

2 teaspoons soy sauce

Place the flour in a shallow bowl. In another shallow bowl, combine the eggs, 2 tablespoons soy sauce, and water. In a third bowl, combine the bread crumbs, sesame seeds, paprika, garlic salt, salt, and pepper. Coat the chicken pieces with flour. Dip them in the egg mixture and then in the crumb mixture to coat well.

In a large heavy skillet, heat ¼ inch of oil for frying. Add the cutlets and fry on both sides until tender, 3 to 5 minutes per side. Keep warm.

To make the sauce, combine the ingredients in a small saucepan and heat gently. Or combine them in a microwave-safe container and microwave on high for 2 minutes.

If you are not serving immediately, the chicken can be refrigerated. Reheat the chicken at 325°F for about 20 minutes. Serve the chicken with the sauce on the side.

Nancy Shanley Schnyer
HARWINTON LIBRARY FRIENDS
HARWINTON, CONNECTICUT

GREEN-CHILI CHICKEN CASSEROLE

MAKES 6 TO 8 SERVINGS

A delicious use for leftover chicken, turkey, or beef. Probably not the best choice for kids, but great for those who like their food on the spicy side.

2 tablespoons butter

1 medium-size onion, diced

16 ounces fresh mushrooms, sliced

1 tablespoon all-purpose white flour

1 cup chicken broth

1 carton (16 ounces) sour cream

1 to 2 cups chopped canned green chilies

1 package (9½ ounces) 6-inch corn tortillas, quartered

3 cups shredded, cooked chicken

8 ounces Monterey Jack cheese, grated

Preheat the oven to 350°F.

Melt the butter in a medium-size saucepan over medium heat. Add the onion and mushrooms and sauté until limp, about 5 minutes. Blend in the flour. Stir in the chicken broth and continue to stir and cook until thickened. Remove from the heat and stir in the sour cream and chilies.

In a greased 2-quart casserole dish, layer the tortillas, chicken, sauce, and cheese, ending with a layer of cheese on top. Bake for 35 to 40 minutes, until heated through. Serve hot.

Adapted from a recipe submitted by Lori Baird
HOPKINTON COOKIE EXCHANGE
HOPKINTON, NEW HAMPSHIRE

Turkey-Almond Casserole

Ever find yourself with a house full of guests after a holiday? This casserole of turkey, mushrooms, water chestnuts, and almonds is delicious and elegant—and makes good use of leftover cooked turkey or chicken.

¼ cup (½ stick) butter

¼ cup all-purpose white flour

1 cup chicken broth

¾ cup milk

2 tablespoons sherry

½ teaspoon salt

¼ teaspoon pepper

4 cups cubed cooked turkey or chicken

1 can (4 ounces) sliced mushrooms, drained

1 can (8 ounces) sliced water chestnuts, drained

⅔ cup slivered or whole almonds

1 medium-size onion, minced

Paprika

Preheat the oven to 350°F. In a medium-size saucepan, melt the butter over low heat. Blend in the flour. Cook until smooth and bubbly, stirring constantly. Stir in the broth and milk. Heat to boiling, reduce the heat, and simmer until thick. Remove from the heat and stir in the sherry, salt, and pepper.

In a 2-quart baking dish, spread half the turkey. Top with the mushrooms, water chestnuts, almonds, and onion. Arrange the remaining turkey on top. Cover with the sauce. Sprinkle with the paprika and bake for about 45 minutes or until heated through.

Rebecca Phipps McGee
Chebeague Parents Association
Chebeague Island, Maine

WILD RICE AND TURKEY CASSEROLE

MAKES 6 TO 8 SERVINGS

We loved this extravagant combination of wild rice, mushrooms, turkey, and almonds. A very special way to use holiday leftovers.

1 cup wild rice

¼ cup (½ stick) butter

16 ounces mushrooms, sliced

½ cup chopped onion

1¼ cups heavy cream

3 cups diced cooked turkey

½ cup blanched sliced almonds

3 cups chicken broth

Salt and pepper to taste

Wash the rice thoroughly. Place in a large saucepan and cover with water. Bring to a boil, then remove from the heat and set aside for 1 hour. Drain.

Preheat the oven to 350°F. Grease a 2-quart casserole dish.

In a large skillet, melt the butter. Add the mushrooms and onion and sauté until browned, about 8 minutes. Add to the rice, along with the remaining ingredients, and mix well. Spoon into the casserole and bake for about 1 hour, until the rice is tender.

Adapted from a recipe submitted by Bobby Head
STOW HISTORICAL SOCIETY
STOW, MASSACHUSETTS

Hot Turkey Salad

MAKES 5 TO 6 SERVINGS

Easy, very quick, and a tasty way to use up leftover Thanksgiving turkey. Works with chicken, too. If you are feeling adventurous, consider adding a can of pineapple chunks or a cup of seedless grapes to the casserole. If you are watching your diet, by all means feel free to substitute cracker or cereal crumbs for the crushed potato chips, and use low-fat mayonnaise.

2 cups cubed cooked turkey

2 cups sliced celery

½ cup toasted sliced almonds

2 teaspoons minced onion

2 tablespoons lemon juice

1 cup mayonnaise

½ cup grated cheese (Cheddar, American, etc.)

1 cup crushed potato chips

Preheat the oven to 350°F. Combine the turkey, celery, almonds, onion, lemon juice, and mayonnaise. Toss lightly to mix and pile into a 1½-quart casserole dish. Sprinkle with the cheese and chips. Bake for 20 minutes. Serve hot.

Patricia Kirk-Hodges
UNITARIAN UNIVERSALIST CHURCH OF CARIBOU
CARIBOU, MAINE

Turkey Casserole
Makes 4 to 6 servings

For those who just can't get enough turkey and stuffing at the holiday meal, a simple casserole to blend the two with a creamy cheese sauce.

1½ cups stovetop stuffing mix

1 can (10¾ ounces) condensed cream of mushroom soup

½ cup milk

½ cup sour cream

1 cup grated Cheddar cheese (sharp is recommended)

4 cups cubed cooked turkey

Prepare the stuffing according to the package directions. Preheat the oven to 350°F.

In a medium-size saucepan, combine the soup, milk, sour cream, and cheese. Heat until the cheese is melted.

In a 9-inch by 13-inch baking dish, layer the sauce, turkey, and stuffing mix, ending with the stuffing mix on top. Heat for 30 to 40 minutes or until hot and bubbly.

Adapted from a recipe submitted by Gladys Anderson
Willington Baptist Church
Willington, Connecticut

MAIN DISHES WITH MEAT

IN THIS MELTING POT of a chapter, we have a veritable smor-
gasbord of flavors—from Swedish meatballs to Greek shish
kebabs, from Italian stuffed shells to a Danish omelet. These
dishes reflect both our wide-ranging ethnic heritage and our willing-
ness to adapt new ideas and new flavors into our own cooking.

There are recipes here for beef, pork, and lamb, as well as ham,
bacon, and sausage, with a preponderance of recipes that require
ground beef. When cooking for a big crowd, ground beef is an economical choice that can be stretched if you end up feeding more
people than you expected.

If there is one theme that unites this chapter, it is surely how
quickly many of these dishes can be whipped together. Most can be
made ahead and cooked at your convenience. Some do simmer on
the back of the stove or bake for more than an hour; during that
time, you are free to be elsewhere, getting ready for the guests who
are sure to enjoy your efforts.

CRANBERRY POT ROAST
MAKES 8 SERVINGS

We've seen pot roasts flavored with horseradish and pot roasts flavored with rum. But this cranberry-and-spice version is a tasty twist on an old Yankee favorite.

2 tablespoons all-purpose white flour

4 pounds beef pot roast (boneless chuck or rump roast)

3 tablespoons solid vegetable shortening

1 can (16 ounces) whole-berry cranberry sauce

8 whole cloves

1 cinnamon stick

Salt and pepper to taste

Rub the flour into the roast. Melt the shortening in a Dutch oven. Brown the roast in the shortening, turning it to brown all sides. Reduce the heat and add the remaining ingredients. Cover and simmer for at least 3 hours, turning once or twice during the cooking. When the meat is tender, remove from the pan. Strain the drippings and discard the spices. Allow the drippings to cool and skim off the fat that rises to the surface. Reheat the meat in the degreased sauce, then bring to the table to carve, serving the sauce on the side.

Eunice M. Grohowski
HARWINTON LIBRARY FRIENDS
HARWINTON, CONNECTICUT

Island Teriyaki

Makes 4 to 6 servings

A wonderfully flavorful recipe—great for a barbecue!

½ cup soy sauce

¼ cup brown sugar

2 tablespoons olive oil

1 teaspoon ground ginger

¼ teaspoon cracked pepper

2 garlic cloves, minced

1½ pounds beefsteak (sirloin, London broil, etc.)

In a shallow glass baking dish, combine the soy sauce, brown sugar, olive oil, ginger, pepper, and garlic. Add the beef, turning until it is well coated with the marinade. Set aside to marinate for 2 hours at room temperature or longer in the refrigerator. Broil or cook on a grill to desired doneness.

Rise Caron
Harwinton Library Friends
Harwinton, Connecticut

This is ev'ry Cook's Opinion,
No sav'ry Dish without an Onyon;
But lest your kissing should be spoyl'd,
Your Onyons must be th'roughly boyl'd.

—Jonathan Swift, 17th-century poet

SPICED CURRIED BEEF
MAKES 10 TO 12 SERVINGS

Made with stew beef or another low grade of beef, this is a good, inexpensive dish that will feed at least 10 people. Serve it with condiments (chutney, sliced bananas, chopped tomatoes, raisins, coconut, or chopped hard-boiled eggs) on separate plates.

2 tablespoons olive oil

3 to 4 medium-size onions, chopped

4 pounds stew beef, cut in 1-inch cubes

1 can (28 ounces) Italian tomatoes (do not drain)

2 teaspoons salt

½ teaspoon chili powder

4 tablespoons curry powder

2 tablespoons vinegar

1½ teaspoons white sugar

Tomato juice (optional)

Hot cooked rice

In a Dutch oven, heat the oil over medium heat. Add the onions and sauté until golden, about 10 minutes. Remove the onions from the pan and set aside. In the same oil (adding more, if necessary), brown the meat. Return the onions to the pan along with the tomatoes, salt, and chili powder. Cover and simmer for 30 minutes. Blend the curry with the vinegar and sugar and add to the pan. Cover and simmer for 2 hours. Add tomato juice if extra liquid is needed. Serve over rice.

Val Rugge
EAST DOVER BAPTIST CHURCH
EAST DOVER, VERMONT

Swedish Meatballs

MAKES 6 TO 8 SERVINGS

An excellent version of an ever-popular buffet dish.

2 slices white bread

¾ cup milk

1 small onion, finely chopped

2 eggs, lightly beaten

¼ teaspoon sugar

Salt and pepper to taste

2 pounds ground beef

½ cup all-purpose white flour

2 tablespoons margarine or vegetable oil

In a mixing bowl, soak the bread in the milk. Add the onion, eggs, sugar, and salt and pepper. Add the ground beef and mix well. Using two spoons or wet hands, form the meat mixture into balls between the size of Ping-Pong balls and golf balls. Roll in the flour.

Heat the margarine in a large skillet. Fry the meatballs until golden brown. You will have to fry them in several batches. As the meatballs brown, transfer them to a shallow baking pan and keep warm in a 300°F oven.

Sylvia M. Brown
FIRST UNIVERSALIST CHURCH OF ESSEX
ESSEX, MASSACHUSETTS

SWEET-AND-SOUR MEATBALLS

MAKES 6 TO 8 SERVINGS

Delicious! Cranberries add a New England touch to these tasty morsels. Leftovers, if there are any, will keep well in the freezer.

2 pounds lean ground beef

1 cup cornflake crumbs

⅓ cup dried parsley

2 eggs, lightly beaten

2 teaspoons soy sauce

¼ cup ketchup

2 teaspoons minced onion

2 tablespoons solid vegetable
   shortening

1 can (16 ounces) whole-berry
   cranberry sauce

1 bottle (12 ounces) chili sauce

2 teaspoons brown sugar

1 teaspoon lemon juice

Combine the beef with the cornflake crumbs, parsley, eggs, soy sauce, ketchup, and onion and mix well. Using two spoons or wet hands, form the meat mixture into balls between the size of Ping-Pong balls and golf balls.

Preheat the oven to 350°F.

Heat the shortening in a large skillet. Fry the meatballs until they are golden brown. You will have to fry them in several batches. As the meatballs brown, transfer them to a shallow baking pan.

When the meatballs are browned, make the sauce. Combine the remaining ingredients and pour over the meatballs. Bake for 20 to 30 minutes and serve hot.

Doris C. Newman
GOSHEN HISTORICAL SOCIETY
GOSHEN, NEW HAMPSHIRE

MEATBALLS IN ONION GRAVY
MAKES 4 SERVINGS

A very easy recipe that offers a good time-saving alternative to the task of hand-rolling meatballs. Serve over mashed potatoes, noodles, or rice.

1 envelope onion soup mix

1 tablespoon all-purpose white flour

2 cups water

½ teaspoon Worcestershire sauce

1 pound ground beef

1 egg, slightly beaten

1 teaspoon dried oregano

1 to 2 garlic cloves, minced

½ cup rolled oats

½ cup milk

¼ teaspoon salt

In a large skillet, combine the soup mix, flour, water, and Worcestershire sauce. Bring to a boil over moderate heat.

In a mixing bowl, combine the beef, egg, oregano, garlic, oats, milk, and salt and mix well. Drop by the rounded teaspoonful into the simmering gravy. Cook for about 5 minutes, then turn the meatballs over. Cover and simmer for another 5 minutes.

Adapted from a recipe submitted by Shirley E. Tucker
ST. PETER'S EPISCOPAL CHURCH
OXFORD, CONNECTICUT

Barbecued Meat Loaves
Makes 4 servings

A huge hit! Kids love having their own mini loaves, and the basting helps keep the top from getting too crusty. Especially good with mashed potatoes and buttered carrots.

MEAT LOAVES

1 pound lean ground beef

1 egg, lightly beaten

¼ cup fine dry bread crumbs or cornflake crumbs

1 tablespoon dried parsley

¼ cup water

2 tablespoons chopped onion

2 tablespoons prepared horseradish

1 teaspoon salt

⅛ teaspoon pepper

SAUCE

½ cup chili sauce

3 tablespoons ketchup

1 teaspoon Worcestershire sauce

½ teaspoon dry mustard

Dash Tabasco sauce

Preheat the oven to 350°F. Grease a shallow baking pan.

Combine all the ingredients for the meat loaves. Mix well and shape into four oblong loaves. Place these in the baking pan; do not allow them to touch. Combine the sauce ingredients and spread over the tops and sides of the loaves. Bake for about 45 minutes, basting the loaves two or three times with the drippings that accumulate.

Leslie Zimmer
St. Agatha's Church
Milton, Massachusetts

Meat Loaf with Onion Stuffing
Makes 6 to 8 servings

*The onion stuffing makes this a nice change of pace for a family dinner—
and the chili sauce makes a wonderful topping!*

MEAT LOAF
1½ pounds ground beef or turkey

½ pound ground pork

4 slices of bread, soaked in warm
    water, then squeezed

1 onion, minced

1 tablespoon salt

¼ teaspoon pepper

2 eggs, beaten

STUFFING
3 tablespoons vegetable oil

3 onions, finely chopped

1½ cups fresh soft bread crumbs

1 teaspoon ground or dried sage

½ teaspoon salt

⅛ teaspoon pepper

2 tablespoons chopped fresh parsley

1 egg, beaten

2 teaspoons water

½ cup chili sauce

Preheat the oven to 350°F.

Combine the meats, bread, minced onion, salt, pepper, and eggs. Mix thoroughly. Reserve about one-third of the meat mixture and use the remainder to line the bottom and sides of a 9-inch by 5-inch loaf pan.

To make the stuffing, heat the oil in a large skillet over medium-low heat. Add the onions and sauté until golden, about 10 minutes. Add the bread crumbs, sage, salt, pepper, and parsley and sauté until evenly browned. Remove from the heat and mix in the egg and the water.

Fill the center of the loaf pan with the stuffing mixture. Cover with the remaining meat. Top with the chili sauce. Bake for 45 minutes.

Adapted from a recipe submitted by Marian McAllister
Daughters of St. Bernard, St. Bernard's Church
Rockland, Maine

RUTH'S LASAGNA
MAKES 8 TO 10 SERVINGS

Highly recommended! The prepared sauce makes it quicker and easier to fix than most lasagna recipes, and the results are better, our tester reports, than many restaurant versions. A good do-ahead dinner, too.

16 ounces dried lasagna noodles

1¼ pounds chuck, chopped

1 bottle (26 ounces) spaghetti sauce with mushrooms

1 tablespoon white sugar

1½ pounds cottage cheese

3 eggs, lightly beaten

¼ teaspoon cayenne pepper

¾ pound mozzarella cheese, shredded

Grated Parmesan cheese

1 cup milk

Cook the lasagna noodles according to the package directions, being sure to add a teaspoon of oil to the cooking water. Rinse and drain.

In a nonstick skillet, brown the meat and drain off any excess fat. Heat the sauce and add the meat to the sauce along with the sugar.

Combine the cottage cheese, eggs, and cayenne.

Preheat the oven to 350°F. To assemble the lasagna, spoon a thin layer of sauce on the bottom of a 9-inch by 13-inch pan. Place a layer of noodles, another thin layer of sauce, a layer of the cottage cheese mixture, then the mozzarella. Repeat until the pan is filled. End with a final layer of sauce and Parmesan cheese. Gently pour milk over the top. Cover with foil and bake for 1 hour. Uncover and let stand for 5 to 10 minutes before cutting into serving-size pieces.

Fred Swallow
EAST DOVER BAPTIST CHURCH
EAST DOVER, VERMONT

PARTY CASSEROLE

MAKES 6 TO 8 SERVINGS

A simplified—but delicious—lasagna for cooks who like to get out of the kitchen fast. This easy-to-prepare dish can be made ahead and refrigerated until you're ready to bake it.

8 ounces medium-wide spinach noodles

1 to 1½ pounds ground beef

1 onion, finely chopped

2 cans (8 ounces each) tomato sauce

½ teaspoon dried oregano

1 package (8 ounces) cream cheese, at room temperature

¼ cup sour cream

1 cup cottage cheese

3 scallions, finely chopped

1 teaspoon salt

Dash pepper

¼ cup grated Parmesan cheese (optional)

Cook the noodles according to the package directions. Drain and set aside.

In a nonstick skillet, brown the meat and the onion. Add the tomato sauce and oregano. Taste and adjust the seasonings, if desired.

Combine the cream cheese, sour cream, cottage cheese, scallions, salt, and pepper.

Preheat the oven to 350°F. To assemble the casserole, grease a 9-inch by 13-inch baking dish. Layer half the noodles, all the cream cheese mixture, the remaining noodles, and the meat sauce. Top with the Parmesan cheese, if desired. Bake for 20 to 30 minutes. Serve hot.

Adapted from a recipe submitted by Shirley Martin
CHURCH OF THE EPIPHANY
SOUTHBURY, CONNECTICUT

ITALIAN SHELLS

MAKES 6 TO 8 SERVINGS

Italian food is always popular at a potluck. Watch these well-seasoned shells disappear from the table. This is another convenient do-ahead dish that can be pulled out of the refrigerator and baked just before serving.

1 package (12 ounces) jumbo shells

1 pound ground beef

1 pound hot Italian sausage, casings removed

1 carton (15 ounces) ricotta or low-fat cottage cheese

16 ounces mozzarella cheese, shredded (about 3 cups)

Garlic powder, oregano, basil, salt, and pepper to taste

1 jar (14 ounces) spaghetti sauce

Grated Parmesan cheese

Chopped fresh parsley, to garnish

Cook the shells according to the package directions. Drain, then cover with cold water and set aside.

In a nonstick skillet, brown the meats. Drain off the excess fat. Then add the ricotta and mozzarella and the seasonings to taste.

Preheat the oven to 350°F. Lightly grease a 9-inch by 13-inch baking pan. Remove the shells from the water, fill with the meat-and-cheese mixture, and place in the baking pan. Cover with the sauce. Sprinkle with Parmesan cheese and parsley. Bake for 40 minutes. Serve hot.

Ellen Moore
ST. BRENDAN'S CATHOLIC WOMAN'S CLUB
COLEBROOK, NEW HAMPSHIRE

CRUNCHY HAMBURGER CASSEROLE
MAKES 6 TO 8 SERVINGS

A casserole classic with noodles, ground beef, cream of mushroom soup, and French-fried onions. Quick, easy, and really good.

2 cups uncooked egg noodles

1 pound ground beef

1 can (10¾ ounces) condensed cream of mushroom soup

1 can (14½ ounces) tomatoes, drained

¾ cup shredded cheese (Cheddar, Colby, Monterey Jack, etc.)

¾ cup diced green bell pepper (optional)

Salt and pepper to taste

1 can (2.8 ounces) French-fried onions

Cook the noodles according to the package directions. Drain well.

In a nonstick skillet, brown the meat. Drain off any excess fat.

Preheat the oven to 350°F. Combine the noodles, beef, soup, tomatoes, cheese, and green pepper. Add salt and pepper to taste. Pour into a greased 9-inch by 13-inch baking dish. Cover and bake for 40 minutes. Uncover and sprinkle the onions on top. Bake for an additional 5 minutes. Serve hot.

Terry York
CHEBEAGUE PARENTS ASSOCIATION
CHEBEAGUE ISLAND, MAINE

Baby (Back Ribs) on Board

*D*o your stews spill or your tortes topple en route to your potluck destination? Here are some pointers for getting your gourmet creation from here to there in one piece:

❧ Keep a couple of medium-size boxes around the house. Place your casserole dish inside and fill the box with either crumpled newspaper or popcorn—air-popped with no butter (it's a terrific munchie after you arrive). The stuffing keeps the dish from sliding around.

❧ If you frequent potluck suppers, you may want to invest in a pie basket. They're great for carting cookies and bars, breads, serving spoons—even pies!

❧ One potlucker who had to transport a seven-layer matzo cake down a bumpy New England road during mud season came up with an ingenious idea for transporting layer cakes: After the cake layers have cooled, remove them from the pans and wrap them well in plastic wrap. Place the frosting in a covered container. Assemble and frost your cake once you arrive.

❧ Pour liquids into containers that can be closed tightly. You may want to transport the soup or beverage in a sturdy bowl and serve it from a prettier one.

STOVETOP HAMBURGER CASSEROLE
MAKES 6 SERVINGS

A quick and easy recipe that would also be good as a stuffing for peppers. For variety—or lower fat content—substitute chicken for the hamburger, or omit both the beef and the chicken and serve it as a vegetarian dish. To stretch this recipe to feed a bigger crowd, cook more rice.

1½ pounds lean ground beef

1 onion, chopped

1 can (16 ounces) stewed tomatoes

1 can (10¾ ounces) condensed tomato bisque or tomato soup plus ½ can water

1 package (16 ounces) frozen mixed vegetables

2 cups cooked rice (1 cup uncooked)

Salt and pepper to taste

In a large nonstick skillet, brown the meat with the onion. Drain off any excess fat. Add the stewed tomatoes and tomato bisque plus water. Heat thoroughly. Add the vegetables and cook for 3 to 6 minutes, until heated through. Add the rice and simmer a few minutes until hot. Season to taste with salt and pepper.

Madeline Boucher
ST. BRENDAN'S CATHOLIC WOMAN'S CLUB
COLEBROOK, NEW HAMPSHIRE

HAMBURGER HOT DISH

MAKES 6 TO 8 SERVINGS

Wild rice and water chestnuts make this delightfully different from the usual hamburger casserole and an excellent choice for a potluck. Our testers loved it!

1 cup uncooked wild rice

1 pound ground beef

1 cup beef broth or bouillon

1 large onion, chopped

½ cup chopped carrots

1 cup chopped celery

1 cup chopped mushrooms

1 can (8 ounces) sliced water
chestnuts, rinsed and drained

1 can (10¾ ounces) condensed cream
of mushroom soup

Cook the wild rice according to the package directions.

Preheat the oven to 350°F. In a nonstick skillet, brown the ground beef. Drain off any excess fat. Combine with the rice and all the remaining ingredients in a 9-inch by 13-inch baking dish. Bake, uncovered, for about 30 minutes or until heated through.

Vera Shinner

WOMEN'S ALLIANCE, FIRST PARISH CONGREGATION UNITARIAN CHURCH
KENNEBUNK, MAINE

Beef 'n' Biscuit Casserole

Makes 4 to 5 servings

Outstanding! A creamy, cheesy chili mixture baked between biscuit layers. A great supper to rustle up midweek, when time is short and the kids are starved. The rare leftovers are excellent, too.

1 pound ground beef

½ cup chopped onion

¼ cup diced green bell pepper

1 can (8 ounces) tomato sauce

2 teaspoons chili powder

½ teaspoon garlic salt

1 can (8 ounces) refrigerator buttermilk biscuits

1½ cups grated Cheddar cheese

½ cup sour cream

1 egg, slightly beaten

Preheat the oven to 375°F. In a large nonstick skillet, brown the ground beef with the onion and green pepper. Drain off any excess fat. Stir in the tomato sauce, chili powder, and garlic salt. Let simmer.

Separate the biscuit dough into 10 biscuits; split each in half. Press 10 biscuit halves over the bottom of an ungreased 8-inch or 9-inch square baking pan. In a bowl, mix ½ cup of the cheese with the sour cream and egg.

Remove the meat mixture from the heat and stir in the sour cream mixture. Spoon over the biscuit dough. Arrange the remaining biscuit halves on top. Sprinkle with the remaining 1 cup of cheese. Bake for 25 to 30 minutes, until golden brown.

Bill Pahl
Handel Society, Dartmouth College Department of Music
Hanover, New Hampshire

SEVEN-LAYER DINNER
MAKES 4 TO 6 SERVINGS

A perfect one-pot, family-style meal. To save time, you can substitute canned or frozen peas or green beans for some or all of the green pepper, celery, or mushrooms.

1 pound ground beef

4 medium-size potatoes, peeled and sliced

1 cup sliced onions

½ cup uncooked rice

1 can (15 ounces) diced tomatoes

1 green bell pepper, sliced

1 stalk celery, sliced

1 cup sliced mushrooms

4 slices bacon

Cold water

In a large nonstick skillet, brown the ground beef. Drain off any excess fat. Preheat the oven to 350°F.

Line a 3-quart or 4-quart casserole with the potatoes. Spread the onions over the potatoes, then add the ground beef. Sprinkle the rice over the beef. Pour the tomatoes over all and top with the vegetables. Place the bacon on top of the casserole. Add enough cold water to just cover the casserole. Cover and bake for 1¾ hours.

Carolyn Kelly
OUR LADY OF GOOD HOPE CATHOLIC WOMEN'S CLUB
CAMDEN, MAINE

Beef Curry

MAKES 6 TO 8 SERVINGS

A good hot-and-spicy dish that's even better reheated the next day. Use firm baking apples, such as Golden Delicious, so they don't turn to mush, and serve with rice and a tossed salad for a complete meal.

3 tablespoons olive oil

4 medium-size onions, chopped

4 garlic cloves, minced

2 pounds extra-lean ground beef

1 can (6 ounces) tomato paste

½ to 1 cup red wine

3 tablespoons Worcestershire sauce

2 tablespoons minced fresh gingerroot

1 bay leaf

4 tablespoons curry powder

5 whole cloves, crushed

1 teaspoon paprika

1 teaspoon black pepper

1 teaspoon ground turmeric (optional)

3 large apples, peeled, cored, and chopped

In a large skillet, heat the olive oil. Add the onions and garlic and sauté until limp, about 8 minutes. Then add the ground beef and sauté until browned. Add the tomato paste, wine, Worcestershire sauce, and seasonings. Add the apples. Simmer, covered if desired, for 15 to 30 minutes. Add water, if needed. Adjust the seasonings to taste. Remove the bay leaf before serving.

Douglas L. Armstrong
THEODORE PARKER UNITARIAN UNIVERSALIST CHURCH
WEST ROXBURY, MASSACHUSETTS

JOE'S GOULASH
MAKES 10 SERVINGS

A pleasing combination of beef, sausage, eggplant, and zucchini, slowly cooked in a tomato sauce, adds up to a hearty and tasty dinner when served over rice or noodles. Our testers added extra garlic and found it "simply delicious"!

1 pound ground beef

1 pound hot Italian sausage (link or patty)

1 pound sweet Italian sausage (link or patty)

2 tablespoons olive oil

3 medium-size zucchini, sliced

1 small eggplant, cubed

3 green bell peppers, cubed

2 onions, chopped

1 garlic clove, minced, or 1 teaspoon garlic powder (or more to taste)

2 cans (14½ ounces each) tomatoes

1½ teaspoons salt

2 teaspoons pepper

1 teaspoon chili powder

2 tablespoons white sugar

In a large Dutch oven, brown the ground beef and the sausages over medium heat. Remove with a slotted spoon and drain off the excess fat. Add the olive oil and heat. Add the vegetables and sauté until soft, about 10 minutes. Return the meat to the pan along with the remaining ingredients. Simmer, uncovered, for 1½ to 2 hours. If it seems dry, add more tomatoes. Serve over rice or noodles.

Joe Barker
THETFORD ACADEMY ALUMNI ASSOCIATION
THETFORD, VERMONT

Veal Patties
Makes 6 to 8 servings

Ask the butcher to grind the meat twice to achieve the best texture for these moist and tasty patties. They can be prepared a day ahead and reheated just before serving.

1½ pounds ground veal

1 cup dry bread crumbs

1 cup evaporated milk

2 eggs, slightly beaten

1 medium-size onion, chopped

1 tablespoon minced parsley

1 tablespoon minced celery

Salt and pepper to taste

3 tablespoons solid vegetable shortening

1 can (10¾ ounces) condensed cream of mushroom soup plus 1 can water

1 teaspoon curry powder

2 tablespoons butter

16 ounces mushrooms, sliced

1 teaspoon Kitchen Bouquet (optional)

In a large bowl, combine the veal, bread crumbs, evaporated milk, eggs, onion, parsley, celery, and salt and pepper. Shape into 8 patties or 16 balls. Melt the shortening in a large pot. Add the meat and cook until browned. Drain off excess fat.

Mix together the soup, water, and curry powder and pour the mixture over the meat. Cover and simmer over medium-low heat for about 40 minutes.

Meanwhile, melt the butter in a large frying pan over medium heat. Add the mushrooms and sauté until golden. Add the sautéed mushrooms and Kitchen Bouquet to the veal mixture. Add a little water if the sauce is too thick.

Nanette Parmelee Bopp
Walpole Historical Society
Walpole, New Hampshire

Barbecued Spareribs
Makes 4 servings

Very good! You can use the same dish for marinating and baking; just let it stand at room temperature for 5 minutes on its way from refrigerator to oven.

2 pounds country-style pork spareribs (preferably boneless)

Meat tenderizer (optional)

3 tablespoons brown sugar

2 tablespoons white sugar

3 tablespoons cider vinegar

3 tablespoons soy sauce

⅛ teaspoon garlic powder

½ cup chicken broth

Place the ribs in a shallow baking pan. Rub the meat tenderizer into the ribs, if using. In a small saucepan, mix together the sugars, vinegar, soy sauce, garlic powder, and chicken broth. Heat to just boiling. Pour over the ribs. Cover and refrigerate overnight.

Preheat the oven to 325°F. Bake the ribs and liquid for about 1 hour, turning the meat once.

Irene Patrick
Gustaf Adolph Lutheran Church
New Sweden, Maine

Apple-Glazed Pork Tenderloin

Makes 6 to 8 servings

What a wonderful way to prepare pork for company! This is simple but elegant and has a wonderful flavor. It can be left to marinate overnight, then slipped in the oven when the guests walk in the door. They'll love it!

2 whole pork tenderloins (each about ¾ pound)

½ cup bourbon

½ cup unfiltered apple cider

¼ cup firmly packed brown sugar

⅛ teaspoon cinnamon

Place the pork tenderloins in a glass baking dish. Mix the remaining ingredients and pour over the tenderloins. Cover with plastic wrap and refrigerate for 8 hours or more, turning the meat several times. (If you need more marinade, add ¼ cup more cider.)

Preheat the oven to 325°F. Place the baking dish with the meat and marinade in the oven and bake for 1¼ hours or until the internal temperature of the meat reaches 160°F (medium well) to 170°F (well-done). While the meat bakes, baste with the marinade every 10 or 15 minutes. Let stand for 10 to 15 minutes before carving.

Mary Gagnon
St. Isaac Jogues Church
East Hartford, Connecticut

Sweet-and-Sour Pork

Makes 6 servings

Fabulous! Lots of sauce and lots of flavor. Serve the ribs over plenty of rice for sopping up the extra sauce.

3 pounds country-style pork ribs, cut in 1½-inch pieces

3 tablespoons all-purpose white flour

1 cup diced celery

1 cup chopped green bell pepper

1 medium-size onion, chopped

1 can (20 ounces) pineapple chunks in juice (do not drain)

½ cup maple syrup

¼ cup vinegar

⅓ cup soy sauce

Preheat the oven to 400°F. Place the ribs in a large baking pan and bake for 30 minutes, stirring occasionally. Reduce the oven temperature to 350°F. Remove the ribs from the pan with a slotted spoon. Pour off the drippings, leaving about ¼ cup in the baking pan. Blend the flour into the remaining drippings until the mixture is smooth. Return the meat to the pan, along with the remaining ingredients, and bake for 1½ hours, basting every 20 minutes.

Helen K. Houston
Boscawen Historical Society
Boscawen, New Hampshire

CRANBERRY PORK CHOPS

MAKES 4 SERVINGS

Very simple and very tasty. Children like them, too.

4 thick-cut pork chops

1 can (16 ounces) whole-berry cranberry sauce

1 tablespoon honey

¼ teaspoon ground cloves

4 orange slices with peel, to garnish (optional)

Preheat the oven to 350°F. In a large skillet, brown the pork chops. Place the chops in a baking dish. Mix together the cranberry sauce, honey, and cloves. Pour over the pork chops. Cover and bake for 1 hour. Garnish with the orange slices.

Lawnie Roberge
STOW HISTORICAL SOCIETY
STOW, MASSACHUSETTS

PORK CHOP CASSEROLE

MAKES 4 SERVINGS

Quick, easy, and very good. A great choice to prepare ahead of time and bake at the last minute.

3 to 4 potatoes, peeled and thinly sliced

4 carrots, thinly sliced

1 to 2 onions, thinly sliced

4 pork chops

Salt and pepper to taste

1 can (10¾ ounces) condensed cream of celery soup plus 1 can water

Preheat the oven to 375°F. Lightly grease a 9-inch by 13-inch baking dish.

Layer the potatoes, carrots, and onions in the baking dish. Place the chops on top. Sprinkle with salt and pepper. Mix the soup with the water and pour over the chops. Cover and bake for 1½ hours. Serve hot.

Eva Fontaine
BOSCAWEN HISTORICAL SOCIETY
BOSCAWEN, NEW HAMPSHIRE

Pork Chops with Rice

Makes 6 servings

This one-dish meal is easy to prepare, and the pork chops are very tender. All in all, definitely a hit.

6 or more pork chops

1 package (3 ounces) Shake 'n Bake for Pork

½ cup chopped onion

1 can (6 ounces) sliced mushrooms, drained

2 cups cooked rice

2 cups chicken broth

½ teaspoon salt

1 tomato, sliced

Preheat the oven to 425°F. Coat the pork chops with the Shake 'n Bake. Place in a large Dutch oven or oven-proof skillet. Bake for 35 minutes.

Remove the chops from the Dutch oven and set aside. Place the Dutch oven over medium heat and add the onion and mushrooms. Sauté in the drippings until limp, about 4 minutes. Stir in the rice, chicken broth, and salt. Arrange the pork chops over the rice. Place the tomatoes on the chops. Sprinkle any remaining Shake 'n Bake on top and sprinkle with a little water. Return the chops to the oven and bake for about 15 minutes.

Charlotte Simmons
Willington Baptist Church
Willington, Connecticut

SHISH KEBABS
MAKES 6 TO 8 SERVINGS

This traditional way to prepare lamb is simple and simply wonderful, especially if you can cook it outside on a grill. Serve on or off the skewers with rice, a green salad, and pita bread that has been oiled, sprinkled with garlic, and toasted on a grill or in a toaster oven.

3 pounds leg of lamb or shoulder, cut in 1½-inch cubes

1 cup olive oil

⅓ cup lemon juice

¼ teaspoon crushed rosemary

2 garlic cloves, minced

¼ teaspoon salt

¼ teaspoon pepper

1 green bell pepper, cut in 1½-inch squares

1 red bell pepper, cut in 1½-inch squares

1 large onion, cut in 1½-inch squares

Cherry tomatoes

Place the lamb in a large shallow baking dish. Combine the olive oil, lemon juice, rosemary, garlic, salt, and pepper. Pour over the lamb, cover, and marinate overnight in the refrigerator, turning once or twice.

Just before serving, preheat the broiler or prepare a fire in the barbecue. Arrange the meat and vegetables on separate skewers. (The meat takes longer to cook than the vegetables do.)

Broil or grill, turning and brushing with the marinade every few minutes. The meat will be done in about 10 minutes, the vegetables in 5 to 6 minutes. Serve at once.

Linda Skinner
NEW ENGLAND HISTORIC GENEALOGICAL SOCIETY
BOSTON, MASSACHUSETTS

HOT PEPPERED LAMB

MAKES 4 SERVINGS

Faced with leftovers from Sunday's roast leg of lamb? This well-spiced dish, served over white or brown rice, is sure to be a hit.

¼ cup (½ stick) butter

⅓ cup chopped sweet or hot peppers

2 medium-size onions, chopped

1 cup chopped fresh mushrooms

2 garlic cloves, minced

½ teaspoon curry powder

½ teaspoon salt

Black pepper to taste

1½ cups diced cooked lamb

In a large skillet over medium heat, melt the butter. Add the peppers and onions and sauté until limp, about 4 minutes. Add the remaining ingredients and sauté over high heat until the lamb is heated through and the mushrooms are golden, 4 to 5 minutes.

Charles Kuntz

CHEBEAGUE PARENTS ASSOCIATION

CHEBEAGUE ISLAND, MAINE

Chinese Rice

MAKES 4 TO 6 SERVINGS

A quick, easy, and very good recipe that can be made with leftover ham, beef, or pork—or with no meat at all.

2 tablespoons vegetable oil

1 cup chopped cooked meat

4 cups cooked white rice (2 cups uncooked)

½ cup canned sliced mushrooms, drained

1½ tablespoons chopped scallions

1 red bell pepper, diced

2 tomatoes, diced

1 hard-boiled egg, sliced

2 to 3 tablespoons soy sauce (or more to taste)

2 to 3 tablespoons brown sugar

¼ teaspoon celery seeds

In a large heavy skillet, heat the oil over medium heat. Add the meat and brown slowly. Then add the remaining ingredients and cook for 5 to 7 minutes, stirring often. Serve hot.

Marie Gosselin
ST. BRENDAN'S CATHOLIC WOMAN'S CLUB
COLEBROOK, NEW HAMPSHIRE

Meat Pie

Makes 6 servings

This is especially good made with lamb, but whatever meat you choose, the winning combination of meat and vegetables baked under a biscuit crust is guaranteed to please.

FILLING

3 tablespoons vegetable oil

1½ pounds lamb, beef, pork, or veal, diced

1 large onion, chopped

2 cups peeled and diced potatoes

2 cups diced turnips

1 cup sliced carrots

1 cup water

1 tablespoon salt (or to taste)

⅛ teaspoon pepper

CRUST

1½ cups all-purpose white flour

1 tablespoon baking powder

1 teaspoon salt

3 tablespoons butter or solid vegetable shortening

¾ cup milk (can use skim or low-fat)

Preheat the oven to 275°F. Grease an 8-inch square baking dish.

In a large skillet, heat the oil over medium-high heat. Add the meat and onion and cook until the meat is browned. Drain off any excess fat. Place the meat in the baking dish along with the vegetables, water, 1 tablespoon salt, and pepper. Cover and bake for 2½ hours. (This can be done a day or so in advance and the mixture refrigerated.)

About 45 minutes before serving, preheat the oven to 400°F. Combine the flour, baking powder, and salt for the crust in a mixing bowl. Cut in the butter or shortening until the mixture resembles coarse meal. Add the milk and stir to form a dough. Drop by the spoonful on top of the meat and vegetables, leaving a few openings for steam to escape. Bake for about 30 minutes. Serve hot.

Adapted from a recipe submitted by Lois Sprague
OUR LADY OF GOOD HOPE CATHOLIC WOMEN'S CLUB
CAMDEN, MAINE

Fiesta Beans

MAKES 4 TO 8 SERVINGS

A good and easy supper that can also be left to simmer all day in a Crock-Pot on low heat.

6 slices bacon

½ green bell pepper, chopped

1 large onion, chopped

½ pound boiled ham, slivered

½ cup ketchup

2 cans (16 ounces each) baked beans

¼ cup brown sugar

1 tablespoon Worcestershire sauce

Salt and pepper to taste

Preheat the oven to 350°F. In a large heavy skillet, cook the bacon until crisp. Drain the bacon well, then crumble. Drain all but 2 tablespoons of the bacon grease from the skillet. Add the green pepper and onion and sauté gently for 5 minutes. Add the ham and cook for 2 to 3 minutes more.

In an 8-inch by 12-inch baking dish, combine all the ingredients. Mix well. Bake for 1 to 1¼ hours. Serve hot.

Ann M. Bridge
ST. JAMES EPISCOPAL CHURCH
KEENE, NEW HAMPSHIRE

SHREDDED POTATO AND HAM PIE

MAKES 6 SERVINGS

A great brunch or dinner dish that's easily doubled to feed a larger group and easily adapted to any cook's whim. Try bacon and Swiss cheese, tomato and mozzarella, or sausage and provolone.

4 eggs, slightly beaten

1 cup frozen mixed peas and carrots

1 cup chopped cooked ham

1½ cups shredded Cheddar cheese (6 ounces)

½ cup milk

¼ teaspoon dried minced onion or 1 tablespoon minced fresh onion

2 medium-size potatoes, peeled and shredded (about 2 cups)

Preheat the oven to 350°F. In a mixing bowl, combine the eggs, peas and carrots, ham, 1 cup of the cheese, the milk, and the onion. Mix well. Set aside.

Combine the shredded potatoes and remaining ½ cup cheese. Press the potato mixture onto the bottom and up the sides of an ungreased 9-inch pie plate or 8-inch square baking dish. Pour the filling over the potato mixture. Bake for 45 to 50 minutes or until the center is set. Let stand for 5 minutes before slicing in wedges or squares. Serve warm.

Christine Burritt
HENNIKER CONGREGATIONAL CHURCH
HENNIKER, NEW HAMPSHIRE

DANISH AEGKAGE
(Danish Omelet)
MAKES 3 TO 4 SERVINGS

Very good and very filling. If you wish, add more vegetables, such as zucchini or broccoli, to the frying pan when you are cooking the potatoes. Garnish with lettuce and tomato slices and serve with mimosas for a delightful brunch.

½ pound bacon, cut in 1½-inch pieces

1 small onion, finely chopped

1 medium-size potato, shredded

1 small tomato, chopped

6 eggs, lightly beaten

½ cup milk

Salt (optional) and pepper to taste

1 tablespoon chopped chives

Preheat the oven to 350°F.

In a large ovenproof skillet, cook the bacon until crisp. Remove the bacon to paper towels to drain. Pour off all but 1 tablespoon of the bacon grease. Add the onion, potato, and tomato to the remaining grease and sauté until the potato is tender. Combine the eggs with the milk. Loosen the vegetables from the bottom of the frying pan with a spatula. Then pour the egg mixture over the vegetables. Add the bacon, salt (if desired) and pepper to taste, and chives. Place the pan in the oven and bake for 20 to 30 minutes or until set. It will take longer if there are additional vegetables or if you use skim milk. Slice into wedges and serve hot.

Barbara E. Jensen
ST. PAUL LUTHERAN CHURCH
EAST LONGMEADOW, MASSACHUSETTS

BREAKFAST CASSEROLE
MAKES 6 TO 8 SERVINGS

A great dish for a brunch or when your house is filled with visitors. Just mix up the ingredients the night before, then leave a note for the first one up to put it in the oven. By the time everyone is up and coffee is made, breakfast will be ready.

1 pound breakfast sausage, removed from casings, or bacon

6 slices day-old white bread, cubed

6 eggs, beaten

2 cups milk

1 teaspoon salt

1 teaspoon prepared mustard

1 cup shredded sharp Cheddar cheese

Fry the sausage or bacon until done. Drain well.

Lightly grease a 9-inch by 13-inch baking dish. Place the bread in the dish and top with the meat. Mix together the eggs, milk, salt, mustard, and cheese. Pour over the meat. Refrigerate overnight.

In the morning, preheat the oven to 350°F. Bake the casserole for 50 minutes.

Gloria Burkey
ST. ANDREW LUTHERAN CHURCH
ELLSWORTH, MAINE

Vegetables and Side Dishes

*H*ERE'S A COLLECTION of cooked vegetable dishes that can claim center stage on a dinner plate or buffet table. These are dishes so colorful, and so tasty, you'll be tempted to ignore the main course entirely!

Too often, vegetables are an afterthought, something thrown together after you've decided to broil the chicken or grill the steak. But with a repertoire of these incredibly easy-to-make vegetable combinations, you may be tempted to decide on the vegetable dish first and choose the meat to complement it. The recipes range from simple, single-vegetable dishes made lively with herbs, spices, and nuts to rich combinations stuffed, baked with cheese, or covered with a sour cream sauce. There are recipes for both white and sweet potatoes as well as rice, and of course, plenty of baked beans. When our testers wrote, "No leftovers—the whole family enjoyed this one!" we knew we had some winners on our hands.

BAKED BEANS

MAKES 8 TO 10 SERVINGS

Can you envision a potluck or a ham supper without baked beans? This recipe is a classic. No wonder these beans are a favorite at Boscawen Historical Society potluck dinners.

1 pound dry beans (navy beans, soldier beans, Great Northern beans, etc.)

¾ pound salt pork

3 tablespoons molasses

3 tablespoons brown sugar

½ teaspoon salt

½ teaspoon dry mustard

Wash the beans in a colander or strainer; pick over the beans to remove any pebbles or debris. Put in a large saucepan and add water to cover the beans by an inch. Soak overnight.

In the morning, bring the beans to a boil. Boil until the skins break when you blow across a few beans on a spoon. Place a layer of beans in the bottom of a crockery bean pot. Score the salt pork, cutting through the pork but leaving the rind intact. Place about ½ pound of the salt pork in the pot. Add most of the remaining beans and water. Place the remaining ¼ pound of salt pork in the pot. Cover with the remaining beans. Add the molasses, brown sugar, salt, and mustard. Cover with additional water. Place the lid on the pot.

Bake in a 300°F oven for at least 6 hours, adding water as needed. You may want to use a drip pan under the pot in the oven.

Henrietta I. Kenney
BOSCAWEN HISTORICAL SOCIETY
BOSCAWEN, NEW HAMPSHIRE

Bourbon Baked Beans

Makes 10 to 15 servings

If you'd rather start with the canned variety, try this Kennebunk, Maine, way to doctor them up—and convince everyone you slaved for hours. These are hearty, flavorful, and perfect for a summer cookout.

5 cans (16 ounces each) baked beans

1 tablespoon molasses

¼ teaspoon dry mustard

½ cup chili sauce or ketchup

½ cup bourbon

⅓ cup strong coffee

1 can (15 ounces) crushed pineapple, well drained

½ cup brown sugar

8 slices bacon, to garnish

Mix together the beans, molasses, mustard, chili sauce, bourbon, and coffee. Let stand for 3 hours. Preheat the oven to 300°F, then bake the beans for 30 minutes. Add the pineapple and brown sugar and bake for another 30 minutes.

Meanwhile, fry the bacon until crisp. Drain well. Crumble. Serve the beans garnished with the bacon.

Vera Shinner

Women's Alliance, First Parish Congregation Unitarian Church
Kennebunk, Maine

GREEN BEANS VIENNESE

MAKES 6 SERVINGS

An easy—and very good—side dish that goes especially well with lamb. It can also be made ahead, kept refrigerated, and then reheated at the last minute in the oven or microwave.

1 package (16 ounces) frozen cut green beans

1 tablespoon butter

¼ cup chopped onion

1 tablespoon all-purpose white flour

1 teaspoon salt

Dash pepper

½ cup chicken broth

2 tablespoons snipped fresh parsley

1 tablespoon vinegar

¼ teaspoon dried dillweed

½ cup sour cream

Cook the beans according to the package directions; drain and set aside.

In the same saucepan, melt the butter. Add the onion and sauté over medium heat until limp, about 3 minutes. Stir in the flour, salt, and pepper. Then add the broth, parsley, vinegar, and dill. Cook, stirring constantly, until the sauce is thick and bubbling. Reduce the heat to low and stir in the sour cream. Add the drained beans. Continue to cook until the beans are heated through, but do not boil.

If you want to make this dish in advance, pour the bean mixture into an 8-inch square glass baking dish. Before serving, heat in a microwave on high for about 10 minutes, stirring every few minutes. Or place in a preheated 350°F oven for about 45 minutes, stirring occasionally, until heated through.

Carolyn Marshall
NEW ENGLAND HISTORIC GENEALOGICAL SOCIETY
BOSTON, MASSACHUSETTS

Nutty Brussels Sprouts

Makes 6 servings

Looking for a way to dress up brussels sprouts? The combination of ginger and walnuts makes a lovely complement for this much-maligned vegetable. This recipe can be easily doubled to feed a small crowd.

2 packages (10 ounces each) frozen brussels sprouts

¼ cup (½ stick) margarine or butter

¾ cup chopped walnuts

¾ teaspoon salt

½ teaspoon ground ginger

In a large saucepan, bring 1 inch of salted water to a boil. Add the brussels sprouts and cook until tender-crisp, about 5 minutes. Drain well.

Meanwhile, in a large skillet, melt the margarine over medium-low heat. Add the walnuts, salt, and ginger and cook, stirring occasionally, until the nuts are lightly browned. Add the drained brussels sprouts and toss well. Serve hot.

Susan B. Shields

Women's Alliance, First Parish Congregation Unitarian Church
Kennebunk, Maine

❧

Training is everything. The peach was once a bitter almond; cauliflower is nothing but cabbage with a college education.

—Mark Twain, *Pudd'nhead Wilson* (1896)

❧

CINNAMON CARROTS
MAKES 6 SERVINGS

Tasty and incredibly easy—especially if you use a food processor to slice the carrots and a microwave to cook them. Serve hot in winter or at room temperature on a hot summer day.

1 to 1½ pounds carrots, sliced

⅓ cup butter, at room temperature

½ cup white sugar

1 teaspoon salt

¼ to ½ teaspoon ground cinnamon

⅓ cup boiling water

Preheat the oven to 350°F. Place the carrots in a 1½-quart casserole or baking dish.

Cream together the butter, sugar, salt, and cinnamon. Stir in the boiling water. Pour over the carrots. Bake for 1 hour. Or cook on high in a microwave for 10 minutes.

Jeanette DeJong
EAST DOVER BAPTIST CHURCH
EAST DOVER, VERMONT

*Let the sky rain potatoes; let it thunder
to the tune of "Greensleeves."*
—William Shakespeare, *The Merry Wives of Windsor*

CURRIED CARROTS

MAKES 4 TO 6 SERVINGS

A simple but exotic side dish that enhances the common carrot and is attractive to boot. A real winner!

1 pound carrots, sliced 1 inch thick

2 tablespoons butter

2 to 3 teaspoons curry powder

¼ teaspoon pepper

1 tablespoon lemon juice

1 tablespoon honey

⅓ cup chopped pecans or walnuts

Place the carrots in a saucepan with water to cover, bring to a boil, and simmer for 15 to 20 minutes or until tender. Drain and return the carrots to the pan. Over low heat, add the remaining ingredients. Mix well and serve immediately.

Susan Gagnon
HOPKINTON COOKIE EXCHANGE
HOPKINTON, NEW HAMPSHIRE

SCALLOPED SPINACH

MAKES 6 TO 8 SERVINGS

This traditional favorite is perennially popular at potlucks; watch it disappear from the table. You can easily double the recipe for a hungry crowd.

3 packages (10 ounces each) frozen chopped spinach

½ to 1 package dry onion soup mix

1 cup sour cream

Bread crumbs

Butter

¼ cup grated Parmesan cheese

Preheat the oven to 350°F. Cook and drain the spinach. Combine with the soup mix and sour cream. Spoon into a buttered shallow casserole dish. Cover with the bread crumbs, dabs of butter, and the Parmesan cheese. Bake for about 35 minutes. Serve hot.

Jeanne Jenkins
CHESTER HISTORICAL SOCIETY
CHESTER, NEW HAMPSHIRE

ZUCCHINI PROVENÇAL
MAKES 6 TO 8 SERVINGS

Try this recipe at the end of the summer, when no one wants to look at another zucchini. When you serve it this way, they'll love it!

3 tablespoons olive oil

⅔ cup chopped onion

4 ounces mushrooms, sliced

8 to 10 small zucchini (2½ pounds), sliced ¼ inch thick

⅔ cup grated Parmesan cheese (3 ounces)

2 cans (6 ounces each) tomato paste

1 garlic clove, minced

1 teaspoon salt

⅛ teaspoon pepper

Preheat the oven to 350°F.

Heat the oil in a large saucepan. Add the onion and mushrooms and sauté until the onion is limp, about 3 minutes. Add the zucchini and continue sautéing until the zucchini is just tender, about 4 minutes. Remove from the heat and stir in half the cheese. Add the tomato paste, garlic, salt, and pepper. Mix well. Turn into a 2-quart casserole dish and sprinkle the remaining cheese on top. Bake for 20 minutes or until heated through. Serve hot.

Gloria A. Ogiela
MARK TWAIN LIBRARY
REDDING, CONNECTICUT

Zucchini Pancakes

Makes 4 servings

These fritters are a great way to serve zucchini. They go well with most meats and can even be served as a main course. For added color, replace some of the zucchini with grated carrot.

2 cups grated zucchini

1 teaspoon onion salt or garlic salt

½ cup all-purpose white flour

2 teaspoons baking powder

½ cup grated Cheddar or Colby cheese

2 tablespoons grated Parmesan cheese

1 tablespoon chopped scallions or
    2 tablespoons chopped fresh chives

1 large egg, lightly beaten

1 tablespoon butter or margarine,
    melted

Butter or margarine for frying

Combine the zucchini and onion salt in a colander and let stand for 15 minutes. Squeeze out any remaining liquid.

In a medium-size mixing bowl, combine the flour and baking powder. Mix in the cheeses and scallions. Then add the egg, melted butter, and zucchini and mix lightly.

Heat a small amount of butter or margarine in a griddle or large frying pan over medium heat. Pour the batter onto the griddle to make small pancakes. Brown lightly on each side, about 4 minutes per side. Keep the pancakes warm on a baking sheet, stacked in a single layer, in a 250°F oven until serving.

Frances B. Holmes
HARWINTON LIBRARY FRIENDS
HARWINTON, CONNECTICUT

BAKED SUMMER SQUASH

MAKES 6 SERVINGS

Outstanding! A terrific way to get vegetables into the most reluctant veggie eaters. We put this to the ultimate test—a friend who hates vegetables—and even she liked it. Those who actually like vegetables love this. And it can be mixed a day ahead and stored in the refrigerator until you're ready to bake it.

3 pounds yellow squash or zucchini

½ cup (1 stick) butter, melted

½ cup chopped onion

2 eggs, lightly beaten

1 tablespoon sugar

1 teaspoon salt

½ teaspoon pepper

1 cup fresh bread crumbs

Slice the squash. Boil or steam until tender. Drain, then mash. Preheat the oven to 375°F.

In a mixing bowl, combine the squash with half the melted butter, the onion, eggs, sugar, salt, and pepper. Spoon into a 2-quart casserole dish. Combine the bread crumbs with the remaining butter and sprinkle over the squash. Bake for about 45 minutes and serve hot.

Elaine B. Ciarcia
HARWINTON LIBRARY FRIENDS
HARWINTON, CONNECTICUT

MAPLE-NUT WINTER SQUASH

MAKES 8 TO 10 SERVINGS

Very easy and very tasty—a nice way to dress up a common vegetable for a group gathering.

2 large buttercup or medium-size butternut squash

⅓ cup maple sugar or brown sugar

⅓ cup margarine or butter, at room temperature

½ to ¾ cup chopped nuts (walnuts, pecans, or hickory nuts)

Preheat the oven to 350°F. Cut whole squash in half lengthwise and remove the seeds. Place the squash, cut side down, in a baking dish and bake for 30 to 40 minutes, or until tender. Or cut the squash into chunks, remove the seeds, and steam until tender. Scoop the flesh from the skins and mash. Spoon into a casserole dish.

In a small bowl, blend the sugar and margarine. Add the nuts. Spoon on top of the squash. Return to the oven and bake until the squash is hot and the nuts are toasted, 20 to 30 minutes. Serve hot.

Ann P. Whitcomb
SPRINGFIELD ART AND HISTORICAL SOCIETY
SPRINGFIELD, VERMONT

POTLUCK DISHES FOR THOSE WHO DON'T COOK—BUT WANT TO BRING SOMETHING SPECIAL

*T*HERE ARE PLENTY of people who don't cook or don't have time to cook, so don't feel you have to turn down an invitation to a potluck just because your cooking style runs to frozen dinners and take-out. Here are some ideas for what to bring to your next potluck that go beyond the uninspired bag of tortilla chips and bottled salsa.

✻ Stop at your favorite bakery and buy an assortment of breads and rolls. Bring them in a cloth-lined basket accompanied by a pottery crock filled with butter.

✻ Bring a cheese board. An assortment of at least four different cheeses and crackers or sliced French bread on a wooden board with suitable cheese slicers or knives makes a luxuriously welcome addition to a buffet table.

✻ A platter of beautifully arranged vegetables is always welcome. The dip can be as simple as a bottle of ranch dressing (but transfer it into a pretty serving bowl or cruet). Good choices for a vegetable platter are cucumber rounds, celery and carrot sticks, cherry tomatoes, whole sugar snap or snow pea pods, and green and red pepper strips.

✻ If you are really short on time, a simple fruit bowl with oranges, apples, pears, and bananas makes a fine addition to a dessert table. Or a large bowl filled with mixed nuts in the shell can make a fine dessert for those inclined to munch and talk. Don't forget to provide a nutcracker!

ORANGE-GLAZED SWEET POTATOES
MAKES 6 SERVINGS

A quick, easy, and very good way to prepare sweet potatoes, and you can used canned or fresh potatoes for this recipe. We love it with turkey and roast chicken. Try the sauce over grilled ham steaks or grilled chicken, too. To save time at the last minute, make the sauce a few days ahead and refrigerate until you're ready to use it.

6 sweet potatoes or 1 can (15 ounces) vacuum-packed sweet potatoes (no syrup)

3 tablespoons butter

1 tablespoon cornstarch

1 cup orange juice

⅓ cup white sugar

⅓ cup light brown sugar

Pinch salt

If you are using fresh sweet potatoes, cook in boiling salted water for 30 minutes. Peel. Slice the canned or freshly cooked potatoes in half lengthwise. Place in a casserole dish and set aside.

Preheat the oven to 350°F.

In a small saucepan, melt the butter. Add the cornstarch and stir until dissolved and smooth. Add the orange juice, stirring constantly. Then add the sugars and salt. Cook over medium heat, stirring constantly, until the sauce is thickened.

Pour the sauce over the sweet potatoes. Bake for 30 minutes. Serve hot.

Mary Gagnon
ST. ISAAC JOGUES CHURCH
EAST HARTFORD, CONNECTICUT

Sweet Potato Pie
Makes 6 Servings

We're not sure how this traditional southern dish made it to a New England kitchen, but we're glad it did!

2 cups peeled and diced sweet potatoes

1 carton (4 ounces) egg substitute (or 2 eggs)

1 teaspoon vanilla extract

1 cup white sugar

2 tablespoons margarine or butter

Dash salt

½ cup milk

½ teaspoon ground nutmeg

1 unbaked 9-inch pie shell

Boil the sweet potatoes in water to cover until tender. Drain and mash.

Preheat the oven to 350°F. While the potatoes are still hot, add the egg substitute, vanilla, sugar, margarine, salt, milk, and nutmeg and mix well. Pour into the pie shell. Bake for 40 to 45 minutes or until a knife inserted near the center comes out clean. Allow to sit for at least 10 minutes before serving.

Mittie Nutter
Hopkinton Congregational Church
Hopkinton, New Hampshire

What I say is that, if a man really likes potatoes, he must be a pretty decent sort of fellow.
—A. A. Milne, *Not That It Matters* (1920)

Oven-Roasted Potatoes

Makes 4 to 6 servings

Crispy and flavorful, these are popular with the whole family—there's no need to worry about leftovers! The recipe is easily increased for a larger crowd, too; just multiply the ingredients to serve as many as necessary.

6 large potatoes

½ cup olive oil

Salt and pepper to taste

Garlic powder to taste (optional)

Paprika

Preheat the oven to 400°F. Place a 9-inch by 13-inch pan in the oven to preheat (this prevents sticking).

Peel the potatoes and slice lengthwise about 1 inch thick. Combine with the olive oil, tossing to coat well. Place the potatoes in a single layer in the preheated baking pan. Sprinkle with salt, pepper, and garlic powder, if using. Then sprinkle with paprika. Return the pan to the oven and roast for 15 minutes. Flip the potatoes and roast for another 15 minutes.

NOTE: Instead of using olive oil, you can use the drippings from any roast. Make sure you have at least ½ cup of drippings or liquid in the pan.

May Checho
WINDSOR WOMAN'S CLUB
WINDSOR, CONNECTICUT

Potatoes Boulangère

MAKES 6 TO 7 SERVINGS

You may know this dish by the name of Potatoes Anna. By any name, these deliciously crisp, golden-brown potatoes make an excellent accompaniment for beef, lamb, or pork.

6 medium-size potatoes

½ cup (1 stick) plus 2 tablespoons butter

3 onions, sliced

½ to 1 cup chicken or beef broth

Peel the potatoes and slice ¹⁄₁₆ inch thick. Butter the inside of a large round casserole or 10-inch cast-iron skillet. Preheat the oven to 450°F.

In another skillet, melt the ½ cup butter. Add the onions and sauté until limp, about 5 minutes. Carefully arrange the potato slices in overlapping concentric circles in the buttered baking dish to form a single layer. Top with a layer of onions. Repeat the layers until all the potatoes and onions are used, ending with a layer of potatoes.

Combine the broth and remaining 2 tablespoons butter and bring to a boil. Pour over the potatoes. Bake the potatoes for 25 to 30 minutes, until crisp and golden. Invert onto a serving platter and cut into wedges to serve.

Mary Gagnon
ST. ISAAC JOGUES CHURCH
EAST HARTFORD, CONNECTICUT

Golden Potato Squares
Makes 8 to 10 servings

An easy dish that makes potatoes something special and yet goes with every-thing. Kids love it—and we know some "big kids" who think it's not Thanks-giving until these are on the table.

5 pounds potatoes

⅔ cup butter, melted

1 cup chopped onion

1 can (12 ounces) evaporated milk

4 eggs, beaten

2½ teaspoons salt

¼ teaspoon pepper

2¼ cups shredded Cheddar cheese

Peel the potatoes and place in cold water to prevent discoloration. Set aside. Preheat the oven to 350°F. Grease a 9-inch by 13-inch baking dish.

Melt the butter in a large skillet. Add the onion and sauté until limp, about 5 minutes. Add the milk and bring to a boil. Remove from the heat.

In a large bowl, combine the eggs, salt, and pepper. Beat until frothy. Shred the potatoes and add to the egg mixture. Toss to combine. Add the milk mixture. Set aside ¾ cup of the cheese, add the rest to the potato mixture, and mix well. Spoon the mixture into the prepared baking dish. Bake for 1 hour. Top with the reserved cheese and bake for an additional 30 minutes. Cut into squares and serve hot.

Christine Burritt
Henniker Congregational Church
Henniker, New Hampshire

Easy Cheese-Potato Casserole
Makes 12 to 15 servings

This quick and easy-to-prepare potato dish is the perfect choice for the buffet table. It can be made in advance and stored in the refrigerator until ready to bake. Meat-and-potatoes lovers will enjoy it as a side dish, while vegetarians might find themselves happy with this as the main course.

1 bag (2 pounds) frozen southern-style hash brown potatoes

1 cup finely diced onion

⅓ cup finely diced celery

1 can (10¾ ounces) condensed cream of celery soup

1 carton (16 ounces) sour cream

8 ounces Cheddar cheese, shredded

½ cup (1 stick) butter or margarine, melted

Salt and pepper to taste

1½ cups crushed potato chips or cornflake crumbs

Preheat the oven to 350°F. Grease a 2-quart casserole or 9-inch by 13-inch baking dish.

Thaw the potatoes just enough to break them apart. Combine in a large bowl with the onion, celery, soup, sour cream, Cheddar cheese, melted butter, and salt and pepper to taste. Mix well. Spoon into the baking dish. Top with the crumbs. Bake for 1 hour. Serve hot.

Adapted from a recipe submitted by Judith Daniels
Walpole Historical Society
Walpole, New Hampshire

STUFFED RED PEPPERS

MAKES 4 SERVINGS

Fun to prepare and popular with all ages. As a side dish, figure on one pepper per person. Two per person makes a fine vegetarian main course.

4 red bell peppers

2 tablespoons olive oil

1 medium-size onion, chopped

2 garlic cloves, minced

½ cup chopped mushrooms

2 sprigs fresh parsley, chopped

2 fresh basil leaves, chopped

2 sprigs fresh oregano, chopped

2 sprigs fresh thyme, chopped

1 tablespoon grated fresh ginger

2 cups chopped tomatoes (skins removed)

1½ cups cooked brown rice

½ teaspoon ground cumin

1 teaspoon red wine vinegar

1 tablespoon tamari

½ cup golden raisins

¾ cup grated Cheddar cheese

Salt and pepper to taste

Water or broth

Cut the stem end from the peppers and scoop out the seeds and membranes. Steam over boiling water until just soft, about 2 minutes. Preheat the oven to 375°F.

Heat the oil in a large skillet over medium-high heat. Add the onion, garlic, mushrooms, fresh herbs, and ginger. Sauté until the onion is soft and the herbs are wilted, about 5 minutes. Reduce the heat to medium-low, add the tomatoes, and cook for 5 minutes. Stir in the rice, cumin, vinegar, tamari, raisins, and ¼ cup of the cheese. Add salt and pepper to taste. Stuff this mixture into the peppers. Sprinkle the tops of the peppers with the remaining ½ cup cheese. Place the peppers in an 8-inch square baking dish. Pour in ¼ inch water or broth. Cover the dish with foil. Bake for about 30 minutes or until the rice is heated through. Serve hot.

Lea Bohrer

THE GREENFIELD GOURMET CLUB

GREENFIELD, MASSACHUSETTS

Spinach-Stuffed Tomatoes

Makes 8 servings

When tomatoes are ripening fast and furious, stuffing them with a delicious spinach filling makes for great eating. These are the perfect accompaniment to a grilled steak.

¼ cup (½ stick) butter

2 medium-size onions, chopped

2 garlic cloves, minced

1½ pounds fresh spinach (stems removed), chopped

1⅓ cups dry whole-wheat bread crumbs (4 slices)

2 eggs, beaten

1 teaspoon salt

8 to 10 small tomatoes

In a large skillet, melt the butter over medium heat. Add the onions and garlic and sauté until the onions are limp. Add the spinach and cook until tender and limp, stirring occasionally. Remove from the heat and stir in the crumbs, eggs, and salt. Set aside.

Preheat the oven to 350°F.

Remove the stem ends from the tomatoes and scoop out the seeds. Place in an 8-inch baking dish; you may have to trim the bottoms so the tomatoes stand up. Stuff with the spinach mixture. Bake for 30 minutes. Serve hot.

Kathy Kuntz
Chebeague Parents Association
Chebeague Island, Maine

Raspberried Vegetables
Makes 8 to 10 servings

Looking for a different way to prepare your daily vegetables? We have a recipe for you: steamed vegetables in a sweet-and-sour raspberry sauce! This unusual dish is a cinch to prepare. The sauce can be made ahead, stored in the refrigerator for up to a week, and served warm or cold. You can substitute other vegetables for the ones suggested below.

2 cups fresh or frozen unsweetened raspberries

½ cup orange juice

3 tablespoons cider vinegar

3 to 4 tablespoons honey

3 tablespoons olive oil

¼ to ½ teaspoon salt

1 garlic clove, minced

1 large head cauliflower, cut in bite-size pieces

1 large bunch broccoli, cut in 2-inch pieces

1 pound brussels sprouts, halved if large

In a saucepan, combine the raspberries, orange juice, vinegar, and honey. Bring to a boil, then reduce the heat to medium and cook, uncovered, for 5 minutes. Remove from the heat and cool to room temperature. Stir in the olive oil, salt, and garlic. Taste to adjust the seasonings. Place in a serving bowl and set aside.

Steam the vegetables until just tender. Serve warm or hot with the raspberry sauce drizzled over the top.

Carol Vandertuin
East Dover Baptist Church
East Dover, Vermont

GARDEN DELIGHT

MAKES 6 SERVINGS

A winner! Simple to make, great tasting, and very attractive, too.

¼ cup (½ stick) margarine

1 large onion, sliced

1 medium-size green bell pepper, chopped

8 ounces fresh mushrooms, sliced

2 large ripe tomatoes, chopped

2 teaspoons dried basil

1 teaspoon dried dillweed

¾ cup sour cream or plain yogurt

Salt and pepper to taste

In a large skillet, melt the margarine over medium heat. Add the onion, pepper, and mushrooms and sauté until soft but not brown, about 5 minutes. Add the tomatoes, basil, and dill and cook for 2 minutes. Season the sour cream with the salt and pepper. Stir the sour cream into the vegetables gently but thoroughly. Serve at once.

Frances L. Calder
CHEBEAGUE PARENTS ASSOCIATION
CHEBEAGUE ISLAND, MAINE

HERB RICE

MAKES 6 TO 8 SERVINGS

This lovely rice pilaf makes a delicious accompaniment to chicken.

2 cups uncooked long-grain white rice

2 teaspoons salt

4 chicken bouillon cubes

4 cups water

1 teaspoon dried marjoram

1 teaspoon dried thyme

1 teaspoon dried rosemary

¼ teaspoon dried basil

¼ cup (½ stick) butter or margarine

In a large heavy saucepan, combine all the ingredients. Bring to a boil, reduce the heat, cover, and cook over low heat for about 15 minutes or until the rice is tender and all the liquid has been absorbed. Fluff with a fork.

Nancy J. Rembert
THE CHURCH OF THE GOOD SHEPHERD
ACTON, MASSACHUSETTS

BREADS, MUFFINS, ROLLS, AND PANCAKES

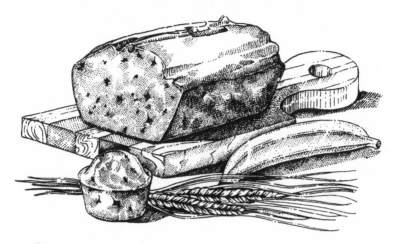

N
EW ENGLAND COOKS draw from a wonderful tradition of baking, and, as you'll note from these recipes, they often have a sweet tooth to inspire them. As we sampled and tasted these wonderful bread recipes, some of us thought that a few of the breads and muffins collected here crossed over into the dessert category. Others insisted that there's nothing out of the ordinary in serving a very sweet bread for breakfast (this is, after all, the region that made famous the custom of serving pie for breakfast). And still others remembered banana bread and other fruit breads being served at the dinner table when they were growing up. The sweet breads stayed.

We have also included one pancake recipe. More recipes for pancakes are to be found in the last chapter, "Recipes to Feed a Crowd." Whether you find the recipes in this chapter appropriate for breakfast, coffee break, dinner, or dessert, we're confident that you will love them.

SWEDISH RYE BREAD
MAKES 3 LOAVES

A popular recipe that comes, appropriately, from New Sweden, Maine, this light rye bread is especially moist. If three loaves are more than your family can use, just halve the recipe and make one large and one small loaf.

2 packages active dry yeast

4 tablespoons white sugar

½ cup warm water

2 cups hot water

1 cup cold water

1 cup milk

3 cups rye flour

9 to 10 cups all-purpose white flour

1 tablespoon salt

½ cup solid vegetable shortening, melted

1 cup (overflowing) molasses

Melted butter or margarine to glaze

In a small bowl, combine the yeast with 2 tablespoons of the sugar and ½ cup warm water. Mix until foamy.

In a very large bowl, combine the hot and cold water with the milk. Let cool. Add the yeast mixture and stir well. Sift the rye flour, 3 cups of the white flour, the salt, and the remaining 2 tablespoons of sugar into the bowl. Stir well. Add the shortening and molasses and stir. Stir in 4 cups or more of the white flour. Turn out onto a floured board and knead. Keep working in more flour; knead for 5 minutes or more until a good solid ball is formed.

Grease your hands, then place the ball of dough into a greased bowl. Cover. Let rise for 1½ hours and punch down. Let rise for another 1½ hours and punch down again.

Divide the dough into thirds. Put into three well-greased 8-inch by 4-inch loaf pans and let rise for another hour. Preheat the oven to 375°F.

Bake for 50 minutes. Brush on melted butter or margarine while the loaves are still warm. Cool for 10 minutes on wire racks, then turn out of the pans to cool completely.

Ruth Carlson
GUSTAF ADOLPH LUTHERAN CHURCH
NEW SWEDEN, MAINE

Dill Bread

Makes 1 loaf

An unusual, very moist yeast bread, redolent of dill. Great served with Italian food, and popular at parties, too.

1 package active dry yeast

¼ cup warm water

1 cup creamed cottage cheese

2 tablespoons honey

1 tablespoon chopped onion

1 tablespoon butter

3 tablespoons dried dillweed, dill seed, or a combination of both

1 teaspoon baking soda

1 egg, slightly beaten

2½ cups all-purpose white flour

Melted butter to glaze

Combine the yeast with the warm water. Set aside.

In a saucepan over low heat, combine the cottage cheese, honey, onion, butter, dill, baking soda, and egg. When the butter is melted, remove from the heat. Stir in the yeast mixture. Gradually add the flour to form a stiff dough. Turn out onto a lightly floured board and knead for 5 to 10 minutes.

Place in a large, well-greased bowl and let rise until doubled in bulk, about 1 hour. Punch down, shape into a loaf, and place in a greased 8-inch by 4-inch loaf pan. Let rise until doubled again, about 40 minutes. Preheat the oven to 350°F.

Bake for 40 to 50 minutes. Brush the top with butter while the bread is still warm.

Marcia Goodnow
FRIENDS OF THE DOVER PUBLIC LIBRARY
DOVER, NEW HAMPSHIRE

Hazel Lee's Oatmeal Bread
Makes 2 loaves

The ladies of Lyme, Connecticut, tell us that the late Mrs. Clarence Lee was locally famous for her homemade bread. After tasting this loaf, we know why!

2 cups rolled oats (not instant or quick-cooking)

2 tablespoons margarine or butter

¾ cup molasses

1 tablespoon salt

2 cups boiling water

2 packages active dry yeast

½ cup warm water (110°F)

5 to 6 cups all-purpose white flour

Combine the oats, margarine, molasses, and salt in a large bowl. Add the boiling water and mix well. Let stand for 1 hour.

Dissolve the yeast in the ½ cup warm water; when bubbly, add to the oat mixture. Work in the flour to make a thick dough. Knead well and continue to add flour until the dough is shiny and no longer sticky. Place in a greased bowl, cover, and set in a warm place to rise until doubled, about 1½ hours.

Divide in half, shape into two loaves, and put into two greased 8-inch by 4-inch loaf pans. Let rise again until well shaped and doubled. Preheat the oven to 350°F.

Bake for 1 hour. Let cool on wire racks for 10 minutes, then turn out of the pans to cool completely. When cool, wrap and store. This bread freezes very well.

FLORENCE GRISWOLD MUSEUM
LYME HISTORICAL SOCIETY
OLD LYME, CONNECTICUT

CARDAMOM COFFEE BRAID

MAKES 16 SERVINGS

This traditional Scandinavian yeast bread is time-consuming to make, but it looks as good as it tastes.

BREAD

1½ cups milk

1 package active dry yeast or 1 cake yeast

¾ cup white sugar

6¼ cups sifted all-purpose white flour

½ cup (1 stick) butter or margarine, at room temperature

2 egg yolks and 1 whole egg

1 teaspoon ground cardamom

¼ teaspoon salt

TOPPING

2 tablespoons milk

6 tablespoons white sugar

Scald the 1½ cups milk and cool to lukewarm. Crumble the yeast into a bowl and add 1 tablespoon of the sugar and the lukewarm milk. Beat in 3 cups of the flour with an electric mixer, beating until smooth. Cover and let rise until light and doubled in bulk, 1 to 1½ hours.

Add the butter, remaining sugar, egg yolks and egg, cardamom, and salt and mix in. Gradually add 3 cups flour. Pour ¼ cup flour on a board, turn out the dough, and knead until smooth and elastic. Use only as much more flour as needed to keep the bread from sticking.

Place the dough in a greased bowl. Cover and let rise until doubled in bulk, 1 to 1½ hours.

Cut risen dough in half for 2 braids. Cut each half into 3 pieces. Roll each piece into a rope 16 inches long. Pinch the 3 ropes together at one end. Braid ropes and pinch other ends together. Place on a greased baking sheet. Make second braid and place on second baking sheet.

Let braids rise until doubled in bulk, about 45 minutes. Preheat the oven to 350°F. Before placing breads in oven, brush each with 1 tablespoon milk and sprinkle with 3 tablespoons sugar. Bake for 30 minutes, until golden brown.

Barbara Anderson
ST. PAUL LUTHERAN CHURCH
EAST LONGMEADOW, MASSACHUSETTS

STUFFED BREAD
MAKES 4 TO 6 SERVINGS (1 LOAF)

Here's a different sort of recipe—bread and sandwich all in one. For an even heartier loaf, increase the amount of meat up to 1 pound and add 10 minutes to the baking time. Surprisingly, this bread can be made from start to finish in about an hour. For a super short-cut, you can substitute thawed frozen bread dough for the homemade dough; then fill and shape it as directed in the recipe, but bake it according to the package directions. Leftovers can be refrigerated and reheated the next day.

3¼ cups all-purpose white flour

1 tablespoon white sugar

1 teaspoon salt

1 package Rapid Rise yeast

1 cup warm water

1 tablespoon margarine, melted

¼ cup Thousand Island dressing (or dressing of your choice)

8 ounces sliced ham, turkey, roast beef, or salami

4 ounces sliced cheese

1 egg white

Caraway or sesame seeds (optional)

In a large bowl, mix 2¼ cups of the flour with the sugar, salt, and yeast. Stir in the warm water and margarine. Mix in only enough of the remaining 1 cup flour to make a soft dough. Turn out onto a floured surface and knead for 4 minutes.

On a greased baking sheet, roll the dough to a rectangle of 10 inches by 14 inches. Spread dressing down the center third of the dough. Top with a layer of sliced meat and cheese. Make cuts in the dough from the filling to the dough edges at 1-inch intervals. Alternating sides, fold the dough strips at an angle over the filling. Brush the top with the egg white and sprinkle with the caraway or sesame seeds, if desired. Cover the loaf with a clean towel.

Preheat the oven to 400°F. Place a large shallow pan on a counter. Half fill it with boiling water. Place the baking sheet over the pan. Let the dough rise for 15 minutes.

Bake for 25 minutes or until done. Cool slightly before serving.

Shirley Kondratowski
WILLINGTON BAPTIST CHURCH
WILLINGTON, CONNECTICUT

SUPER BRAN BREAD
MAKES 2 LOAVES

A perfect substitute for the more traditional brown bread, this goes especially well with baked beans. It's best made with bread flour, which contains more gluten than all-purpose flour.

2 cups All-Bran cereal

⅓ cup solid vegetable shortening

1 cup molasses

1½ cups boiling water

2 eggs

2 cups bread flour

2 teaspoons baking soda

½ teaspoon salt

1 teaspoon ground cinnamon

Preheat the oven to 350°F. Grease two 8-inch by 4-inch loaf pans.

In a large mixing bowl, combine the cereal, shortening, and molasses. Add the boiling water and stir until the shortening is melted. Add the eggs and beat well. Add the remaining ingredients and mix thoroughly. Pour into the prepared pans.

Bake for 35 to 40 minutes or until a tester inserted near the center of the loaves comes out clean. Cool in the pans for 10 minutes before turning out onto wire racks to finish cooling.

Yvonne Menzone
AUBURN GROUP OF WORCESTER COUNTY EXTENSION SERVICE
AUBURN, MASSACHUSETTS

DOUBLE CORN BREAD

MAKES 9 SERVINGS

A traditional New England corn bread with a special bonus of sweet corn kernels. The recipe is quick, easy, and inexpensive to make, and most of the ingredients are probably already on your kitchen shelf.

1 cup all-purpose white flour

1 cup yellow cornmeal

4 teaspoons baking powder

½ teaspoon salt

4 tablespoons white sugar (or more or less to taste)

1 can (11 ounces) corn

Approximately ¾ cup milk

1 egg, slightly beaten

¼ cup (½ stick) butter or margarine, melted

Preheat the oven to 400°F. Grease an 8-inch square baking pan.

In a 1-quart bowl, combine the flour, cornmeal, baking powder, salt, and sugar. Drain the corn, pouring the liquid into a glass measure. Fill the glass measure with milk to make 1 cup. Add to the cornmeal mixture along with the corn kernels, egg, and melted butter. Stir just enough to moisten the dry ingredients. The batter will be lumpy. Spoon into the prepared baking dish.

Bake for 20 to 25 minutes or until a tester inserted near the center comes out clean. Serve warm or cooled.

Mildred K. Ladd
BRENTWOOD HISTORICAL SOCIETY
BRENTWOOD, NEW HAMPSHIRE

Strawberry Bread

Makes 3 loaves

A sweet tea bread that makes three loaves, perfect for holiday gift giving. Or just spread the slices with softened cream cheese and enjoy!

1 cup (2 sticks) butter, at room temperature

1½ cups white sugar

1 teaspoon vanilla extract

¼ teaspoon lemon extract

4 eggs

3 cups all-purpose white flour

1 teaspoon salt

½ teaspoon baking soda

1 teaspoon cream of tartar

1 cup strawberry preserves

½ cup sour cream

1 cup chopped nuts

Preheat the oven to 350°F. Grease three 8-inch by 4-inch loaf pans.

In a mixing bowl, cream the butter, sugar, vanilla, and lemon extract until soft. Add the eggs one at a time, beating well after each addition. In another bowl, sift together the flour, salt, soda, and cream of tartar. In a third bowl, combine the preserves, sour cream, and nuts. Add the preserves mixture alternately with the dry ingredients to the creamed mixture. Spoon into the loaf pans.

Bake for 50 minutes or until a tester inserted in the loaves comes out clean. Cool on racks for 10 minutes before removing from the pans to cool completely.

Phyllis Curtis
Church of the Epiphany
Southbury, Connecticut

APPLE-GINGER QUICK BREAD
MAKES 1 LOAF OR 6 MINI BUNDT CAKES

A pleasant change of pace, especially attractive if baked in mini bundt pans. This bread freezes well, too.

2 cups whole-wheat pastry flour or all-purpose white flour

2 teaspoons baking powder

2 teaspoons ground ginger

1 teaspoon salt

2 large eggs, beaten

½ cup brown sugar

½ cup vegetable oil

3 medium-size tart apples, peeled and cut into ½-inch cubes

½ cup raisins and/or ½ cup unsalted mixed nuts (optional)

Preheat the oven to 350°F. Grease an 8-inch by 4-inch loaf pan or 6 mini bundt pans.

Sift together the flour, baking powder, ginger, and salt; set aside. Combine the remaining ingredients and blend thoroughly. Add the liquid ingredients to the dry ingredients and combine just until blended thoroughly (do not beat). Pour into the prepared pan(s).

Bake the loaf pan for 80 minutes, the mini bundt pans for 60 minutes, or until a tester inserted in the loaves comes out clean. Cool on a rack for 10 minutes before removing from the pans.

Adapted from a recipe submitted by Cecilia Bennett
THEODORE PARKER UNITARIAN UNIVERSALIST CHURCH
WEST ROXBURY, MASSACHUSETTS

Eggnog Almond Tea Loaf

Makes 1 loaf

A lovely tea bread, rich with almonds and spiced with nutmeg and lemon.

2½ cups all-purpose white flour

¾ cup sugar

3½ teaspoons baking powder

1 teaspoon salt

½ teaspoon ground nutmeg

½ teaspoon grated lemon zest

1 cup finely chopped toasted almonds

1 egg, beaten

3 tablespoons vegetable oil

1¼ cups commercial or homemade eggnog

Preheat the oven to 350°F. Grease and flour an 8-inch by 4-inch loaf pan.

In a large mixing bowl, sift together the flour, sugar, baking powder, salt, and nutmeg. Add the lemon zest and almonds and stir to combine. In another bowl, combine the egg, oil, and eggnog. Stir this mixture into the dry ingredients just until well blended. Pour the batter into the prepared loaf pan.

Bake for about 1 hour or until a tester inserted in the center comes out clean. Cool in the pan for 5 minutes, then turn out onto a rack to cool completely.

Libby Yanizyn
Walpole Historical Society
Walpole, New Hampshire

BANANA BREAD

MAKES 1 LOAF

A particularly moist version of an old favorite. Especially good served warm from the oven, with the top still crusty and delicious, or spread with cream cheese for tea sandwiches. This bread freezes well, too.

¼ cup solid vegetable shortening

1 cup white sugar

4 bananas, mashed

1 egg

2 cups all-purpose white flour

1 teaspoon baking soda

Pinch salt

Preheat the oven to 350°F. Grease an 8-inch by 4-inch loaf pan.

Cream together the shortening and sugar. Add the bananas and the egg and stir to combine. Sift together the flour, soda, and salt. Add the sifted dry ingredients to the banana mixture and stir just until combined. The batter will be lumpy. Spoon the batter into the prepared loaf pan.

Bake for 50 to 60 minutes or until a tester inserted in the center comes out clean. Cool in the pan for 10 minutes before turning out onto a wire rack to finish cooling.

Betty Smith
SOUTH CONGREGATIONAL CHURCH
CONCORD, NEW HAMPSHIRE

German Almond Bread

Makes 2 loaves

The sweet flavor of almonds makes this bread the perfect match for a cup of coffee. Almond paste can be found in most supermarkets.

1 cup Grape-Nuts cereal

3 cups milk

1 cup almond paste, cut into small pieces

1 teaspoon butter

2 eggs, beaten

1½ cups white sugar

3½ cups all-purpose white flour

1 teaspoon baking powder

1 teaspoon baking soda

1 teaspoon salt

Combine the cereal and milk and set aside for 1 hour. Preheat the oven to 350°F. Grease two 8-inch by 4-inch loaf pans.

Cream together the almond paste, butter, eggs, and sugar. Add the cereal mixture and mix well. Sift the flour, baking powder, soda, and salt into another bowl. Add to the almond paste mixture and mix thoroughly. Spoon into the prepared loaf pans.

Bake in the preheated oven for 1 hour or until a tester inserted in the center of the loaves comes out clean. Cool for 10 minutes, then turn out of the pans to cool thoroughly on wire racks.

Adapted from a recipe submitted by Renate K. Kempinski
AUBURN GROUP OF WORCESTER COUNTY EXTENSION SERVICE
AUBURN, MASSACHUSETTS

Pumpkin Bread with Orange Spice Glaze
Makes 2 loaves

Kids love this easy quick bread, which tastes something like applesauce cake because of all the spices. If it's a bit too sweet for your taste, try it without the glaze. Great served with coffee, too.

BREAD

¾ cup vegetable oil

4 eggs

1 can (15 ounces) pumpkin purée

2 cups white sugar

¼ cup orange juice

3½ cups all-purpose white flour

2 teaspoons baking powder

2 teaspoons baking soda

1 teaspoon salt

½ teaspoon ground cloves

1 teaspoon ground cinnamon

1 teaspoon ground nutmeg

1½ cups chopped nuts

GLAZE

1 cup confectioners' sugar

¼ teaspoon ground nutmeg

¼ teaspoon ground cinnamon

⅓ cup orange juice

Preheat the oven to 350°F. Grease two 8-inch by 4-inch loaf pans.

In a large mixing bowl, cream together the oil, eggs, pumpkin, and sugar. Stir in the ¼ cup orange juice. In another bowl, sift together the flour, baking powder, soda, salt, cloves, 1 teaspoon cinnamon, and 1 teaspoon nutmeg. Combine with the pumpkin mixture and mix well. Fold in 1 cup of the nuts. Spoon the batter into the prepared pans. Sprinkle the remaining nuts on top.

Bake for 50 to 60 minutes or until a tester inserted near the center comes out clean. Cool in the pans for 10 minutes, then turn out onto wire racks to finish cooling.

Combine all the glaze ingredients. Drizzle over the bread while it is still warm (but not hot).

Adapted from a recipe submitted by Bernice Gladue
Auburn Group of Worcester County Extension Service
Auburn, Massachusetts

THE BEST FRUIT MUFFINS
MAKES 12 MUFFINS

They really are—the best, that is. Be sure to use regular sour cream, not low-fat or nonfat—it makes all the difference in the taste. For fruit, the contributor recommends apples, peaches, blueberries, raisins (and nuts), or candied ginger.

1 cup white sugar

1 egg

1 cup sour cream

¼ cup vegetable oil

1¾ cups all-purpose white flour

1 teaspoon baking soda

½ teaspoon salt

1 cup diced fruit

Preheat the oven to 400°F. Grease 12 muffin cups.

In a food processor, combine the sugar, egg, sour cream, and oil. Pulse until well blended. In a separate bowl, combine the flour, soda, and salt. Add to the food processor and pulse just to blend. Stir in the fruit. Spoon the mixture into the muffin cups, filling them three-quarters full. Bake for 20 minutes or until a tester inserted in the center comes out clean.

Carolyn Muller
ST. PETER'S EPISCOPAL CHURCH
WESTON, MASSACHUSETTS

APRICOT MUFFINS
MAKES 12 MUFFINS

Perfect! Moist and delicious.

1 cup Grape-Nuts cereal (or any granola-type cereal)

½ cup snipped dried apricots

½ cup boiling water

1¾ cups all-purpose white flour

1 tablespoon baking powder

½ teaspoon salt

½ cup brown sugar

½ cup chopped nuts

⅔ cup milk

½ cup oil

1 egg, beaten

Preheat the oven to 375°F. Grease 12 muffin cups or line with paper.

In a small mixing bowl, combine the cereal, apricots, and water. Set aside. Sift the flour, baking powder, and salt into a large mixing bowl, then add the brown sugar and nuts. Set aside. In a third bowl, combine the milk, oil, and egg. Add to the cereal mixture and mix well. Add this mixture to the dry ingredients and stir until just moistened. Spoon into the prepared muffin cups. Bake for 20 to 25 minutes or until a tester inserted in the center comes out clean.

Cynthia A. Miga
ALL SAINTS CHURCH IN PONTIAC
WARWICK, RHODE ISLAND

MAPLE SYRUP–BRAN MUFFINS

MAKES 12 MUFFINS

With maple syrup, pecans, and sour cream, these are bran muffins with a difference! The syrup adds a distinctively sweet flavor. The muffins are at their best served warm from the oven, so a pat of butter can melt in.

1 egg

½ cup sour cream

½ cup maple syrup

¾ cup all-purpose white flour

1 teaspoon baking soda

1¼ cups branflakes

¼ cup raisins

¼ cup chopped pecans

Preheat the oven to 350°F. Grease 12 muffin cups or line with paper.

In a large mixing bowl, beat the egg. Add the sour cream and maple syrup and beat to combine. Set aside. In another bowl, sift the flour with the soda. Add to the egg mixture along with the branflakes and stir just to moisten. The batter will be lumpy. Stir in the raisins and nuts. Spoon into the prepared muffin cups and bake for 20 minutes. Serve hot.

FLORENCE GRISWOLD MUSEUM
LYME HISTORICAL SOCIETY
OLD LYME, CONNECTICUT

KEEP IT CLEAN

WE HEARD ABOUT a woman who, as a child growing up in a small farming community, thought that the hymn "Bringing in the Sheaves" was a song about doing laundry: "Bringing in the Sheets."

Carrot-Zucchini Muffins

Makes 18 to 24 muffins

The yogurt keeps these delightfully moist muffins fresh for days (if you can hold on to them that long), and the nutmeg gives them extra zip. If you don't have time to deal with an abundance of zucchini in season, try running the squash through the food processor and freezing the grated result in 1-cup batches. (Old 8-ounce yogurt containers are perfect for this.) When you're ready to whip up a batch of muffins, just pull the zucchini out of the freezer, defrost, drain off the excess water, and add as directed.

2 eggs, beaten

1 cup plus 2 tablespoons plain yogurt

1 cup canola oil

1 cup grated carrots

1 cup grated zucchini

4 cups all-purpose white flour

1 cup white sugar

2 tablespoons baking powder

1 teaspoon ground nutmeg

1 cup coarsely chopped pecans

Preheat the oven to 375°F. Grease 18 to 24 muffin cups or line with paper.

In a large mixing bowl, mix together the eggs, yogurt, and oil; then stir in the carrots and zucchini. Set aside. In another bowl, sift together the flour, sugar, baking powder, and nutmeg. Add the dry ingredients to the wet mixture and stir until just combined. The batter will be lumpy. Stir in the chopped pecans. Spoon the batter into the prepared muffin cups and bake for 15 to 20 minutes or until a tester inserted in the center comes out clean.

Sue MacEwan
Pilgrim Church
Duxbury, Massachusetts

Zucchini-Oatmeal Muffins
Makes 12 muffins

Confirmed zucchini haters love these outstanding muffins! Nice and crusty on top (even after freezing and reheating in the microwave), moist and delicious on the inside. They don't even need butter.

2 eggs, beaten

1 medium-size zucchini (about 10 ounces), shredded

¼ cup vegetable oil

1 cup plain yogurt

2½ cups all-purpose white flour

1 cup white sugar

½ cup rolled oats (not instant)

1 tablespoon baking powder

1 teaspoon salt

1 teaspoon ground cinnamon

1 cup chopped pecans

Preheat the oven to 400°F. Grease 12 muffin cups or line with paper.

In a large mixing bowl, mix together the eggs, zucchini, oil, and yogurt. Set aside. In another bowl, whisk together the flour, sugar, oats, baking powder, salt, and cinnamon. Add to the zucchini mixture and stir just to moisten. Stir in the pecans. The batter will be lumpy. Spoon into the prepared muffin cups and bake for about 25 minutes or until a tester inserted in the center comes out clean. Do not overbake.

Adapted from a recipe submitted by Connie Mackay
St. Andrew Lutheran Church
Ellsworth, Maine

Butterscotch Rolls

Makes 8 to 12 servings

A very good recipe and very easy to make, best served piping hot from the oven. Be sure to invert the rolls onto a serving plate as soon as they come out of the oven, so you don't lose any of the sauce (and to prevent the rolls from sticking to the pan).

6 to 8 tablespoons (¾ to 1 stick) margarine or butter, melted

1-pound loaf frozen bread dough, thawed just enough to allow slicing

1 package (3 ounces) butterscotch pudding (not instant)

1 to 2 teaspoons cinnamon

½ cup brown sugar

Pour the melted margarine into a 9-inch tube or bundt pan. Break or slice the dough into 2-inch chunks and arrange in the pan. Mix the pudding with the cinnamon and brown sugar. Sprinkle over the dough. Let rise overnight on a kitchen counter.

Preheat the oven to 375°F. Bake for 30 minutes. Remove the pan from the oven and immediately invert onto a serving plate. Serve warm.

Adapted from a recipe submitted by Larry Beswick
Claremont Kiwanis Club
Claremont, New Hampshire

Looks can be deceiving—it's eating that's believing.
—James Thurber, 20th-century humorist

PANCAKE BREAKFAST KNOW-HOW

SOME SAY COFFEE is the most important part of breakfast. Be sure yours is ready when the doors open. Coffee perked in a big urn is notoriously undrinkable. If you can, practice making good coffee in whatever pot you will be using. Or consider lining up a row of drip coffee makers brought from home. That way you can provide both caffeinated and decaffeinated coffees, and the coffee will always be fresh. (But someone will need to monitor the pots constantly and make more as needed.)

⚜ Make up your dry mix (flour, baking powder, salt, and sugar) in advance. During the pancake breakfast, make up ready-to-cook batches as needed. Extra dry mix can be stored in airtight containers for up to a year, but pancake batter already made must be used immediately.

⚜ Sausage holds up better over time than bacon and requires less handling. Parboil the sausage early in the morning or even the night before. Then brown as needed.

⚜ It's a good idea to set out a buffet of baskets of muffins and coffee cakes to appease your hungry breakfast eaters while you make the pancakes to order. This cuts your food costs, as the muffins and coffee cakes are always donated, and you may have to purchase the pancake fixings. It decreases the amount of pancakes (and expensive syrup) you ultimately serve, which eliminates stress on the kitchen staff. It also enables you to make pancakes to order. Finally, it provides a tasty alternative for those who don't like pancakes. When word gets around about the varied spread your organization offers, you will note a steady increase in attendance.

Sweet Milk Pancakes
Makes about 4 servings (18 four-inch pancakes)

Pancakes from scratch taste so much better than those from a mix! The contributor multiplies this recipe for pancake breakfasts served at her church.

1½ cups all-purpose white flour

2½ teaspoons baking powder

¼ teaspoon baking soda

3 tablespoons sugar

2 eggs, slightly beaten

1⅔ cups milk

3 tablespoons vegetable oil

In a large bowl, mix together the flour, baking powder, soda, and sugar. In a small bowl, beat the eggs, then add the milk and oil and blend well. Add the wet ingredients to the dry ingredients, whisking together until smooth. Ladle the batter onto a hot oiled griddle or skillet and cook until browned on both sides. Serve hot.

Cynthia A. Miga
All Saints Church in Pontiac
Warwick, Rhode Island

COOKIES AND BARS

 COOKIES ARE POPULAR with cooks and eaters alike, young and old. For taking to a potluck, nothing beats a batch of cookies lovingly presented in a basket lined with a cheery cloth napkin. The cookies can be made up days in advance—as long as you can hide them from hungry hands.

This particular collection of tried-and-true cookie recipes emphasizes no-fail, easy-to-make drop cookies and bar cookies. You can count on them whether you are preparing a dessert for a party or whipping up a batch for a last-minute bake sale.

Most of these recipes were developed on good old metal baking sheets that have been used for years. If your kitchen is equipped with baking sheets with nonstick coatings, by all means use them and don't bother to grease the sheet, even if the recipe calls for it.

ORANGE CHOCOLATE CHIP COOKIES
MAKES 6 DOZEN

The fresh orange gives a wonderful flavor and provides a nice twist on a traditional recipe. If you like, mix all the other ingredients in a food processor, then add the chocolate chips and nuts by hand at the end.

1 cup (2 sticks) margarine or butter, at room temperature

¼ cup plus 2 tablespoons white sugar

¼ cup plus 2 tablespoons brown sugar

1 teaspoon salt

1 egg

Grated zest of 1 orange

2 cups all-purpose white flour (or substitute part whole-wheat pastry flour)

¼ teaspoon baking soda

Juice of 1 orange

1 to 2 cups semisweet chocolate chips

½ cup chopped walnuts

Preheat the oven to 350°F. Lightly grease 2 baking sheets.

In a mixing bowl, cream together the margarine and sugars. Add the salt, egg, and zest and beat well. Sift together the flour and soda. Add to the creamed mixture with the orange juice, mixing well. Stir in the chips and nuts. Drop by the spoonful onto the greased baking sheets.

Bake for 10 minutes or until lightly browned on the edges. Remove the cookies to wire racks to cool completely.

Ann P. Whitcomb
SPRINGFIELD ART AND HISTORICAL SOCIETY
SPRINGFIELD, VERMONT

MUD PUDDLES
MAKES ABOUT 4 DOZEN

It takes a little practice to get the amount of dough in each tart cup exactly right, but kids of all ages adore these candy-cookie treats.

1 bag (14 ounces) miniature Reese's Peanut Butter Cups

1 cup (2 sticks) margarine or butter, at room temperature

¾ cup brown sugar

¾ cup white sugar

1 teaspoon vanilla extract

1 egg

2¼ cups all-purpose white flour

1 teaspoon baking soda

½ teaspoon salt

½ cup semisweet mini chocolate chips

Preheat the oven to 350°F. Spray miniature muffin pans with non-stick cooking spray. Remove the wrapping from the peanut butter cups.

In a mixing bowl, cream together the margarine and sugars. Add the vanilla and egg and mix until creamy. Sift together the flour, soda, and salt and add to the creamed mixture. Mix well. Stir in the chocolate chips. Place about 1 teaspoon of dough in each muffin cup.

Bake for 10 to 12 minutes, until brown and not too doughy. Immediately push a peanut butter cup into the middle of each cookie. Let cool completely before removing from the pan.

Nancy Burgess
EMMANUEL CHURCH
NEWPORT, RHODE ISLAND

WE KID YOU NOT (OR POTLUCKS R US)

POTLUCK DINNERS are frequently family and friend get-togethers, and so you're likely to spot at least a couple of toddlers navigating among the crowd. And with just a little extra care, the occasion can be fun for the kids, which means the grownups will enjoy themselves more, too.

❧ Make it clear in the invitation whether or not you're expecting children at your dinner so that some poor kid doesn't end up all alone among a dozen adults. A lonely tot becomes a bored tot, who in turn becomes a cranky tot.

❧ Allow the small ones to help out: folding and stacking napkins, distributing paper plates, and calling guests for dinner are all jobs small children can handle.

❧ You may want to set up a "kids only" area with toys, coloring books and crayons, and perhaps some music.

❧ Chances are that the kids will want to play when the adults are ready to eat, so keep food choices for kids simple and avoid anything that needs to be served very hot. Good choices include cheese, peanut butter and jelly, or baloney sandwiches cut into quarters; gelatin and pasta salads; and (of course) ice cream.

❧ Finger foods are popular at potlucks and suitable for small hands, too. Serve foods in small pieces when possible. Tots love carrot sticks with dip and "ants on a log": celery filled with peanut butter and garnished with raisins.

❧ Finally, keep hot dishes away from the edge of the buffet table and turn handles in toward the center of the table where little hands can't reach.

OATMEAL COOKIES

MAKES ABOUT 6 DOZEN

For those who like to take their nutrition in cookie form, these tasty morsels are boosted with good-for-you oats, sunflower seeds, wheat germ, raisins, and walnuts. We think they are particularly good for a hike or a picnic.

1 cup (2 sticks) butter or margarine, at room temperature

½ cup sugar (brown, white, or a combination)

4 eggs

½ cup milk

3 cups all-purpose white flour

2 teaspoons baking soda

1 teaspoon salt

1½ teaspoons ground cinnamon

1 tablespoon brewer's yeast (optional, available in health food stores)

½ cup unsweetened coconut flakes

2 tablespoons toasted wheat germ

½ cup chopped walnuts

3⅓ cups quick or rolled oats (don't use instant)

1½ cups raisins

Preheat the oven to 350°F. Grease two baking sheets.

Cream together the butter and sugar. Add the eggs and milk and beat until creamy. Sift together the flour, soda, salt, and cinnamon. Add to the creamed mixture and beat until smooth. Stir in the brewer's yeast if using, the coconut, wheat germ, walnuts, oats, and raisins. Drop by the rounded teaspoonful onto the baking sheets.

Bake for 10 to 12 minutes or until golden brown. Remove the cookies to wire racks to cool completely.

Isabel Drobney
WILLINGTON BAPTIST CHURCH
WILLINGTON, CONNECTICUT

COCONUT OATMEAL COOKIES
MAKES ABOUT 6 1/2 DOZEN

The coconut adds a distinctive flavor to these delicious morsels.

1 cup (2 sticks) butter, at room
   temperature

1 cup white sugar

1 cup brown sugar

2 eggs

1 teaspoon vanilla extract

2 cups all-purpose white flour

1 teaspoon baking powder

1 teaspoon baking soda

½ teaspoon salt

2 cups quick-cooking oats

1 cup unsweetened coconut

Preheat the oven to 350°F. Grease two baking sheets.

In a mixing bowl, cream together the butter and sugars. Add the eggs and vanilla and beat until creamy. Sift together the flour, baking powder, soda, and salt. Add to the creamed mixture and beat until smooth. Stir in the oats and coconut. Drop by the rounded teaspoonful onto the baking sheets.

Bake for 9 to 12 minutes. Remove to wire racks to cool completely.

Adapted from a recipe submitted by Dorothy M. White
UNITARIAN CHURCH OF BARNSTABLE
BARNSTABLE, MASSACHUSETTS

Molasses Cookies

Makes about 6 dozen

These very tasty cookies have just the right punch of spice and molasses. Our tester said they reminded her of Thanksgiving.

¾ cup solid vegetable shortening

1 cup white sugar

¼ cup molasses

1 egg, slightly beaten

1¾ cups all-purpose white flour

1 teaspoon baking soda

¼ teaspoon salt

1 teaspoon ground cinnamon

¾ teaspoon ground ginger

½ teaspoon ground cloves

Preheat the oven to 350°F. Grease two baking sheets.

In a mixing bowl, cream together the shortening and sugar. Add the molasses and egg and beat until smooth. Sift together the flour, soda, salt, and spices. Add to the creamed mixture and blend well. Drop by the teaspoonful onto the baking sheets. Flatten with a fork dipped in milk.

Bake for 6 to 8 minutes. Remove the sheets from the oven when the cookies are still puffy and light brown. Allow to rest on the cookie sheets for 5 minutes before removing to wire racks to cool completely.

Dorothy M. White
Unitarian Church of Barnstable
Barnstable, Massachusetts

SNAPPY GINGERSNAPS
MAKES ABOUT 6 DOZEN

A fabulous old-fashioned gingersnap recipe that our testers rated topnotch!

¾ cup solid vegetable shortening

1 cup white sugar

¼ cup molasses

1 egg

2 cups all-purpose white flour

2 teaspoons baking soda

½ teaspoon salt

1 tablespoon ground ginger

1 teaspoon ground cinnamon

Preheat the oven to 350°F. Grease two baking sheets.

In a mixing bowl, cream together the shortening and sugar. Add the molasses and egg and beat until smooth. Sift together the flour, soda, salt, and spices. Add to the creamed mixture and blend well. Drop by the teaspoonful onto the baking sheets, keeping the cookies 2 inches apart.

Bake for 10 to 15 minutes. Allow to rest on the baking sheets for 5 minutes before removing to wire racks to cool completely.

Yvonne Menzone
AUBURN GROUP OF WORCESTER COUNTY EXTENSION SERVICE
AUBURN, MASSACHUSETTS

*An I had but one penny in the world,
thou shouldst have it to buy gingerbread.*

—William Shakespeare, *Love's Labour's Lost*

FAIRY GOLD COOKIES
MAKES ABOUT 5 DOZEN

An inexpensive cookie that's easy to make from ingredients already in the house. Excellent with coffee or milk. If they don't all disappear on the first day, you'll find the flavor gets even better with age!

1 cup solid vegetable shortening

1 cup brown sugar

1 egg

1 teaspoon baking soda

¼ cup hot water

2¾ cups all-purpose white flour

In a mixing bowl, cream together the shortening and sugar. Add the egg and beat until smooth. Add the baking soda dissolved in the hot water. Add the flour in thirds, beating well after each addition. Chill thoroughly.

Preheat the oven to 350°F. Grease two baking sheets.

Form the chilled dough into balls about the size of walnuts and place 2 inches apart on the baking sheets. Flatten with a fork.

Bake for about 10 minutes. Remove to wire racks to cool completely.

Mary Ann Hermance
BOSCAWEN HISTORICAL SOCIETY
BOSCAWEN, NEW HAMPSHIRE

SUGAR COOKIES
MAKES ABOUT 5 DOZEN

A very good cookie with excellent flavor and texture. Kids love rolling the balls in the sugar and squishing them down on the baking sheet.

1 cup (2 sticks) butter or margarine, at room temperature

1 cup white sugar

1 cup brown sugar

¼ cup milk

4 eggs

1 teaspoon grated lemon zest or 1 teaspoon lemon juice

4 cups all-purpose white flour

2 teaspoons baking powder

2 teaspoons baking soda

1 teaspoon salt

1 teaspoon ground nutmeg

½ teaspoon ground cinnamon

¼ teaspoon ground cloves

White sugar or unsweetened coconut

In a mixing bowl, cream together the butter and sugars. Add the milk, eggs, and lemon zest or juice and beat until smooth. Sift together the flour, baking powder, soda, salt, and spices and add to the creamed mixture, beating well. Chill thoroughly.

Preheat the oven to 350°F. Grease two baking sheets.

Form the chilled dough into balls about the size of walnuts. Roll the balls in the sugar or coconut. Place 2 inches apart on the baking sheets. Flatten with a fork.

Bake for 10 to 12 minutes, then remove to wire racks to cool completely.

Isabel Drobney
WILLINGTON BAPTIST CHURCH
WILLINGTON, CONNECTICUT

HONEY DROPS
MAKES ABOUT 3 DOZEN

These are wonderful! *The honey and the apricot jam are a winning combination that makes the sandwich cookies flavorful but not overly sweet. Surprisingly fast to put together, a plate of these makes an attractive gift. They freeze well, too—but unless you hide them in the back of the freezer or use an unmarked container, you'll be lucky if there are any left to give away!*

1 cup solid vegetable shortening

1 cup brown sugar

2 eggs

6 tablespoons honey

1 teaspoon vanilla extract

3½ cups all-purpose white flour

2 teaspoons baking soda

½ teaspoon salt

Apricot jam

In a mixing bowl, cream together the shortening and sugar. Add the eggs, honey, and vanilla and beat until smooth. Sift the flour with the soda and salt. Add the flour mixture to the creamed mixture, beating well. Chill thoroughly.

Preheat the oven to 350°F.

Form the chilled dough into balls about the size of walnuts and place the balls 2 inches apart on ungreased baking sheets.

Bake for 10 to 12 minutes. Remove to wire racks to cool slightly. While still warm, make cookie sandwiches with the apricot jam as the filling.

Harriet Martin
WOMAN'S FELLOWSHIP OF FIRST CHURCH
STERLING, MASSACHUSETTS

Lois Ann's Rhubarb Cookies
Makes 3 to 4 dozen

Apple is a good substitute if you don't have access to fresh rhubarb, but the rhubarb adds a pleasant tartness and texture.

½ cup solid vegetable shortening

1 cup brown sugar

1 egg

2 cups all-purpose white or whole-wheat pastry flour

2 teaspoons baking powder

Dash salt

½ teaspoon ground nutmeg

½ teaspoon ground cloves

1 teaspoon ground cinnamon

¼ cup milk

1 cup diced rhubarb (or apple)

½ cup raisins

1 cup chopped walnuts

Preheat the oven to 350°F. Grease two baking sheets.

In a mixing bowl, cream together the shortening and sugar. Add the egg and beat until smooth. Sift together the flour, baking powder, salt, and spices. Add the flour mixture to the creamed mixture with the milk; beat until smooth. Mix in the fruit and nuts. Drop by the teaspoonful onto the baking sheets.

Bake for about 12 minutes or until lightly browned. Remove to wire racks to cool completely.

Ann P. Whitcomb
Springfield Art and Historical Society
Springfield, Vermont

SWEDISH SPRITZ COOKIES

MAKES ABOUT 4 DOZEN

A delightful cookie that's especially popular at Christmastime.

1 cup (2 sticks) butter, at room
   temperature

⅔ cup white sugar

3 egg yolks

1 teaspoon vanilla or almond extract

2½ cups all-purpose white flour, sifted

Cream the butter. Add the sugar, egg yolks, and vanilla and beat well. Stir in the flour. Form the dough into four balls. Chill thoroughly.

Preheat the oven to 375°F.

Working with one ball of dough at a time, put the dough in a cookie press and press out various designs and shapes onto ungreased baking sheets.

Bake for 10 minutes or until golden brown. Remove to wire racks to cool completely.

Pauline Bauer
GUSTAF ADOLPH LUTHERAN CHURCH
NEW SWEDEN, MAINE

HO, HO, WHO?

IT WAS AROUND Christmastime, and a Sunday school teacher was asking her class of two- and three-year-olds who was up in heaven. In addition to God and Jesus, one of the children offered, "Santa Claus?"

Forgotten Cookies

MAKES ABOUT 3½ DOZEN

Incredibly easy, this is a great recipe for busy people because you just turn off the oven and leave the cookies unattended. Because meringues don't hold up well in humid weather, they are best made in winter. We know people who consider these treats the very best part of the holiday season.

2 egg whites
¾ cup white sugar
1 teaspoon vanilla extract
1 cup semisweet chocolate chips
1 cup chopped nuts

Preheat the oven to 400°F. Line two baking sheets with waxed paper.

Beat the egg whites until foamy. Gradually add the sugar and vanilla and continue beating until very stiff. Fold in the chips and nuts. Drop by the teaspoonful onto the baking sheets. Place in the oven and turn off the heat. Leave in the oven for 2 hours or more, until completely dry. Store in an airtight container.

Cynthia LaPointe
CLAREMONT LIONESS CLUB
CLAREMONT, NEW HAMPSHIRE

SOUR CREAM TWISTS

MAKES 2 DOZEN

Our tester's family went crazy over these rich, buttery twists. Amazingly easy to make, they're especially good right out of the oven, but they keep well, too.

COOKIE

2 cups sifted all-purpose white flour

½ teaspoon salt

1 cup (2 sticks) butter or margarine

¾ cup sour cream

1 egg yolk

FILLING

¾ cup white sugar

¾ cup finely chopped walnuts

1 teaspoon ground cinnamon

1 egg white (optional)

In a mixing bowl, combine the flour and salt. Cut in the butter until the mixture resembles coarse crumbs. Add the sour cream and egg yolk and blend well. Shape the dough into a ball. Sprinkle lightly with flour. Wrap in plastic and chill for 2 hours or up to 3 days.

Preheat the oven to 350°F. Lightly spray two baking sheets with non-stick cooking spray. Make the filling by combining the sugar, walnuts, and cinnamon in a small bowl.

Divide the dough into thirds. Roll each ball into a flat circle. Sprinkle a third of the filling on each circle. Cut into wedges, like a pie. Roll each wedge up from the wide end to the tip. Place on the baking sheets. Brush with egg white to glaze, if desired.

Bake for 25 to 30 minutes. Remove to wire racks to cool completely.

Jo-Ann M. Huguenin
WILLINGTON BAPTIST CHURCH
WILLINGTON, CONNECTICUT

CHOCOLATE CHIP SQUARES

MAKES ABOUT 2½ DOZEN

The classic chocolate chip bar cookie, this is easy to make and very good.

¾ cup solid vegetable shortening

½ cup white sugar

1½ cups brown sugar

2 egg yolks

1 tablespoon water

1 teaspoon vanilla extract

2 cups all-purpose white flour

1 teaspoon baking powder

¼ teaspoon baking soda

¼ teaspoon salt

1 package (6 ounces) semisweet
  chocolate chips

2 egg whites

Preheat the oven to 350°F. Grease a 10-inch by 15-inch baking sheet.

In a large mixing bowl, cream together the shortening, white sugar, and ½ cup of the brown sugar. Add the egg yolks, water, and vanilla and blend well. Sift together the flour, baking powder, soda, and salt. Add to the creamed mixture and blend well. Pat onto the baking sheet to form a thin cookie-crust base. Sprinkle on the chocolate chips.

Beat the egg whites until stiff. Fold in the remaining 1 cup brown sugar. Spread on top of the chips.

Bake for 25 to 30 minutes or until a tester inserted in the center comes out clean. Cool completely before cutting into squares.

Polly Long
LADIES AID SOCIETY, GILSUM CONGREGATIONAL CHURCH
GILSUM, NEW HAMPSHIRE

TURTLE COOKIES

MAKES 2 DOZEN

A fast seller at bake sales, these are very rich and very sweet.

CRUST LAYER

2 cups all-purpose white flour

½ cup (1 stick) butter, at room
   temperature

1 cup brown sugar, firmly packed

1 cup whole pecans

CARAMEL LAYER

⅔ cup butter

½ cup brown sugar

1 cup semisweet chocolate chips

Preheat the oven to 350°F.

To make the crust, combine the flour, ½ cup butter, and 1 cup brown sugar. Pat firmly into a 9-inch by 13-inch baking pan. Sprinkle the pecans over the crust.

To make the caramel layer, combine the ⅔ cup butter and ½ cup brown sugar in a small saucepan and boil for 30 seconds to 1 minute. Or put in a deep microwave-safe container and cook on high for 2 to 3 minutes, until bubbly. Pour over the nuts.

Bake for 18 to 22 minutes or until the top is bubbly. Remove from the oven and sprinkle the chips on top. When the chocolate has melted, swirl it in with the tip of a knife. Cut into squares when completely cooled.

Suzanne Weed
ST. PETER'S EPISCOPAL CHURCH
OXFORD, CONNECTICUT

Maple-Pecan Squares

Makes 2 dozen

A wonderful use of fresh maple syrup! When we served these at a party, they were gobbled up in no time.

CRUST

1½ cups all-purpose white flour

¼ cup brown sugar

½ cup (1 stick) butter, at room
  temperature

FILLING

⅔ cup brown sugar

1 cup maple syrup

2 eggs, beaten

2 tablespoons all-purpose white flour

¼ teaspoon salt

½ teaspoon vanilla extract

1 cup chopped pecans

Preheat the oven to 350°F. Grease a 9-inch by 13-inch baking pan.

Make the crust by combining the 1½ cups flour, ¼ cup brown sugar, and butter. Blend with a fork until the mixture has the consistency of cornmeal. Pat into the baking pan. Bake for 15 minutes.

Meanwhile, make the filling by combining the ⅔ cup brown sugar and the maple syrup in a saucepan and simmering for 5 minutes. Pour this over the beaten eggs, stirring constantly. Stir in the 2 tablespoons flour, salt, and vanilla. Pour over the partially baked crust. Sprinkle with the nuts.

Return the pan to the oven and bake for 20 to 25 minutes more. Cool completely before cutting into squares.

Ann Hebert
St. Brendan's Catholic Woman's Club
Colebrook, New Hampshire

LEMON SQUARES
MAKES 1 DOZEN

So easy to make, with ingredients already in the cupboard, and always the first to disappear from any holiday gift assortment.

1 cup all-purpose white flour

¼ cup confectioners' sugar

½ cup (1 stick) butter or margarine

2 eggs

1 cup white sugar

¼ teaspoon salt

½ teaspoon baking powder

2 tablespoons lemon juice

Confectioners' sugar or coconut

Preheat the oven to 350°F.

Mix together the flour and ¼ cup confectioners' sugar. Cut in the butter until the mixture has the consistency of cornmeal. Press the mixture evenly on the bottom of an ungreased 9-inch square pan. Bake for 20 minutes.

Meanwhile, beat the eggs, white sugar, salt, baking powder, and lemon juice together until light and fluffy. Pour over the hot, partially baked crust. Return to the oven and bake for 25 minutes. Cool completely. Dust with confectioners' sugar or coconut. Cut into squares.

Adapted from a recipe submitted by Lorraine Record
GOOD SHEPHERD LUTHERAN CHURCH
RUTLAND, VERMONT

Date Squares

Makes 12 to 15

An easy version of an old favorite.

FILLING

8 ounces dates, finely chopped

1 cup water

½ cup white sugar

1 tablespoon all-purpose white flour

CRUST

1¼ cups quick-cooking oats

1½ cups all-purpose white flour

1 cup brown sugar

1 teaspoon baking soda

¾ cup (1½ sticks) butter or
    margarine, at room temperature

In a small saucepan, combine all the filling ingredients. Cook over low heat for 5 to 7 minutes, until thickened. Set aside for 10 to 15 minutes to allow the dates to soften fully.

Preheat the oven to 350°F.

To make the crust, mix together the oats, flour, brown sugar, and soda. With a fork, blend the butter into the oat mixture. Divide in half and press half into the bottom of an ungreased 9-inch by 13-inch baking pan. Spread the date filling on top. Sprinkle with the remaining oat mixture.

Bake for 30 minutes. Cool completely before cutting into squares.

Gladys Anderson
WILLINGTON BAPTIST CHURCH
WILLINGTON, CONNECTICUT

MARJIT'S HALLONRUTAR
(Currant Jelly Cookies)
MAKES ABOUT 20

This authentic Swedish bar cookie is simply wonderful, and an excellent addition to any buffet or potluck.

1 pound (4 sticks) butter, at room temperature

½ cup white sugar

3½ cups all-purpose white flour

2 teaspoons almond extract

1 to 1½ cups currant jelly

Preheat the oven to 325°F. Lightly grease a baking sheet or spray with nonstick cooking spray.

Combine the butter, sugar, flour, and almond extract and mix until thoroughly blended. Form the mixture into two balls, one containing two-thirds of the dough, the other containing one-third. On a lightly floured board, roll out the larger ball of dough into a ⅛-inch-thick to ¼-inch-thick rectangle that measures about 8 inches by 12 inches. Transfer to the baking sheet. Spread the jelly on the dough. Roll out the remaining piece of dough and cut into ½-inch strips. Arrange on the diagonal over the jelly. Bake for 30 to 45 minutes. Cool completely before cutting into squares.

Janet M. Erickson
GUSTAF ADOLPH LUTHERAN CHURCH
NEW SWEDEN, MAINE

SADIE ANSON'S SCOTTISH SHORTBREAD
MAKES 6 DOZEN

Mrs. Anson, a long-time member of the Emmanuel Church, brought this recipe with her from Scotland. Best made with real butter, these are rich and delicious. Be careful not to overwork the dough, however, or the cookies will be tough. Rice flour can be found in most health food stores.

1 pound (4 sticks) butter, at room temperature

1 cup white sugar

3½ cups all-purpose white flour

½ cup rice flour

Preheat the oven to 350°F. Cream the butter with the sugar. Add the flours and blend well. Roll out the dough directly onto an ungreased 10-inch by 15-inch baking sheet. Trim the edges and prick all over with a fork. Bake for 15 minutes, then reduce the oven temperature to 300°F and continue baking for 30 minutes. Cut into squares while still warm.

Elsie Power
EMMANUEL CHURCH
NEWPORT, RHODE ISLAND

BOETERKOEK
MAKES 12 TO 16

A rich and easy shortbread from Holland.

1 cup (2 sticks) butter

1 cup white sugar

1 egg

2 teaspoons almond extract

2 teaspoons baking powder

2 cups all-purpose white flour

Preheat the oven to 350°F. Melt the butter. Stir in the sugar, egg, and almond extract. Sift together the baking powder and flour and stir into the mixture. Spread into an ungreased 9-inch pie plate and bake for 25 minutes. Cut into wedges while warm.

Deborah K. Nowers
UNITARIAN UNIVERSALIST PARISH OF MONSON
MONSON, MASSACHUSETTS

CAKES

WHEN WE READ one recipe that called for butter "the size of an egg," we knew we had collected some wonderfully authentic old-style recipes. Better yet, many of these can be prepared quickly from ingredients you're likely to have on hand, so they're perfect when you need a last-minute contribution to a potluck or just want to try something a little different for the family dinner.

There are classic recipes here for apple cakes, blueberry cake, pound cakes, and Boston Cream Pie. The Poor Man's Cake is a deliciously dense cake that was also known as a Depression Cake. Of course, no gathering of cake recipes would be complete without chocolate, and this collection is no exception. One hint: Just wait until you taste the Chocolate Cheesecake!

Easy Pound Cake

Makes 10 to 12 servings

We think you'll enjoy this classic pound cake, and baking it in the bundt pan makes for an attractive presentation. If you're not fond of almond flavoring, omit that and increase the vanilla to 1½ teaspoons.

½ pound (2 sticks) butter, at room temperature

½ pound (1 cup plus 2 heaping tablespoons) white sugar

½ pound (4 large) eggs

1 teaspoon vanilla extract

½ teaspoon almond extract

½ pound (2 scant cups sifted) all-purpose white flour

1 teaspoon baking powder

Confectioners' sugar

Preheat the oven to 325°F. Butter a bundt pan.

Cream together the butter and sugar. Add the eggs, one at a time, mixing well after each addition. Mix in the vanilla and almond extracts. Sift together the flour and baking powder. Add to the creamed mixture and beat until well blended. Spoon into the prepared pan.

Bake for 50 minutes or until a tester inserted near the center comes out clean. Cool in the pan for 10 minutes before turning out onto a wire rack to cool completely. Dust with confectioners' sugar just before serving.

Lee Huber
Friends of the Dover Public Library
Dover, New Hampshire

CHOCOLATE CREAM POUND CAKE

MAKES 6 TO 8 SERVINGS

We really enjoyed this loaf cake, which is lighter than most pound cakes. It is heavenly served with sliced strawberries and dusted with confectioners' sugar. According to the contributor, "If you can resist eating it, this cake will keep fresh and moist for as long as a week if cooled thoroughly and wrapped airtight in plastic wrap and foil."

1 cup heavy cream

2 eggs

1 teaspoon vanilla extract

1½ cups all-purpose white flour

1 cup white sugar

⅓ cup unsweetened cocoa powder

2 teaspoons baking powder

¾ teaspoon salt

Confectioners' sugar

Preheat the oven to 350°F. Butter an 8-inch by 4-inch loaf pan and dust with white sugar.

In a large mixing bowl, beat the cream until stiff. Beat in the eggs and vanilla. Combine the flour, white sugar, cocoa, baking powder, and salt and sift over the cream. Stir to blend thoroughly. Spoon the batter into the loaf pan.

Bake for 55 minutes or until the cake just begins to pull away from the pan. Cool in the pan for 10 minutes, then turn out onto a wire rack to finish cooling. Before serving, dust liberally with confectioners' sugar.

Libby Yanizyn
WALPOLE HISTORICAL SOCIETY
WALPOLE, NEW HAMPSHIRE

LEMON LOAF CAKE

MAKES 12 SERVINGS

A wonderful recipe! Extremely easy and inexpensive to make (most of the ingredients are already on hand in the average kitchen) and perfect as an afternoon tea cake or even for dessert. Try serving it with a fruit compote and vanilla ice cream—heavenly!

¼ cup solid vegetable shortening

1 cup white sugar

Grated zest of 1 lemon

¼ cup milk

2 eggs

1½ cups all-purpose white flour

1 teaspoon baking powder

½ teaspoon salt

Juice of 1 lemon

½ cup white sugar

Preheat the oven to 350°F. Grease an 8-inch by 4-inch loaf pan.

In a mixing bowl, cream together the shortening, 1 cup sugar, and lemon zest. Mix together the milk and eggs; add to the shortening mixture. Sift together the flour, baking powder, and salt. Add to the liquid ingredients. Mix just enough to moisten.

Pour into the loaf pan and bake for 1 hour or until a tester inserted in the cake comes out clean. While the cake is still hot, combine the lemon juice with the remaining ½ cup sugar. Heat until the sugar melts. Pour over the hot cake. When absorbed, remove the cake from the pan and cool on a wire rack.

Annabel Hill Bates
THETFORD ACADEMY ALUMNI ASSOCIATION
THETFORD, VERMONT

BUTTERMILK COFFEE CAKE

MAKES 12 TO 15 SERVINGS

Very moist, and great with coffee. This can be made the night before and served the next morning, but it's even better hot from the oven.

3 cups all-purpose white flour

1 cup white sugar

1 cup brown sugar

½ teaspoon salt

1½ teaspoons ground nutmeg

1 cup vegetable oil

2 eggs

1 teaspoon baking soda

1½ cups buttermilk

½ cup chopped nuts

1 teaspoon ground cinnamon (or more to taste)

Preheat the oven to 350°F. Grease a 9-inch by 13-inch baking pan.

In a large mixing bowl, combine the flour, sugars, salt, nutmeg, and oil by hand or on the lowest speed of a mixer. Reserve ½ cup for the topping. To the flour mixture left in the mixing bowl, add the eggs, soda, and buttermilk. Mix on the lowest speed until just blended. Pour into the baking dish. Sprinkle with the reserved topping, the nuts, and the cinnamon.

Bake for 40 minutes or until a tester inserted near the center comes out clean. Cool for at least 10 minutes before serving, or serve completely cooled.

Cynthia A. Miga
ALL SAINTS CHURCH IN PONTIAC
WARWICK, RHODE ISLAND

Grammy Clade's Coffee Cake

MAKES 9 SERVINGS

A popular contribution to church suppers and other potlucks, this is also a special treat for a family breakfast. The topping has a delicious caramel flavor.

CAKE

1 cup white sugar

⅓ cup solid vegetable shortening

1 egg

⅔ cup milk

1 teaspoon vanilla extract

1⅔ cups all-purpose white flour

2½ teaspoons baking powder

TOPPING

3 tablespoons butter, melted

3 tablespoons heavy cream

5 tablespoons light brown sugar

¾ cup chopped walnuts

Preheat the oven to 350°F. Grease a 9-inch square baking pan.

In a large mixing bowl, cream together the sugar and shortening. Add the egg and beat until light. Mix in the milk and vanilla. Sift together the flour and baking powder, add to the mixture, and beat until smooth. Pour into the pan and bake for 25 to 30 minutes or until a tester inserted near the center of the cake comes out clean.

To make the topping, combine the topping ingredients. Sprinkle on the warm cake. Place under the broiler until the topping bubbles (about 5 minutes), then remove the cake immediately. Cool in the pan on a wire rack. Serve warm or completely cooled.

Gladys Nicoll
CHESTER HISTORICAL SOCIETY
CHESTER, NEW HAMPSHIRE

ANGEL GINGERBREAD

MAKES 6 TO 8 SERVINGS

Incredibly moist and flavorful, this is truly a heavenly dessert—not a speck of ginger in the recipe, yet the finished product radiates ginger! Highly recommended.

⅓ cup sugar

¼ cup solid vegetable shortening

1 egg, beaten

½ cup molasses

1 cup all-purpose white flour

1 teaspoon salt

½ teaspoon ground nutmeg

½ teaspoon ground cinnamon

¼ teaspoon ground cloves

½ cup boiling water

Preheat the oven to 350°F. Grease an 8-inch square baking pan.

In a mixing bowl, cream together the sugar and shortening. Add the egg and molasses and beat until smooth. Sift together the flour, salt, and spices and add to the molasses mixture. Mix well. Then add the boiling water and beat until smooth. Pour into the baking pan.

Bake for 30 minutes or until a tester inserted near the center comes out clean. Serve warm or completely cooled. Whipped cream makes a lovely accompaniment.

Mary (Molly) Lawrence
EMMANUEL CHURCH
NEWPORT, RHODE ISLAND

OLD-FASHIONED GINGERBREAD
MAKES 6 TO 8 SERVINGS

A variation on the same theme, this is an authentic, hundred-year-old recipe that's wonderful served warm with a scoop of French vanilla ice cream or sprinkled with confectioners' sugar.

¼ cup (½ stick) butter or margarine, at room temperature

½ cup sugar

1 egg

½ cup buttermilk

1 teaspoon baking soda

1½ cups all-purpose white flour

¼ teaspoon salt

1 teaspoon ground cinnamon

1 teaspoon ground ginger

½ teaspoon ground cloves

½ cup molasses

Confectioners' sugar

Preheat the oven to 375°F. Grease and flour an 8-inch square baking pan.

In a mixing bowl, cream together the butter and sugar until light and fluffy. Add the egg and beat for 1 minute. Combine the buttermilk and soda and set aside. In a separate bowl, sift the flour with the spices. Add the flour mixture to the sugar mixture, blending well but not beating. Stir in the buttermilk, then the molasses. Pour into the pan.

Bake for 30 to 35 minutes or until a tester inserted near the center of the cake comes out clean. Cool in the pan for 20 minutes, then turn out onto a plate. Sprinkle with confectioners' sugar, if desired.

Fay Linden
FIRST PARISH IN NEEDHAM, UNITARIAN UNIVERSALIST
NEEDHAM, MASSACHUSETTS

MINNIE'S SHORTCAKE
MAKES 12 SERVINGS

A traditional shortcake recipe that the parishioners of All Saints Church use at their annual strawberry shortcake supper each June.

2 cups all-purpose white flour

5 teaspoons baking powder

1 teaspoon salt

5 tablespoons solid vegetable shortening

1 egg

¾ cup milk

2 tablespoons sugar

Preheat the oven to 425°F. Grease 12 muffin cups.

Sift together the flour, baking powder, and salt. Set aside.

In a small saucepan, melt the shortening. Remove from the heat and add the egg, milk, and sugar. Mix well. Pour into the flour mixture and stir to combine. Spoon into the muffin cups.

Bake for 12 minutes, until golden. When cooled, split the shortcakes. Top with sweetened berries and a dollop of whipped cream.

Cynthia A. Miga
ALL SAINTS CHURCH IN PONTIAC
WARWICK, RHODE ISLAND

THE ULTIMATE POTLUCK DESSERT

*T*HE ULTIMATE potluck cake was a pioneer stack cake, which was often served at weddings. The guests would each bring a cake layer—any flavor—to make the wedding cake. The layers were held together with applesauce. The popularity of the bride was gauged by the height and number of stacks made. Today, you might encounter a stack cake in Appalachia, where the layers are likely to be made of ginger cake.

Boston Cream Pie

Makes 8 servings

All New Englanders know that Boston Cream Pie is not a pie at all, but a cake. And this version is so easy to make!

CAKE LAYER

¼ cup solid vegetable shortening

1 cup white sugar

1 egg

1¾ cups all-purpose white flour

4 teaspoons baking powder

⅛ teaspoon salt

1 cup milk

1 teaspoon vanilla extract

CREAM FILLING

2 tablespoons plus 2 teaspoons all-purpose white flour

6 tablespoons white sugar

1 egg

½ cup milk

Pinch salt

½ teaspoon vanilla extract

Chocolate frosting

Preheat the oven to 350°F. Grease and flour two 8-inch round cake pans.

Cream the shortening with the 1 cup sugar. Add 1 egg and beat until blended. Sift the 1¾ cups flour together with the baking powder and ⅛ teaspoon salt. Add to the creamed mixture alternately with the milk. Stir in the vanilla. Divide the batter between the cake tins.

Bake for 20 minutes or until a tester inserted near the center of the cake comes out clean. Cool in the pans for 10 minutes, then turn out onto wire racks to finish cooling.

To make the filling, combine the flour with the sugar in a small saucepan. Add the egg, milk, and salt. Cook over low heat, stirring constantly, until the filling is smooth and thick. Stir in the vanilla. Chill in the refrigerator.

To assemble, spread the filling between the cooled cake layers and top with the frosting.

Adapted from a recipe submitted by Carol Frederick
Chester Historical Society
Chester, New Hampshire

Apple Cake

MAKES 12 TO 15 SERVINGS

Very light and not overly sweet. The poppy seeds add delicious texture. This is a good choice for a morning coffee cake, but we also liked it as a dessert, served with whipped cream or vanilla ice cream.

4 eggs

2 teaspoons vanilla extract

1 cup (2 sticks) butter, melted

1½ cups white sugar

2 cups all-purpose white flour

4 teaspoons baking powder

½ teaspoon salt

2 teaspoons ground cinnamon

4 teaspoons poppy seeds

6 to 8 apples, peeled, cored, and sliced (Golden Delicious, Rome, Northern Spy, etc.)

Preheat the oven to 350°F. Grease a 9-inch by 13-inch baking pan.

Beat together the eggs, vanilla, butter, and sugar. Sift together the flour, baking powder, salt, and cinnamon. Add to the egg mixture along with the poppy seeds and blend well. Gently fold in the apples. Pour into the prepared pan.

Bake for 45 to 50 minutes or until a tester inserted near the center comes out clean. Let cool in the pan. Serve warm or completely cooled.

Adapted from a recipe submitted by Malita Brown
UNITARIAN UNIVERSALIST PARISH OF MONSON
MONSON, MASSACHUSETTS

Apple-Pie Cake

Makes 6 to 8 servings

Our tester called this "incredibly easy for something so good." We loved the combination of apple-pie spices, apples, and pecans in the cake. This superb coffee cake makes a great dessert served warm with ice cream.

½ cup (1 stick) margarine or butter

¾ cup white sugar

1 egg, slightly beaten

1 cup all-purpose white flour

1 teaspoon baking powder

½ teaspoon salt

1 teaspoon ground cinnamon

½ teaspoon ground nutmeg

¼ teaspoon ground cloves

⅛ teaspoon vanilla extract

2 cups peeled, cored, and chopped apples

½ cup chopped pecans

Preheat the oven to 350°F. Thoroughly grease a 9-inch pie pan.

In a large saucepan, melt the margarine. Or melt the margarine by heating it in a large microwave-safe mixing bowl in the microwave for 30 seconds on high. Remove from the heat and blend in the sugar and egg. Sift together the flour, baking powder, salt, and spices; add to the mixture and beat until smooth. Stir in the vanilla, apples, and pecans. Spread into the pie pan.

Bake for 40 to 45 minutes or until a tester inserted near the center comes out clean. Serve warm, directly out of the pan.

Florence Griswold Museum
Lyme Historical Society
Old Lyme, Connecticut

WHOLE-WHEAT APPLESAUCE CAKE

MAKES 12 SERVINGS

A very good spice cake that's easy to make and not overly sweet. This cake is lower in fat than most, and the whole wheat adds to the fiber and nutrition.

½ cup canola oil

½ cup white sugar

1 egg, beaten

1 jar (15 ounces) applesauce

2 teaspoons baking soda

½ cup boiling water

2½ cups whole-wheat flour

1 teaspoon ground cinnamon

1 teaspoon ground cloves

1 teaspoon ground allspice

1 cup raisins

½ cup pecans, chopped

Preheat the oven to 350°F. Grease an 8-inch by 12-inch baking pan.

Cream together the oil and sugar. Blend in the egg and applesauce. Dissolve the soda in the water. Sift together the flour and the spices. Alternately add the water and flour mixtures to the applesauce mixture and beat until smooth. Stir in the raisins and pecans. Pour the mixture into the pan.

Bake for 35 to 40 minutes or until a tester inserted near the center comes out clean. Serve warm or cooled, directly out of the pan.

Adapted from a recipe submitted by Gary Martin
NORTH PARISH CHURCH OF NORTH ANDOVER, UNITARIAN UNIVERSALIST
NORTH ANDOVER, MASSACHUSETTS

Grandmother's Blueberry Cake

MAKES 8 SERVINGS

An easy and delicious cake that tastes like a blueberry muffin.

¼ cup (½ stick) butter
1 cup white sugar
1 egg
1 teaspoon baking soda
½ cup milk
2½ cups all-purpose white flour
2 teaspoons cream of tartar
1 teaspoon lemon juice
1 teaspoon vanilla extract
1 pint blueberries

Preheat the oven to 350°F. Grease and flour a 9-inch by 13-inch baking pan.

Cream together the butter and sugar. Add the egg and beat well. Dissolve the soda in the milk. Sift together the flour and cream of tartar. Add the flour mixture to the butter mixture alternately with the milk, beating well after each addition. Add the lemon juice and vanilla extract. Fold in the berries. Spoon into the baking pan.

Bake for about 45 minutes. Serve warm or completely cooled, directly out of the pan.

Bernice Gladue
AUBURN GROUP OF WORCESTER COUNTY EXTENSION SERVICE
AUBURN, MASSACHUSETTS

CRANBERRY SWIRL COFFEE CAKE

MAKES 8 TO 10 SERVINGS

Kids and adults both love this—be prepared for lots of requests for the recipe! Serve it with coffee, of course, but also as a snack or dessert. One family we know has happily settled on this as the centerpiece of their traditional Christmas morning breakfast. If you don't have a big sweet tooth, try using just half of the glaze recipe.

CAKE

½ cup (1 stick) butter or margarine

1 cup white sugar

2 eggs

1 cup sour cream

½ teaspoon almond extract

2 cups all-purpose white flour

1 teaspoon baking powder

1 teaspoon baking soda

½ teaspoon salt

1 cup whole-berry cranberry sauce

½ cup chopped nuts

GLAZE

¾ cup confectioners' sugar

2 tablespoons warm water

½ teaspoon almond extract

Preheat the oven to 350°F. Grease a 9-inch tube pan.

Cream together the butter and sugar. Add the eggs while beating on medium speed of a mixer. Add the sour cream and ½ teaspoon almond extract and beat until smooth. Add the flour, baking powder, soda, and salt and mix just until combined. Pour half the batter into the prepared pan. Evenly distribute half the cranberry sauce by the spoonful around the pan. Swirl the sauce into the batter with the tip of a knife. Pour in the remaining batter. Distribute the remaining cranberry sauce by the spoonful around the pan. Sprinkle with the nuts. Swirl in the sauce and nuts with the tip of a knife.

Bake for about 45 minutes or until a tester inserted in the cake comes out clean. Cool in the pan on a wire rack for about 10 minutes, then invert onto the rack. Mix together the glaze ingredients and pour over the still-warm cake. Let cool completely.

Adapted from a recipe submitted by Carol A. Norman
UNITARIAN CHURCH OF BARNSTABLE
BARNSTABLE, MASSACHUSETTS

Hawaiian Wedding Cake

Makes 12 to 15 servings

We're delighted that this pineapple cake made its way to New England. It's quick, easy, and absolutely delicious—great for a party. The cake itself is so moist and full of flavor that it would be almost as good without the frosting.

CAKE

2 cups all-purpose white flour

1½ cups white sugar

1 cup unsweetened coconut

2 teaspoons baking soda

1 can (20 ounces) crushed pineapple, with juice (do not drain)

2 eggs, beaten

1 cup chopped nuts

FROSTING

½ cup (1 stick) butter or margarine, at room temperature

1 package (8 ounces) cream cheese, at room temperature

1½ cups confectioners' sugar

2 teaspoons vanilla extract

Preheat the oven to 350°F. Grease a 9-inch by 13-inch baking pan.

To make the cake, sift the flour and soda into a large mixing bowl. Add the remaining ingredients and mix by hand. Pour into the baking pan.

Bake for 45 minutes or until a tester inserted near the center comes out clean. Cool completely.

To make the frosting, combine all the ingredients and beat until smooth. Smooth over the completely cooled cake.

Sally Foley
Daughters of St. Bernard, St. Bernard's Church
Rockland, Maine

POOR MAN'S CAKE

MAKES 12 TO 15 SERVINGS

An old-fashioned dessert that was especially popular in the 1930s and is sometimes known as Depression Cake. Notice how low in fat this recipe is! Try it with a cream cheese frosting.

2 cups brown sugar

2 cups hot water

1 teaspoon salt

2 tablespoons solid vegetable shortening

1 package (15 ounces) raisins

1 teaspoon ground cinnamon

1 teaspoon ground cloves

3 cups all-purpose white flour

1 teaspoon baking soda dissolved in 2 teaspoons hot water

Preheat the oven to 350°F. Grease a 9-inch by 13-inch baking pan.

In a large saucepan, combine the brown sugar, water, salt, shortening, raisins, and spices. Bring to a boil, then remove from the heat and let cool to room temperature. Sift together the flour and soda, add to the batter, and mix well. Pour into the pan.

Bake for about 30 minutes or until a tester inserted near the center comes out clean. Cool in the pan.

Ruth Gagen
BRENTWOOD HISTORICAL SOCIETY
BRENTWOOD, NEW HAMPSHIRE

Chocolate Chip Cupcakes
Makes 15 to 18 cupcakes

You can call these muffins, or you can call them cupcakes. Whatever you call them, serve them warm from the oven, while the tops are still crisp and the chocolate is meltingly delicious. Then just watch the kids go for 'em!

2 cups all-purpose white flour

⅓ cup white sugar

⅓ cup brown sugar

1 tablespoon baking powder

1 egg, beaten

½ cup milk

⅓ cup margarine or butter, melted

½ cup sour cream or plain yogurt

1 cup semisweet chocolate chips

½ cup chopped nuts (optional)

Preheat the oven to 400°F. Grease 15 to 18 muffin cups or line with paper liners.

In a large mixing bowl, sift together the flour, sugars, and baking powder. In a small bowl, beat together the egg, milk, margarine, and sour cream. Stir into the dry ingredients and mix only until the dry ingredients are moistened. Fold in the chocolate chips and nuts, if using. Spoon into the muffin cups.

Bake for 15 to 20 minutes. These are best served warm.

Cynthia A. Miga
All Saints Church in Pontiac
Warwick, Rhode Island

⁂

Come, butter, come
Come, butter, come;
Peter stands at the gate
Waiting for a butter cake,
Come, butter, come.
—Old English nursery rhyme

⁂

Root Beer Cake

MAKES 6 TO 8 SERVINGS

Moist and light, the way good cake should be, and perfect for a child's birthday party. If the whipped cream frosting doesn't appeal, try making your favorite cream cheese frosting, substituting root beer extract for the vanilla.

CAKE

2 cups white sugar

¾ cup solid vegetable shortening

3 cups cake flour

2 teaspoons baking powder

1 teaspoon salt

1 cup root beer

1 teaspoon root beer extract

5 egg whites

FROSTING

1 cup heavy cream

¾ cup confectioners' sugar

1 teaspoon root beer extract

Preheat the oven to 350°F. Grease and flour two 9-inch round cake pans.

In a large mixing bowl, cream together the sugar and shortening until light. Sift together the dry ingredients and add to the creamed mixture, along with the root beer and extract. Beat well. In a separate bowl, beat the egg whites until stiff but not dry. Fold into the cake batter. Pour into the cake pans.

Bake for about 35 minutes or until a tester inserted near the center comes out clean. Cool in the pans for 10 minutes before turning out onto wire racks to cool. When the cake is completely cool, frost.

To make the frosting, beat the cream with the sugar and extract until stiff. Spread between the layers and on top of the cooled cake.

Adapted from a recipe submitted by Libby Yanizyn
WALPOLE HISTORICAL SOCIETY
WALPOLE, NEW HAMPSHIRE

CHOCOLATE CHEESECAKE
MAKES 12 SERVINGS

This recipe is stupendous! The light chocolate cheesecake with the darker chocolate bits, dark crust, and white topping is truly eye-catching, and the flavor is out of this world. Too rich for everyday, but wonderful for a special occasion.

CRUST

½ cup (1 stick) butter

2 cups ground chocolate wafer cookies

FILLING

4 packages (8 ounces each) cream cheese, at room temperature

1 cup white sugar

1 tablespoon rum

1 teaspoon vanilla extract

3½ ounces semisweet or bittersweet chocolate, melted

Pinch salt

4 large eggs

¼ cup mini semisweet chocolate chips

TOPPING

2 cups sour cream

¼ cup white sugar

1 teaspoon almond extract

Preheat the oven to 350°F.

To make the crust, melt the butter and mix with the cookie crumbs in a food processor. Press onto the bottom and up the sides of a 10-inch springform pan.

To make the filling, combine the cream cheese and sugar and beat for 2 minutes or until soft. Add the rum, vanilla, melted chocolate, and salt and blend thoroughly. Add the eggs, one at a time, beating on the lowest speed until just incorporated. (Do not overbeat once the eggs have been added.) Stir in the chocolate bits. Pour into the crust.

Bake for 40 to 50 minutes. Remove from the oven and let stand for 10 minutes while you prepare the topping.

Mix the topping ingredients together and spread over the cake. Return the cake to the oven to bake for 10 minutes. Put in the refrigerator immediately to prevent cracking. Serve chilled.

Adapted from a recipe submitted by Dorothy Johnson
CHURCH OF THE EPIPHANY
SOUTHBURY, CONNECTICUT

MOLASSES SPONGE CAKE
MAKES 15 SERVINGS

This is a great dessert—even better served warm with whipped cream.

1 egg

½ cup white sugar

½ cup solid vegetable shortening

1 cup molasses

2½ cups all-purpose white flour

2 teaspoons baking soda

Pinch salt

½ to 1 teaspoon ground allspice

1 cup boiling water

Whipped cream (optional)

Preheat the oven to 325°F. Grease a 9-inch by 13-inch pan.

In a large mixing bowl, combine the egg, sugar, shortening, and molasses. Beat until thoroughly combined. Sift together the flour, soda, salt, and allspice. Add to the molasses mixture and beat until well combined. While still beating, gradually add the boiling water. Beat until well combined. Pour into the baking pan.

Bake for 30 to 35 minutes. Serve warm with whipped cream.

Gladys Anderson
WILLINGTON BAPTIST CHURCH
WILLINGTON, CONNECTICUT

Oreo Ice Cream Cake

Makes 12 servings

A great summer dessert that's especially popular with the younger set.

CAKE

16 ounces Oreo cookies, crushed

½ cup (1 stick) butter or margarine, melted

½ gallon mint chocolate chip ice cream, softened

FUDGE TOPPING

½ cup (1 stick) butter or margarine

2 ounces unsweetened baking chocolate

1 cup white sugar

1 can (12 ounces) evaporated milk (not skim)

1 container (8 ounces) Cool Whip

To make the cake, stir the cookies into the melted butter. Place in a 9-inch by 13-inch baking dish. Freeze.

Spread the ice cream on top of the frozen crushed cookies and return to the freezer to freeze solid.

To make the topping, combine the ½ cup butter, chocolate, sugar, and evaporated milk in a heavy saucepan. Cook for 10 minutes, stirring constantly, until thick. Cool. Spread over the ice cream and freeze solid. Top with Cool Whip, wrap well to prevent freezer burn, and return to the freezer until you are ready to serve.

Barbara Birmingham
CHURCH OF THE EPIPHANY
SOUTHBURY, CONNECTICUT

ORANGE CREAM CAKE
MAKES 8 SERVINGS

A refreshing summer dessert that starts with either a homemade or store-bought cake, which is then filled with a delicious orange custard sauce.

2 eggs, slightly beaten

1 cup white sugar

Juice and grated zest of 1 orange

Juice and grated zest of 1 lemon

½ pint heavy cream

1 two-layer (8-inch or 9-inch) sponge cake

In the top of a double boiler, mix the eggs, sugar, and juice and zest of the orange and lemon. Cook over boiling water for about 10 minutes, or until the custard sauce is thickened, stirring occasionally. Cool thoroughly.

Whip the cream. Fold the cooled custard sauce into the cream. Cut the sponge cake into four layers. Fill and frost with the custard filling. Chill for several hours or overnight.

Dot Colbeth
CHEBEAGUE PARENTS ASSOCIATION
CHEBEAGUE ISLAND, MAINE

Eggs are very much like small boys.
If you overheat them or overbeat them,
they will turn on you,
and no amount of future love will right the wrong.
—Anonymous

SNOWBALL CAKE

MAKES 6 TO 8 SERVINGS

Delicious, fast, and fun to make. A light, refreshing dessert for a summer gathering.

2 envelopes (3 ounces each) unflavored gelatin

1 cup boiling water

1 cup white sugar

1 can (20 ounces) crushed pineapple, drained

Juice of 1 lemon

3 envelopes (1.3 ounces each) whipped topping mix

1 angel food cake (10 ounces), torn into bite-size pieces

1 can (3½ ounces) coconut

Sprinkle the gelatin over the boiling water. Stir until dissolved. Add the sugar, pineapple, and lemon juice. Stir well and refrigerate until slightly thickened.

Prepare two envelopes of the topping mix according to the package directions. Stir into the gelatin mixture.

Place a layer of cake pieces in a 2½-quart mold or bowl. Then add a layer of the gelatin mixture. Repeat the layers until all the cake and gelatin mixture are used. Refrigerate for at least 1 hour.

Prepare the remaining envelope of whipped topping according to the package directions. Unmold the cake onto a serving plate. Frost with the whipped topping. Sprinkle with the coconut.

Ruth Southwick
WILLINGTON BAPTIST CHURCH
WILLINGTON, CONNECTICUT

PIES

Yankees may not be eating much pie for breakfast these days, but we sure are enjoying it for dessert, especially at church suppers. It's the one item you can usually count on eating. Sometimes the choice is just pumpkin or apple, but often a table is covered with every kind of pie imaginable.

This chapter begins with some luscious no-bake pies and ends with a surprise—a mock apple pie made not with crackers, but with zucchini. You have to taste it to believe it! In between, there are recipes for apple pie, lemon meringue pie, pumpkin pie, pecan pie, maple-walnut pie—all the classics—plus a luxurious peanut butter pie, a scrumptious pineapple meringue pie, and other nontraditional but oh-so-good pies.

BLACKBERRY CREAM CHEESE PIE
MAKES 6 TO 8 SERVINGS

A beautiful summer pie that's assembled in no time if you make the syrup a day ahead.

5 cups blackberries

½ cup water

3 tablespoons cornstarch

⅔ cup white sugar

1 tablespoon lemon juice

2 packages (3 ounces each) cream cheese, at room temperature

1 tablespoon milk

1 teaspoon grated lemon zest

1 baked 8-inch or 9-inch pie shell

Whipped cream and/or additional berries, to garnish (optional)

In a medium-size saucepan, combine 3 cups of the berries with the water. Bring to a boil. Let cool, then strain to remove the seeds. Return the syrup to the saucepan. Stir in the cornstarch, sugar, and lemon juice. Bring to a boil, stirring, and boil for 2 minutes. Cool.

When the syrup is cool, blend the cream cheese, milk, and lemon zest until smooth. Spread evenly in the baked pie shell. Top with the remaining 2 cups uncooked berries. Pour the cooled, thickened syrup evenly over the berries. Refrigerate for 1 hour or more.

Just before serving, decorate with whipped cream and/or additional fresh berries.

Virginia Cabana
EAST DOVER BAPTIST CHURCH
EAST DOVER, VERMONT

CHERRY CREAM PIE
MAKES 6 TO 8 SERVINGS

Easy to make and wonderfully versatile. Try it with any type of fruit pie filling or with fresh or frozen fruit—strawberries or raspberries, for instance—over the cream cheese base.

1 package (8 ounces) cream cheese, at room temperature

½ cup confectioners' sugar, sifted

½ teaspoon almond extract

½ pint whipping cream

1 baked 8-inch or 9-inch graham cracker pie shell

1 can (16 ounces) cherry pie filling

Blend the cream cheese, sugar, and almond extract until smooth. Whip the cream until stiff. Fold the whipped cream into the cream cheese mixture. Pour into the baked pie shell. Top with the pie filling. Chill for at least 1 hour before serving.

Wilma Meyer
EAST DOVER BAPTIST CHURCH
EAST DOVER, VERMONT

FOR WHOM THE BELL TOLLS

EIGHT-YEAR-OLD Michael was getting ready for his debut as altar boy at church, and he was quite nervous. One of his duties during the Mass was to ring the bells when the priest raised the Eucharist. Sunday arrived, and his big moment came. Michael watched as the priest raised the chalice. At that very moment, Michael realized that he was on one side of the altar and the bells were on the other. The priest, still holding the chalice in the air, whispered to him, "The bells!" Michael panicked, remembering that he wasn't supposed to cross the altar during Mass. Then he did the only thing he could do: he took a deep breath and in his loudest voice yelled, "Ding-a-ling-a-ling, ding-a-ling-a-ling!"

Peach-Yogurt Pie

Makes 8 servings

A delicious summer treat, this tastes like a lighter version of cheesecake. If you prefer it lighter still, use low-fat cream cheese and nonfat yogurt.

1 package (3 ounces) peach-flavored gelatin

¼ cup water

2 egg yolks, slightly beaten

2 packages (3 ounces each) cream cheese, at room temperature

2 cartons (8 ounces each) peach yogurt

2 tablespoons sugar

1 medium-size peach, peeled

1 tablespoon lemon juice

1 baked 9-inch graham cracker pie shell

Unsweetened whipped cream (optional)

Fresh mint sprigs, to garnish (optional)

In a small saucepan, combine the gelatin and water and stir until the gelatin is moistened. Add the egg yolks. Cook over medium heat, stirring constantly, until the gelatin is dissolved and the mixture is slightly thickened. Beat in the cream cheese and yogurt until smooth. Slightly chill the mixture, stirring occasionally.

When the gelatin mixture is partially set—so it's the consistency of unbeaten egg whites—fold the sugar into the mixture.

If desired, reserve a few slices of the peach for a garnish. Chop the remainder of the peach, toss with the lemon juice to prevent discoloration, and fold into the gelatin mixture. Pour the mixture into the baked pie shell. Chill for several hours or overnight, until set. If desired, garnish the pie with peach slices, whipped cream, and sprigs of fresh mint.

Adapted from a recipe submitted by Alice Veraguth
East Dover Baptist Church
East Dover, Vermont

RHUBARB PIE

MAKES 12 SERVINGS

A good recipe to try on those who think they don't like rhubarb; the sweet strawberry-rhubarb flavor and the soft pudding make an enticing combination. It's a good thing this recipe makes two pies—they won't last long!

3 cups chopped fresh or frozen rhubarb

¾ cup white sugar

1 package (3 ounces) strawberry gelatin

1 package (3 ounces) instant vanilla pudding

1½ cups milk

1 container (8 ounces) Cool Whip

2 baked 8-inch graham cracker pie shells

In a medium-size saucepan, combine the rhubarb with the sugar. Let stand for 10 minutes to make its own juice. Cook over low heat for 10 minutes, until the rhubarb is tender. Stir in the strawberry gelatin until completely dissolved. Set in the refrigerator to cool for about 30 minutes.

When the rhubarb mixture has cooled and jelled slightly, mix together the vanilla pudding and the milk. Fold in the Cool Whip. Swirl in the rhubarb sauce; do not beat. Pour into the graham cracker shells. Refrigerate for at least 3 hours before serving.

Gladys Anderson
WILLINGTON BAPTIST CHURCH
WILLINGTON, CONNECTICUT

Fudge Pie
Makes 8 servings

Chocolate lovers will find this rich chocolate pie irresistible. It's guaranteed to disappear from the dessert table—fast! For a smashing presentation, top with sliced strawberries and glaze with a little melted jelly.

6 tablespoons (¾ stick) butter or margarine

1 cup plus 2 tablespoons white sugar

2 ounces unsweetened chocolate, melted

1 teaspoon vanilla extract

¾ cup pasteurized egg substitute

1 baked 9-inch pie shell

In a large mixing bowl, cream together the butter and sugar. Add the melted chocolate and vanilla and beat well. Add the egg substitute, ¼ cup at a time, and beat for a full 5 minutes after each addition. Pour into the baked pie shell and refrigerate for 1 day before serving.

Adapted from a recipe submitted by Marian McKelvy
Harwinton Library Friends
Harwinton, Connecticut

Peanut Butter Pie
Makes 6 to 8 servings

Very rich and, our tester and her guests report, "unbelievably awesome!"

4 ounces cream cheese, at room temperature

1 cup confectioners' sugar

⅓ cup crunchy peanut butter

⅓ cup milk

1 container (8 ounces) Cool Whip

1 baked 9-inch graham cracker pie shell

In a large mixing bowl, cream together the cream cheese and sugar. Add the peanut butter and milk and beat well. Fold in the Cool Whip. Pour into the baked pie shell. Freeze until firm. Remove from the freezer a few minutes before serving.

Virginia (Gee Gee) Dyer
Chebeague Parents Association
Chebeague Island, Maine

AUNT FLORENCE'S APPLE PIE
MAKES 6 TO 8 SERVINGS

A classic apple pie, with just the right amount of sweetness. Our testers liked a mixture of apple varieties in this one, with a couple of McIntosh apples thrown in for flavor.

Unbaked pastry for double-crust
   9-inch pie

¼ cup brown sugar

¾ cup white sugar

2 tablespoons all-purpose white flour

¼ teaspoon ground cinnamon

¼ teaspoon ground nutmeg

⅛ teaspoon salt

6 cups peeled, cored, and sliced apples

¼ cup cream or milk

1 tablespoon milk

1 tablespoon margarine

1 tablespoon white sugar

Preheat the oven to 400°F. Prepare the pastry and fit the bottom crust into a 9-inch pie pan.

In a small bowl, combine the brown sugar, ¾ cup white sugar, flour, spices, and salt. Spread one-third of the apples in the pie pan; sprinkle with one-third of the sugar mixture. Repeat the layers twice more. Pour the cream into the center of the apples. Cover with the top crust. Brush the crust with milk, dot with the margarine, and sprinkle with the 1 tablespoon sugar.

Bake for 1 hour. Cool slightly before serving warm, or serve completely cooled.

Cheryl R. Buxbaum
CHEBEAGUE PARENTS ASSOCIATION
CHEBEAGUE ISLAND, MAINE

SUGARLESS APPLE PIE
MAKES 6 TO 8 SERVINGS

What a great alternative to the traditional apple pie! Be sure to use firm baking apples. Golden Delicious, Granny Smith, Jonathan, Jonagold, Rome, and Northern Spy are all good choices.

Unbaked pastry for double-crust 10-inch pie

6 to 8 large apples, peeled, cored, and sliced

2 tablespoons cornstarch

½ cup apple juice or water

8 ounces frozen unsweetened apple juice concentrate, thawed

½ teaspoon ground cinnamon

Preheat the oven to 425°F. Fit the bottom crust into a 10-inch pie pan. Arrange the apples in the pie shell.

Mix the cornstarch with the apple juice in the top of a double boiler. Add the apple juice concentrate and cinnamon and cook until thickened, stirring constantly. Remove from the heat and pour over the apples. Cover the pie with the top crust. Cover the edges of the pie with aluminum foil to prevent browning. Place the pie on a baking sheet to catch any spills.

Bake for 25 minutes. Reduce the heat to 350°F and bake for another 30 minutes. During the last 15 minutes of baking, remove the foil. Cool slightly before serving warm, or allow to cool completely.

Shirley Kondratowski
WILLINGTON BAPTIST CHURCH
WILLINGTON, CONNECTICUT

BAVARIAN APPLE TART
MAKES 6 TO 8 SERVINGS

This one's a keeper! Rich and delicious, it looks and tastes like a lot more work than it really is.

PASTRY

¼ cup (½ stick) butter or margarine, at room temperature

⅓ cup white sugar

¼ teaspoon vanilla extract

1 cup all-purpose white flour

FILLING

1 package (8 ounces) cream cheese, at room temperature

¼ cup white sugar

1 egg, slightly beaten

½ teaspoon vanilla extract

TOPPING

⅓ cup white sugar

½ teaspoon ground cinnamon

4 cups peeled, cored, and sliced apples

¼ cup slivered almonds

Preheat the oven to 450°F. Grease a 9-inch springform pan.

To make the pastry, cream the butter with the ⅓ cup sugar and ¼ teaspoon vanilla. Add the flour. Press onto the bottom and up the sides of the pan.

To prepare the filling, beat the cream cheese and ¼ cup sugar until smooth. Mix in the egg and ½ teaspoon vanilla and beat until smooth. Pour into the pastry.

To prepare the topping, combine the ⅓ cup sugar and cinnamon. Toss with the apples. Arrange on top of the cream cheese mixture. Sprinkle the almonds on top.

Bake for 10 minutes. Reduce the heat to 400°F and continue baking for 25 minutes more. Cool completely before removing the rim from the pan.

Hannelore Classen
ST. ANDREW LUTHERAN CHURCH
ELLSWORTH, MAINE

CRANBERRY SURPRISE PIE

MAKES 6 TO 8 SERVINGS

A quick, company's-coming pie that makes its own crust and tastes like a macaroon cookie with cranberries. Serve it during the holidays, when cranberries are most available, with a dollop of whipped cream.

2 cups raw cranberries (fresh or frozen)

½ cup sliced almonds

1½ cups white sugar

2 eggs

¾ cup (1½ sticks) butter, melted

1 teaspoon almond extract

1 cup all-purpose white flour

Whipped cream

Preheat the oven to 325°F. Grease a 10-inch pie plate.

Wash the cranberries, leaving some water on them. Combine the cranberries with the almonds in the pie plate. Sprinkle with ½ cup of the sugar.

In a mixing bowl, cream the remaining 1 cup sugar with the eggs and butter. Stir in the almond extract. Add the flour and mix well. The batter will be thin. Pour over the cranberries.

Bake for 35 to 45 minutes or until a tester inserted near the center of the crust comes out clean. Let cool slightly before serving warm, or serve completely cooled, with a dollop of whipped cream on each slice.

Mary Lou Murphy
NEW ENGLAND HISTORIC GENEALOGICAL SOCIETY
BOSTON, MASSACHUSETTS

LEMON MERINGUE PIE

MAKES 6 TO 8 SERVINGS

A very sweet pie that's an old favorite. Make this on a dry winter day; meringue doesn't fare well in hot, humid weather.

LEMON FILLING

1½ cups white sugar

1½ cups water

½ teaspoon salt

½ cup cornstarch mixed with ⅓ cup water

4 egg yolks, slightly beaten

½ cup lemon juice

3 tablespoons butter

1 teaspoon grated lemon zest

MERINGUE

4 egg whites

½ teaspoon cream of tartar

¼ teaspoon salt

½ cup white sugar

1 baked 9-inch pie shell

To make the filling, combine the 1½ cups sugar, 1½ cups water, and ½ teaspoon salt in a heavy saucepan or the top of a double boiler. Bring to a boil. Mix the cornstarch with the ⅓ cup water and add to the boiling mixture slowly, stirring constantly. Cook until thickened and clear. Remove from the heat. Stir in the egg yolks and lemon juice. Return the mixture to the heat and stir until it begins to bubble. Remove from the heat and stir in the butter and lemon zest. Cover and cool until lukewarm.

To make the meringue, combine the egg whites, cream of tartar, and ¼ teaspoon salt and beat until frothy. Gradually add the ½ cup sugar, beating until glossy peaks form when you lift the beater.

Preheat the oven to 325°F. Pour the filling into the pie shell. Pile on the meringue, spreading to touch the edge of the crust. Bake for 15 minutes, or until lightly browned. Cool on a rack for 1 hour. Chill for at least 4 hours before serving. This is best served the day it is made.

If you prefer not to make a meringue with raw egg whites, substitute whipped cream for the egg white topping. Pipe sweetened whipped cream onto the pie just before serving.

Adapted from a recipe submitted by Susan W. Gillespie
NEW ENGLAND HISTORIC GENEALOGICAL SOCIETY
BOSTON, MASSACHUSETTS

Pineapple Meringue Pie

MAKES 6 TO 8 SERVINGS

A wonderful dessert that makes a great change from the familiar lemon meringue pie.

FILLING

2 tablespoons cornstarch

½ teaspoon salt

½ cup white sugar

2 egg yolks, beaten

2 cans (8 ounces each) crushed pineapple, drained

MERINGUE

2 egg whites

½ teaspoon cream of tartar

¼ teaspoon salt

¼ cup white sugar

1 baked 9-inch pie shell

In a heavy saucepan or the top of a double boiler, combine the cornstarch, ½ teaspoon salt, and ½ cup sugar. Stir in the egg yolks over low heat and continue cooking until the mixture is thick and clear. In a separate saucepan, heat the pineapple to simmering. Add to the cornstarch mixture and stir thoroughly. Set aside.

To make the meringue, combine the egg whites, cream of tartar, and ¼ teaspoon salt and beat until frothy. Gradually add the sugar, beating until glossy peaks form when you lift the beater.

Preheat the oven to 325°F. Pour the filling into the pie shell. Pile on the meringue, spreading to touch the edge of the crust. Bake for 15 minutes, or until lightly browned. Cool on a rack for 1 hour. Then chill for at least 4 hours before serving. This is best served the day it is made.

If you prefer not to make a meringue with raw egg whites, substitute whipped cream for the egg white topping. Pour the filling into the pie shell and chill for at least 1 hour before serving. Pipe sweetened whipped cream onto the pie just before serving.

Adapted from a recipe submitted by Waneta Cleaves
CHEBEAGUE PARENTS ASSOCIATION
CHEBEAGUE ISLAND, MAINE

RASPBERRY-RHUBARB PIE
MAKES 8 SERVINGS

An excellent pie that's equally good made with blueberries instead of raspberries. Serve with whipped cream.

3 cups chopped fresh rhubarb

1¼ cups white sugar

3 tablespoons all-purpose white flour

Pinch salt

2 cups fresh or frozen raspberries

Unbaked pastry for double-crust 9-inch pie

1 tablespoon butter

In a bowl, combine the rhubarb with 1 cup of the sugar, the flour, and salt. Allow to stand for about 10 minutes. In a separate bowl, combine the berries with the remaining ¼ cup sugar.

Preheat the oven to 450°F. Line a 9-inch pie pan with pastry for the bottom crust. Pour the rhubarb into the shell. Drain the raspberries and add to the rhubarb. Dot with the butter. Cover with the top crust.

Bake for 15 minutes. Then reduce the heat to 325°F and bake for 30 more minutes, or until the pie is golden brown.

Mary Gomez
CHEBEAGUE PARENTS ASSOCIATION
CHEBEAGUE ISLAND, MAINE

Promises and Pie-Crust are made to be broken.
—Jonathan Swift, *Polite Conversation*

Pumpkin Pie

Makes 8 Servings

Wonderfully spicy and full of flavor. Serve with ice cream, a wedge of Cheddar, or fresh whipped cream.

1 cup brown sugar, firmly packed

¾ teaspoon salt

¾ teaspoon ground nutmeg

½ teaspoon ground cinnamon

½ teaspoon ground cloves

¼ teaspoon ground ginger

1½ cups cooked or canned pumpkin purée

1 cup milk, scalded

3 eggs

1 unbaked 10-inch pie shell

Preheat the oven to 400°F.

In a large mixing bowl, combine the sugar, salt, and spices. Stir in the pumpkin. Gradually add the milk.

Separate one of the eggs. Beat together the two whole eggs and 1 egg yolk. Add to the pumpkin. In a separate bowl, beat the egg white until stiff. Fold into the pumpkin mixture.

Pour into the pie shell. Bake for 35 to 45 minutes, or until set. Serve warm or cooled.

Adapted from a recipe submitted by Gladys Anderson
Willington Baptist Church
Willington, Connecticut

≈≈≈

We have pumpkin at morning
And pumpkin at noon.
If it were not for pumpkin
We would be undoon.

—Anonymous

≈≈≈

Pecan Pie
Makes 8 servings

A fabulous version of a classic American dessert. Delicious!

1 cup pecans

1 unbaked 9-inch pie shell

3 eggs

½ cup white sugar

1 cup light or dark corn syrup

⅛ teaspoon salt

1 teaspoon vanilla extract

¼ cup (½ stick) butter, melted

Preheat the oven to 350°F. Line a 9-inch pie plate with the pie shell. Arrange the pecans on the bottom of the unbaked pie shell.

In a medium-size mixing bowl, beat the eggs. Add the sugar, corn syrup, salt, vanilla, and butter. Pour over the pecans.

Bake for 50 to 60 minutes. The nuts will rise to the top and form a crusted layer. Serve warm or cooled.

Edith Morris
Woman's Fellowship of First Church
Sterling, Massachusetts

Madison Avenue Baptism

*L*ittle Debbie hadn't yet been baptized, so she wasn't permitted to partake of the Holy Communion at her church. Some of the other parents allowed their children to snatch a piece of bread as it was passed, but Debbie's mother stood firm, and that had led to several battles between mother and daughter. One summer Sunday, Debbie again asked her mother if she could participate in the Communion. By the exasperated expression on her mother's face, Debbie knew it was the wrong question to ask, and quickly added, "Oh, I know—I haven't been advertised yet."

Chess Pie

Makes 6 to 8 servings

Similar to a traditional pecan pie, but much lighter and not as sweet. Under the pecans, the consistency is almost like that of a custard pie.

¼ cup (½ stick) butter, at room temperature

½ cup white sugar

1 cup brown sugar

⅛ teaspoon salt

3 eggs

1 teaspoon vanilla extract

2 tablespoons all-purpose unbleached flour

½ cup cream

1 cup chopped pecans

1 unbaked 9-inch pie shell

Preheat the oven to 375°F.

In a mixing bowl, cream the butter with the sugars and salt. Beat in the eggs, one at a time. Stir in the remaining ingredients. Pour into the pie shell.

Bake for 35 to 40 minutes or until a tester inserted near the center of the pie comes out clean. Serve warm or cooled completely.

Virginia B. Augerson
New England Historic Genealogical Society
Boston, Massachusetts

Maple-Walnut Pie

Makes 6 to 8 servings

Maple and walnut are heavenly together, especially with whipped cream!

3 eggs

¾ cup brown sugar

2 tablespoons all-purpose unbleached flour

1¼ cups pure maple syrup

¼ cup (½ stick) butter or margarine, melted

1 cup chopped walnuts

1 unbaked 9-inch pie shell

Preheat the oven to 375°F.

In a mixing bowl, beat together the eggs, brown sugar, flour, maple syrup, and butter. Stir in the nuts. Pour into the pie shell.

Bake for 40 to 45 minutes or until a tester inserted near the center of the pie comes out clean. Serve warm or completely cooled.

Marge Long
WOMAN'S FELLOWSHIP OF FIRST CHURCH
STERLING, MASSACHUSETTS

Toll House Pie

An easy recipe that everyone loves. It tastes like a giant Toll House cookie. Go all the way and serve it warm with a scoop of ice cream.

2 eggs

½ cup all-purpose unbleached flour

½ cup white sugar

½ cup brown sugar, firmly packed

1 cup (2 sticks) butter, melted and cooled

1 cup semisweet chocolate chips

1 cup chopped walnuts

1 unbaked 9-inch pie shell

Preheat the oven to 325°F.

In a mixing bowl, beat the eggs until foamy. Add the flour and sugars and beat until blended. Blend in the butter. Stir in the chips and nuts. Pour into the pie shell.

Bake for 1 hour. Serve warm or cooled completely.

Elizabeth Wheeler
EAST DOVER BAPTIST CHURCH
EAST DOVER, VERMONT

SURPRISE "APPLE" PIE

MAKES 6 TO 8 SERVINGS

Surprise! Now you know what to do with that overwhelming crop of zucchini: just smuggle it in pie crusts to unsuspecting friends.

Unbaked pastry for double-crust
  9-inch pie

4 to 5 cups peeled and sliced zucchini

2 tablespoons lemon juice

Dash salt

1 cup white sugar

3 tablespoons all-purpose white flour

1½ teaspoons ground cinnamon

1½ teaspoons cream of tartar

Preheat the oven to 400°F. Line a 9-inch pie plate with the bottom crust.

Blanch or steam the zucchini for 5 to 10 minutes, until tender. Drain well. Pour the lemon juice and sprinkle the salt over the zucchini.

In a separate bowl, combine the sugar, flour, cinnamon, and cream of tartar. Mix with the zucchini. It will be watery. Pour into the pie shell. Cover with the top crust.

Bake for 40 minutes. Let cool. The filling will thicken as it cools.

Doreen Connor
WILLINGTON BAPTIST CHURCH
WILLINGTON, CONNECTICUT

FRUIT DESSERTS AND PUDDINGS

EVERY ONE of these desserts has an affinity for whipped cream! Collected in this chapter are spoon desserts—fruit salads, puddings, cobblers. Many—like the wonderful old-fashioned Ambrosia or the flavorful Peach Cobbler—are modern variations on old-time delights, sure to bring back memories. Others, like the Brownie Pudding Cake or Layered Strawberry Dessert, are particularly popular with the younger set.

One of the best things about these recipes is that virtually all of them can be prepared quickly, with very little effort (though some then need to sit for a while before serving). But they are not intended to be *eaten* quickly! These are delicious, comforting, homey desserts, meant to be savored. You can't nibble on a lemon soufflé while you are on the run, as you might a cookie. These are desserts to linger over at the table, in the company of friends and family.

EASY PINEAPPLE DESSERT
MAKES 8 SERVINGS

Bring out the wine goblets or the fancy glass sherbet dishes to serve this in; no one will guess how easy this dessert was to make.

2 packages (3 ounces each) instant vanilla pudding

2 cups milk

1 can (20 ounces) crushed pineapple, with juice (do not drain)

Cool Whip

Combine the pudding and milk according to the package directions. Fold in the pineapple. Spoon into dessert bowls. Top with Cool Whip. Refrigerate overnight.

Cora LaRochelle
AUBURN GROUP OF WORCESTER COUNTY EXTENSION SERVICE
AUBURN, MASSACHUSETTS

AMBROSIA
MAKES 8 TO 12 SERVINGS

An old-fashioned dessert that hasn't lost an ounce of appeal over the years, Ambrosia is extremely easy to prepare and makes a light, refreshing dessert.

2 cups drained and chopped oranges

2½ cups (half of a 10-ounce bag) miniature marshmallows

1 cup chopped pecans

2 cups drained crushed pineapple

1 cup coconut

1 carton (16 ounces) sour cream

Mix together all the ingredients. Chill in the refrigerator.

Elisabeth S. Pratt
UNITARIAN UNIVERSALIST PARISH OF MONSON
MONSON, MASSACHUSETTS

Layered Strawberry Dessert

Makes 8 servings

Kids adore this. The contributor says this delicious combination of straw-
berries and pineapple serves eight, but our tester witnessed four kids, all of
them under the age of ten, devouring an entire recipe.

2 packages (3 ounces each)
   strawberry-flavored gelatin

1 cup boiling water

1 package (16 ounces) frozen sliced
   strawberries, thawed and drained

½ cup chopped walnuts

2 cans (8 ounces each) crushed
   pineapple, drained

1 carton (16 ounces) sour cream

In a medium-size mixing bowl, dissolve the gelatin in the boiling water.
Let cool until slightly thickened.

Divide the gelatin between two
bowls. Set one in the refrigerator.
Add the strawberries, walnuts, and
pineapple to the other bowl, then
pour into a 2-quart mold or square
baking dish. Stir well. Place in the
freezer for 30 to 40 minutes or until
set. Remove from the freezer and smooth the sour cream over the gelatin.
Pour the remaining refrigerated bowl of gelatin over the sour cream and
place the mold in the refrigerator until the gelatin is completely set.

Madeleine Fisher
Unitarian Universalist Parish of Monson
Monson, Massachusetts

Is There Going to Be Enough?

*I*T TAKES A LOT of experience to trust in the very idea of potlucks—that there will be enough food brought in to feed everyone. Some hosts guarantee the success of their parties by ensuring that there is enough of all the important stuff—beverages, main course, and dessert. Such a host will make one large main course and one large dessert and have extra beer, wine, and juice to cover any contingency.

The main course should be a dish that is easily frozen if there are leftovers. So don't make a big pasta salad, but consider making a tray of lasagna. Soups and stews are also good choices. If you have a big tin of cookies or brownies tucked away, you are assured that there will be dessert. And if your table is laden with desserts from your guests, you can save your efforts for your family to enjoy later in the week—or freeze them for your next potluck.

It's also a good idea to have a few cans of juice tucked away in the refrigerator. Guests often tote a six-pack of beer to these informal gatherings, forgetting that the kids need liquid refreshment, too!

Unless you travel with a crowd that is guaranteed to arrive on time, some bowls of pretzels, chips with salsa, and vegetables with dip will get the party off to an easy start.

FRUKTSOPPA
(Fruit Soup)
MAKES 10 TO 12 SERVINGS

A Swedish dessert soup that's easy to make and very good. Try serving it over vanilla ice cream, too.

1 box (8 ounces) dried apricots

1 box (6 ounces) seedless raisins

1 box (12 ounces) pitted prunes

4 to 5 apples, peeled, cored, and sliced in wedges

10 cups water

1 cup white sugar

¼ cup quick-cooking tapioca

Cream or whipped topping

In a large saucepan, combine the fruit and water. Bring to a boil and simmer for 30 minutes. Add the sugar and tapioca and simmer for another 15 minutes. Serve warm or cooled, with cream or whipped topping.

Edith Ostlund
GUSTAF ADOLPH LUTHERAN CHURCH
NEW SWEDEN, MAINE

LEMON DELIGHT
MAKES 6 SERVINGS

A delightful soufflé that makes an elegant and refreshing finish to any meal.

1 cup white sugar

¼ cup all-purpose white flour

⅛ teaspoon salt

2 tablespoons butter, melted

Juice and grated zest of 2 lemons

3 eggs, separated

1½ cups milk

Preheat the oven to 350°F. Grease a 1½-quart soufflé dish.

In a large mixing bowl, combine the sugar, flour, and salt and mix well. Add the butter, lemon juice, and lemon zest. Blend with a whisk. Add the egg yolks and milk and beat until light.

In a separate bowl, beat the egg whites until stiff. Fold into the lemon mixture. Pour into the soufflé dish. Set the soufflé dish in a large pan and place in the oven. Fill the pan with hot water. Bake for 1 hour. Serve immediately.

Carolyn Muller
ST. PETER'S EPISCOPAL CHURCH
WESTON, MASSACHUSETTS

French Cherry Dessert

Makes 4 servings

Simple to make, and very good. For a large group, triple the recipe and bake in a 9-inch by 13-inch pan.

½ cup white sugar

2 tablespoons butter, at room temperature

½ cup milk

¾ cup all-purpose white flour

1½ teaspoons baking powder

1 can (16 ounces) pitted sweet or sour cherries, drained (reserve the liquid)

1 tablespoon white sugar (if using sour cherries)

Whipped cream or confectioners' sugar (optional)

Preheat the oven to 350°F. Grease a 1-quart baking dish.

Combine the ½ cup sugar, butter, milk, flour, and baking powder in a mixing bowl and beat until smooth. Pour into the baking dish. Spoon the cherries on top.

Combine the reserved cherry liquid and 1 tablespoon sugar and boil to reduce the volume by half. Pour over the cherries.

Bake for 25 minutes or until golden brown. The cherries will sink to the bottom and the dough will rise to the top. Serve with whipped cream or a dusting of confectioners' sugar, if desired.

Adapted from a recipe submitted by Ruth Clark
St. Peter's Episcopal Church
Oxford, Connecticut

Peach Cobbler

Makes 6 to 8 servings

Easy to make, this old-fashioned dessert is always popular. It can be made with other fruits as well as peaches. We've seen some similar recipes in 19th-century cookbooks that went by the name of "bird's nest pudding" or "crow's nest pudding." The finished dish does bear a resemblance to a bird's nest, as least in the eyes of some.

½ cup (1 stick) butter or margarine

3 cups peeled and sliced fresh peaches

2 cups white sugar

Sprinkling of ground nutmeg or ground cinnamon

1 cup all-purpose white flour

2 teaspoons baking powder

¾ cup milk

Whipped cream (optional)

Preheat the oven to 400°F.

Melt the butter and pour into a 9-inch by 13-inch baking pan. Add the peaches. Sprinkle 1 cup of the sugar over the peaches. Dust with a little nutmeg or cinnamon.

In a medium-size mixing bowl, combine the remaining 1 cup sugar with the flour, baking powder, and milk. Beat until smooth. Pour over the peaches.

Bake for 45 minutes or until the top is golden. Cool for 10 minutes or longer and serve with whipped cream, if desired.

Gladys Anderson
Willington Baptist Church
Willington, Connecticut

Pots de Crème

MAKES 4 SERVINGS

Quick to prepare, elegant, and so popular you may want to double the recipe.

1 package (6 ounces) semisweet chocolate chips

2 tablespoons sugar

¼ cup pasteurized egg substitute

1 teaspoon vanilla extract

1 to 2 tablespoons fruit or nut liqueur (optional)

¾ cup milk

Strawberries, raspberries, mandarin oranges, or nuts, to garnish (optional)

Combine the chocolate chips, sugar, egg substitute, vanilla, and liqueur, if using, in a blender. Heat the milk just to the boiling point (but do not boil) and add to the blender. Blend all the ingredients until smooth, about 1 minute on high. Pour into 4 custard cups and refrigerate for at least 6 hours before serving. If desired, garnish each cup with fruit or nuts.

Susan Gagnon
HOPKINTON COOKIE EXCHANGE
HOPKINTON, NEW HAMPSHIRE

Is There Going to Be Enough? Part 2

WE KNOW ONE HOSTESS who always worries about whether there will be enough food at her parties. She and a fellow worrier have devised a system they claim works without fail. When one calls the other to worry about food quantities, the other always responds with "You have more than enough. Cut the quantities in half!"

Brownie Pudding Cake

Makes 10 to 12 Servings

Is this a pudding or a cake? As the dessert bakes, the cake rises to the top, leaving a fudgy layer of pudding below. An easy, excellent dessert that everyone loves. Serve warm, topped with whipped cream or ice cream.

3 cups all-purpose white flour

6 tablespoons unsweetened cocoa powder

2 tablespoons baking powder

2¼ cups white sugar

1½ teaspoons salt

1½ cups milk

6 tablespoons vegetable oil

1 tablespoon vanilla extract

TOPPING

2¼ cups brown sugar

¾ cup unsweetened cocoa powder

5¼ cups boiling water

Preheat the oven to 350°F. Butter a 9-inch by 13-inch baking pan.

Into a large mixing bowl, sift together the flour, 6 tablespoons cocoa, baking powder, sugar, and salt. Combine the milk, oil, and vanilla and add to the dry ingredients. Beat until smooth. Pour into the baking pan.

In a medium-size bowl, combine the brown sugar, ¾ cup cocoa, and boiling water. Mix until smooth. Gently pour over the batter. Bake for 35 minutes. Serve warm.

Adapted from a recipe submitted by Yvonne Menzone
Auburn Group of Worcester County Extension Service
Auburn, Massachusetts

Chocolate Pudding Dessert

Makes 12 servings

Easy, rich, delicious, and quickly devoured at any potluck.

6 egg whites

¾ teaspoon cream of tartar

Dash of salt

2 cups white sugar

2 cups crushed Waverly crackers

¾ cup finely chopped walnuts

1 package (3 ounces) instant chocolate pudding mix

2 cups milk

1 container (8 ounces) Cool Whip

Preheat the oven to 350°F. In a large bowl, beat together the egg whites, cream of tartar, and salt until stiff. Add the sugar and beat again. Fold in the crushed crackers and chopped walnuts. Spread this meringue mixture evenly in a greased 9-inch by 13-inch baking dish and bake for 18 to 20 minutes or until slightly brown. (Be careful not to overbake.) Remove from the oven and allow to cool.

Combine the pudding mix and milk and prepare the pudding according to the package directions.

When the meringue base is cool, spread the pudding over it. Then spoon the Cool Whip evenly over the top of the pudding. Chill in the refrigerator for at least an hour. Cut into squares and serve.

William R. Price
St. Patrick's Church
Milford, New Hampshire

Chocolate Eclair Dessert
Makes 12 servings

So easy, and so good. Make the dessert the day before serving, so it has time to chill.

FILLING

2 packages (3 ounces each) instant French vanilla pudding

3½ cups milk

1 container (8 ounces) Cool Whip

TOPPING

2 cups confectioners' sugar

2 ounces semisweet chocolate, melted

2 tablespoons butter or margarine, at room temperature

2 tablespoons milk

LINING

1 package (16 ounces) graham crackers

To make the filling, combine the pudding and milk. Beat until thick. Fold in the Cool Whip. Set aside.

To make the topping, combine the topping ingredients and beat until smooth. Set aside.

Line an ungreased 9-inch by 13-inch baking pan with whole graham crackers. Add half the filling mixture. Cover with a layer of graham crackers. Cover with the remaining filling and top with more graham crackers. Spread the topping over all. Chill overnight.

Adapted from a recipe submitted by Margaret A. Everly
St. Andrew Lutheran Church
Ellsworth, Maine

RECIPES TO
FEED A CROWD

*A*LL THE RECIPES in this cookbook have fed a crowd at one time or another. Some recipes were made in small quantities and were one of many, many dishes on a sumptuous buffet table. Others were made in multiple batches or multiplied by skilled cooks who can eyeball a quantity of food and work out the proportions for a quantity recipe in their heads. But in this chapter, the math and the guesswork have already been done. These are recipes to feed a crowd—desserts made on sheet pans, pancakes for all-you-can-eat breakfasts, plus salads, breads, even meat loaf. Whether you're preparing for a family reunion or planning a fundraiser for the local volunteer fire department, you'll find something here to fit the bill.

You say you need to make corn bread for forty? No problem—we have just the recipe for you.

PARTY MIX

MAKES 40 TO 50 SERVINGS

People love this stuff! It's good for parties and snacks. Packaged in a decorative container, Party Mix can be given as a gift at Christmastime.

2 cups (4 sticks) margarine, melted

1 tablespoon celery salt

¼ cup Worcestershire sauce

1 tablespoon garlic salt or garlic powder

1 box (12 ounces) Quaker Oats Crunch Corn Bran

1 box (12 ounces) Rice Chex

1 box (12 ounces) Corn Chex

1 can (5 ounces) chow mein noodles

16 ounces raw or roasted peanuts

Preheat the oven to 225°F. Combine the margarine with the celery salt, Worcestershire sauce, and garlic salt. Combine the remaining ingredients and pour the margarine mixture over them. Mix thoroughly. Pour into one large or two smaller roasting pans and bake for 1 hour, covered. Uncover and bake for another hour. Stir occasionally. Cool completely before storing in an airtight container.

Jodie Raymond
CLAREMONT LIONESS CLUB
CLAREMONT, NEW HAMPSHIRE

GREEK CHEESE TRIANGLES

MAKES ABOUT 72 TRIANGLES

Golden brown, flaky-crisp, with a tasty filling, these appetizers are delicious! Filo can be tricky to work with, so don't try these when you're in a hurry, but they're a delicious treat for a special occasion. These are best if you use a light hand with the butter and let the filling sit for an hour or so, allowing the flavors to meld, before making up the triangles.

1 pound filo dough, thawed if frozen (available in the freezer section of most supermarkets)

8 ounces feta cheese, crumbled

8 ounces ricotta cheese

2 eggs, beaten

2 tablespoons chopped fresh dill

1 cup (2 sticks) unsalted butter

Remove the filo from the refrigerator several hours before using, but keep it securely wrapped in plastic.

In a medium-size bowl, combine the feta, ricotta, eggs, and fresh dill. Melt the butter in a small saucepan and skim off the foam.

Unwrap the filo, unfold it, and cover it with a damp (not wet) towel. Use the sheets one at a time because they dry out quickly. Cut each sheet of filo into thirds lengthwise. Brush each of the three strips with melted butter. Fold each strip in half lengthwise and brush the upper surface of each with more butter. Place a teaspoon of cheese filling on a bottom corner of each strip. Starting at the bottom, fold each strip of filo as you would a flag so that the cheese is completely enclosed in a triangle. Brush the top of each folded triangle with butter.

Place the completed triangles on an unbuttered baking sheet and repeat with the remaining filo and filling.

Preheat the oven to 350°F and bake the triangles for 20 minutes or until golden brown. These can be made ahead, frozen, and reheated for serving.

Susan Mulford
NEWTON KINGDOM HALL
BELMONT, MASSACHUSETTS

Broccoli-Cheese Soup

MAKES 16 TO 20 SERVINGS

Easy and well loved by many.

¼ cup (½ stick) margarine

1 onion, chopped

5 cups water

5 chicken bouillon cubes

2 packages (10 ounces each) frozen chopped broccoli

1 package (8 ounces) medium egg noodles

5 cups milk

32 ounces Velveeta cheese, cubed

Pepper to taste

In a large kettle, melt the margarine over medium heat. Add the onion and sauté until tender, about 4 minutes. Add the water and bouillon cubes; stir to dissolve. Bring to a boil. Add the frozen broccoli and simmer for 5 minutes. Add the noodles and simmer for 5 minutes. Add the milk and Velveeta and simmer until the cheese is melted. Season to taste with pepper.

Elaine Proulx

NORTH PARISH CHURCH OF NORTH ANDOVER, UNITARIAN UNIVERSALIST

NORTH ANDOVER, MASSACHUSETTS

SUNSHINE SALAD

MAKES 75 TO 100 SERVINGS

The ladies of Gilsum, New Hampshire, know how to cook for a crowd. They tell us this salad is a great complement to the ham and beans they serve at the town's annual rock swap supper.

1 package (1½ pounds) lemon gelatin (1-gallon size)

1 quart boiling water

2 to 3 tablespoons vinegar

1 quart cold water

3 cans (20 ounces each) crushed pineapple, with juice

1 pound carrots, grated

In a large bowl, combine the gelatin with the boiling water. Stir until thoroughly dissolved. Add the vinegar and cold water. Then add the pineapple and carrots. Rinse in cold water three or four glass 9-inch by 13-inch baking pans, depending on how far you want the recipe to stretch, and pour in the gelatin mixture. Chill for at least 4 hours, preferably overnight. Cut into squares to serve.

Mildred McHoul
LADIES AID SOCIETY, GILSUM CONGREGATIONAL CHURCH
GILSUM, NEW HAMPSHIRE

Rock Swap Glop
Makes about 6 quarts

Judging by the name of their coleslaw dressing, nobody can accuse the Gilsum Ladies Aid Society of being overly pretentious! For the annual rock swap dinner, the contributor follows this recipe—making more than enough dressing for 25 to 30 pounds of coleslaw.

5 quarts mayonnaise
1 jar (8 ounces) spicy mustard
½ cup lemon juice
½ cup cider vinegar
Approximately 1½ cups milk
Salt and pepper to taste

Combine the mayonnaise, mustard, lemon juice, and vinegar and mix well. Thin with milk until you have a good consistency. Add salt and pepper to taste. Pour over the coleslaw and refrigerate until ready to serve.

Rosemarie Calhoun
Ladies Aid Society, Gilsum Congregational Church
Gilsum, New Hampshire

Vacancies

A GROUP OF FIRST-GRADERS was presenting a Christmas pageant for all the parents of the church. During one scene in Bethlehem, Mary and Joseph were to go from door to door searching for a place to stay for the night. At each door, they were *supposed* to be turned away by the innkeeper, who would tell them, "I'm sorry, there's no room at the inn." When the time came on the night of the performance, little Mary and Joseph walked downstage and knocked at the door. "Is there room at the inn?" they asked the innkeeper. Instead of turning them away, the little boy—who felt sorry for Jesus's parents—replied, "Sure, come on in."

COLESLAW

MAKES ABOUT 20 SERVINGS

For those who prefer their coleslaw in slightly *smaller quantities, here's a tasty alternative from Rockland, Maine.*

1 medium-large green cabbage,
   shredded (preferably by hand)

½ cup chopped onion

¼ cup chopped green bell pepper

¼ cup chopped red bell pepper

½ cup shredded carrot

1 cup white sugar

¾ cup cider vinegar

1 tablespoon salt

2 tablespoons vegetable oil

2 tablespoons olive oil

Rinse the cabbage under cold running water. Drain. In a large bowl, mix the cabbage with the onion, green and red peppers, and shredded carrot. Combine the sugar, vinegar, salt, and oils and pour over the vegetables. Mix well. Chill in the refrigerator until serving time.

Hildy Plante
DAUGHTERS OF ST. BERNARD, ST. BERNARD'S CHURCH
ROCKLAND, MAINE

Curried Turkey Pasta Salad

Makes 20 servings

The crowds are guaranteed to flock to this deliciously different pasta salad made with turkey, pineapple, and a creamy, not-too-spicy curry dressing. This is great picnic food.

1 fresh turkey breast (6 to 7 pounds)

1 carrot, sliced

1 celery stalk, sliced

1 medium-size onion, sliced

2 packages (16 ounces each) rotini

3 cans (20 ounces each) crushed pineapple, with juice

¼ bunch celery, cut into bite-size pieces

2 cups mayonnaise

2 cups sour cream

2 tablespoons curry powder

Place the turkey breast in a 12-quart pot, cover with water, and add the sliced carrot, celery, and onion. Cover the pot and bring to a boil; then reduce the heat and simmer for about 1½ hours, or until the turkey is done. Remove the turkey from the broth and allow to cool. When cool, remove the skin and bones and cut the turkey into bite-size pieces.

Remove the vegetables from the broth with a slotted spoon and add enough water to equal about 10 quarts. When the liquid returns to a boil, add the rotini and cook for 10 to 12 minutes. Do not overcook. Drain and cool the rotini.

Drain the pineapple, reserving the juice. In a large bowl, combine the pineapple, celery, and turkey, mixing thoroughly. Add the rotini and mix again.

To make the dressing, combine ¼ cup of the reserved pineapple juice with the mayonnaise, sour cream, and curry powder. Add to the pasta salad and mix again completely. Refrigerate until serving time.

Linnea H. Landraitis
Theodore Parker Unitarian Universalist Church
West Roxbury, Massachusetts

CHEESE MEAT LOAF

MAKES 25 SLICES

A favorite every time! If you're not feeding a crowd, freeze one loaf (either before or after baking) for later use.

2½ pounds ground beef

1 cup grated Cheddar cheese

⅔ cup chopped onion

3 tablespoons chopped green bell pepper

2½ cups dry bread crumbs

1 tablespoon salt

¼ teaspoon dried thyme

Dash garlic salt

3 eggs, beaten

2½ cups tomato purée

Preheat the oven to 350°F.

In a large bowl, mix together the beef, cheese, onion, green pepper, bread crumbs, salt, thyme, and garlic salt. Combine the eggs and tomato purée and blend into the meat mixture. Turn into two 8-inch by 4-inch loaf pans. Bake for 1 hour.

Alvina B. Thomson
NORTH PARISH CHURCH OF NORTH ANDOVER, UNITARIAN UNIVERSALIST
NORTH ANDOVER, MASSACHUSETTS

MEAT LOAF FOR 65

MAKES 65 SERVINGS

A recipe that's been the basis for its share of church suppers in Lancaster, Massachusetts.

20 pounds ground beef

10 cups rolled oats

10 cups grated carrots

5 cups minced onions

24 eggs, beaten

5 tablespoons Worcestershire sauce

3 tablespoons salt

2 teaspoons pepper

Preheat the oven to 350°F.

Mix together all the ingredients in a large bowl. Form into two 10-inch-long loaves and place in a large roasting pan or form into eight loaves and place in eight 8-inch by 4-inch loaf pans. Bake the long loaves for 1¼ hours; bake the small loaves for 50 to 60 minutes.

Katherine E. Perkins
THE FEMALE CHARITABLE SOCIETY, FIRST CHURCH OF CHRIST
LANCASTER, MASSACHUSETTS

CORN BREAD FOR A CROWD

MAKES 40 TO 50 SERVINGS

A good recipe to feed a group—written by someone who clearly has done just that! Corn bread makes a great accompaniment for ham and beans or any kind of chili.

3 cups all-purpose white-flour

5 cups stone-ground cornmeal

⅞ cup (14 tablespoons) white sugar

3 tablespoons plus 1 teaspoon baking powder

2 teaspoons salt

4 eggs, beaten

4 cups milk

12 tablespoons (1½ sticks) butter, melted

Preheat the oven to 425°F. Grease an 11½-inch by 19½-inch pan.

Combine the flour, cornmeal, sugar, baking powder, and salt in a large bowl and mix thoroughly with a whisk.

In another large bowl, beat the eggs with the milk. Add the butter and mix thoroughly. Add to the dry ingredients and stir just until moistened. Pour into the pan.

Bake for about 30 minutes or until a tester inserted near the center comes out clean. Do not overbake. Serve warm or cooled.

Linnea H. Landraitis
THEODORE PARKER UNITARIAN UNIVERSALIST CHURCH
WEST ROXBURY, MASSACHUSETTS

APPLE ROLLS

MAKES 3 LOAVES (36 SLICES)

An unusual recipe that's easy to prepare and very good. It is best made with Granny Smith apples—or any other variety that's crisp and tart—and with bread flour, which is high in gluten, rather than all-purpose flour. Serve in thick slices as either a bread or a cake (delicious with a hard sauce drizzled over it). The recipe makes a lot, so if your crowd fails to materialize, freeze the extras right in the baking cans, covered with the original plastic lids. (If you don't have a good supply of leftover coffee cans to use for baking these rolls, standard 8-inch by 4-inch loaf pans, filled half full, work just fine.)

4 cups peeled, cored, and diced apples

1 cup chopped nuts

1 cup white sugar

3 cups bread flour

2 teaspoons baking soda

½ teaspoon salt

¼ teaspoon ground allspice or ground cloves

¼ teaspoon ground nutmeg

¾ teaspoon ground cinnamon

½ cup vegetable oil

2 teaspoons vanilla extract

2 eggs, beaten

In a medium-size bowl, stir together the apples, nuts, and sugar. Let them stand for 1 hour, stirring often. Preheat the oven to 325°F. Grease three 12-ounce coffee cans.

In a large mixing bowl, sift together the flour, soda, salt, and spices. Add the apple mixture and stir well. Then add the oil, vanilla, and eggs and mix well.

Divide the batter among the prepared cans. Cover with a double thickness of foil folded so that it comes down over the sides of the cans at least 2 inches. Bake for 1 hour. Let the cans cool on a wire rack for about 10 minutes before turning the rolls out of the cans to finish cooling. To serve, slice 1 inch thick.

Adapted from a recipe submitted by Dottie Rowe
BRENTWOOD HISTORICAL SOCIETY
BRENTWOOD, NEW HAMPSHIRE

GRIDDLE CAKES FOR 65

MAKES 65 SERVINGS

The First Church of Christ, from which this recipe came, was founded in 1653 (just 33 years after the Pilgrims hit Plymouth Rock). It's housed in the Bulfinch Church, which dates from 1816. This recipe isn't quite that historic, but it is a time-honored one.

20 cups sifted all-purpose white flour

3 cups white sugar

6 tablespoons plus 2 teaspoons baking soda

20 eggs

5 quarts buttermilk (or sour milk)

1¼ cups (2½ sticks) butter or margarine, melted

In a large bowl, combine the flour, sugar, and soda. Mix with a whisk to blend well.

In a large mixing bowl, beat the eggs. Add the buttermilk and melted butter and blend well. Add the dry ingredients and mix well.

Cook the pancakes on a lightly oiled griddle. Serve hot.

Katherine E. Perkins

THE FEMALE CHARITABLE SOCIETY, FIRST CHURCH OF CHRIST
LANCASTER, MASSACHUSETTS

Quick Chocolate Cake

MAKES ABOUT 100 SERVINGS

A very fudgy and moist cake that's great for a crowd because it doesn't dry out quickly. Serve with frosting, whipped cream, or ice cream.

4 cups water

1½ cups vegetable oil

¼ cup vinegar

1½ tablespoons vanilla extract

7 cups all-purpose white flour

¾ cup unsweetened cocoa powder

4 cups white sugar

1½ tablespoons baking soda

2 tablespoons baking powder

1½ teaspoons salt

Preheat the oven to 350°F. Grease an 18-inch by 26-inch sheet pan.

In a large bowl, combine the water, oil, vinegar, and vanilla. Mix well. In a separate bowl, whisk together the flour, cocoa, sugar, soda, baking powder, and salt. Add the dry ingredients to the wet and mix until smooth. Pour into the prepared pan.

Bake for approximately 45 minutes or until a tester inserted near the center comes out clean. Cool in the pan.

Patricia A. Johnson

LADIES AID SOCIETY, GILSUM CONGREGATIONAL CHURCH
GILSUM, NEW HAMPSHIRE

CHOCOLATE SHEET CAKE

MAKES ABOUT 40 SERVINGS

A quick and easy dessert with a frosting that turns to fudge. Terrific for a summer picnic.

CAKE

1 cup (2 sticks) butter or margarine

¼ cup unsweetened cocoa powder

1 cup water

2 cups all-purpose white flour

2 cups white sugar

½ teaspoon salt

1 teaspoon baking soda

2 eggs

½ cup sour cream, buttermilk, or yogurt

FROSTING

½ cup (1 stick) butter or margarine

½ cup unsweetened cocoa powder

5 to 6 tablespoons milk

1 box (1 pound) confectioners' sugar (4½ cups)

1 teaspoon vanilla extract

Preheat the oven to 350°F. Grease an 11-inch by 17-inch baking pan.

In a large saucepan, combine the 1 cup butter, ¼ cup cocoa, and water. Bring to a boil, then cool to room temperature. Add the remaining cake ingredients and beat until smooth. Pour into the prepared pan. Bake for about 22 minutes or until a tester inserted near the center comes out clean.

Meanwhile, make the frosting by combining all the ingredients in a saucepan. Bring to a boil. Pour the warm frosting on the warm cake. Let cool before serving.

Ruth Southwick
WILLINGTON BAPTIST CHURCH
WILLINGTON, CONNECTICUT

CHOCOLATE CHIP OATMEAL SHEET CAKE

MAKES ABOUT 35 SERVINGS

Quick, relatively easy to prepare, and great for kids. For variety, try substituting M&Ms for the chocolate chips.

1¾ cups boiling water

1 cup rolled oats (not instant)

½ cup (1 stick) margarine or butter

1 cup light brown sugar, packed

1 cup white sugar

2 large eggs

1¾ cups sifted all-purpose white flour

1 teaspoon baking soda

½ teaspoon salt

1 tablespoon unsweetened cocoa powder

1 package (12 ounces) semisweet chocolate chips

¾ cup chopped nuts (optional)

Preheat the oven to 350°F. Lightly grease a 15-inch by 10-inch baking pan.

Pour the boiling water over the oats and let stand for 10 minutes. Add the margarine and stir until melted. Add the sugars and stir until dissolved. Add the eggs and mix well. Sift together the flour, soda, salt, and cocoa. Add to the oat mixture and mix well. Pour into the baking pan. Sprinkle the chips and nuts, if using, on top.

Bake for 20 to 25 minutes. Cool completely before serving.

Violet M. Lindon
BRENTWOOD HISTORICAL SOCIETY
BRENTWOOD, NEW HAMPSHIRE

JANIE'S BRIDESMAID SALAD

MAKES 20 SERVINGS

Janie may call this easy-to-prepare dish a salad, but we say it is sweet enough to be served as a dessert. The yellow of the pineapple and the red of the strawberries make a pretty presentation.

2 packages (10 ounces each) frozen strawberries

1 can (14 ounces) sweetened condensed milk

1 container (8 ounces) Cool Whip

1 can (20 ounces) crushed pineapple, with juice

2½ cups (half of a 10-ounce bag) miniature marshmallows, colored variety if available

½ cup chopped nuts (optional)

Partially thaw the berries. Combine in a 12-cup bowl with the condensed milk, Cool Whip, pineapple, and marshmallows. Mix well. Freeze until solid.

Remove from the freezer about 1 hour before serving. Sprinkle with the nuts, if desired.

Ellen Moore
ST. BRENDAN'S CATHOLIC WOMAN'S CLUB
COLEBROOK, NEW HAMPSHIRE

FRUIT BREAD PUDDING

MAKES 25 TO 30 SERVINGS

Flavored with bananas and studded with raisins and pineapple bits, this bread pudding is a rich variation on an old classic.

2 loaves raisin bread

2 cans (12 ounces each) evaporated milk

3 cups whole milk

5 eggs

3 ripe bananas, mashed

1 teaspoon ground cinnamon

1 teaspoon ground nutmeg

1 tablespoon vanilla extract

1 jar (6 ounces) pineapple jam (or substitute another fruit jam)

Preheat the oven to 350°F. Spray a 10-inch by 15-inch pan with non-stick cooking spray.

Cut the bread into bite-size pieces. In a large mixing bowl, combine the bread with the evaporated and whole milk and set aside for 10 minutes. Beat the eggs thoroughly and add to the bread. Add the remaining ingredients and mix well. Pour into the pan.

Bake for 50 minutes or until lightly browned. Serve warm or cooled.

Emma Mazzeo

DAUGHTERS OF ST. BERNARD, ST. BERNARD'S CHURCH
ROCKLAND, MAINE

MELBA ICE CREAM SAUCE
MAKES 20 SERVINGS

Served over ice cream or vanilla pudding, this wonderful combination of peach and raspberry is a good way to make a simple dessert really special.

1 jar (10 ounces) peach preserves
½ cup raspberry preserves
½ cup currant jelly
¼ cup lemon juice

Combine all the ingredients in a medium-size saucepan. Heat until melted. Stir to blend. Cool.

Marguerite R. Curtiss
WOMEN OF THE MOOSE (LOYAL ORDER OF MOOSE)
KEENE, NEW HAMPSHIRE

Index